DEAN ACHESON

AND THE CREATION OF AN AMERICAN WORLD ORDER

ADDITIONAL FORTHCOMING TITLES IN THE
SHAPERS OF INTERNATIONAL HISTORY SERIES

Edited by Melvyn P. Leffler, University of Virginia

Zhou Enlai–Chen Jian
Vyacheslav Molotov–Geoffrey Roberts
Mikhail Gorbachev–Robert English
Madeleine Albright–Peter Ronayne
Henry Kissinger–Jeremi Suri
Ho Chi Minh–Robert K. Brigham
Robert McNamara–Fredrik Logevall
Konrad Adenauer–Ronald Granieri
Yasser Arafat–Omar Dajani
Jimmy Carter–Nancy Mitchell
George Kennan–Frank Costigliola
Fidel Castro–Piero Gleijeses
Vladimir Putin–Allen C. Lynch
Ronald Reagan–Nancy Tucker
Deng Xiaoping–Warren Cohen

DEAN ACHESON

AND THE CREATION OF AN AMERICAN WORLD ORDER

ROBERT J. MCMAHON

SHAPERS OF
INTERNATIONAL
HISTORY

Potomac Books, Inc.
Washington, D.C.

Cover photo: Secretary of State Acheson testifies before a Joint Senate Committee, appealing for additional military aid for Western Europe, August 1949.

Library of Congress Cataloging-in-Publication Data
McMahon, Robert J., 1949–
　Dean Acheson and the creation of an American world order / Robert J. McMahon.
　– 1st ed.
　　p. cm. – (Shapers of international history series)
　Includes bibliographical references and index.
　ISBN 978-1-57488-926-0 (hardcover : alk. paper) – ISBN 978-1-57488-927-7 (pbk. : alk. paper)
　1. Acheson, Dean, 1893–1971. 2. Statesmen–United States–Biography. 3. United States–Foreign relations–1945–1953. 4. Cold War. I. Title.
　E748.A15M35 2009
　973.918092–dc22
　[B]
　　　　　　　　　　　　　　　　　　　2008034904

Potomac Books, Inc.
22841 Quicksilver Drive
Dulles, Virginia 20166

First Edition

10 9 8 7 6 5 4 3 2 1

For Alison

CONTENTS

SERIES EDITOR'S FOREWORD

by Melvyn Leffler

As human beings, we are interested in our leaders. What they say and do has a profound impact on our lives. They can lead us into war or help to shape the peace; they can help promote trade and prosperity or sink us into poverty; they can focus on fighting terror or combating disease, or do both, or neither.

We also know that they are not so strong and powerful as they pretend to be. They are enveloped by circumstances that they cannot control. They are the products of their time, buffeted by technological innovations, economic cycles, social change, cultural traditions, and demographic trends that are beyond their reach. But how they react to matters they cannot control matters a great deal. Their decisions accrue and make a difference.

This series is about leaders who have shaped the history of international relations during the modern era. It will focus on those who were elected to high office and those who were not; it will focus on those who led revolutionary movements and those who sought to preserve the status quo; it will include leaders of powerful states and those of weak nations whose capacity to influence international events extended well beyond the power of the country they led. It will deal with presidents and dictators, foreign secretaries and defense ministers, diplomats and soldiers.

The books in the series are designed to be short, evocative, and provocative. They seek to place leaders in the context of their times. How were they influenced by their family and friends, by their class, their status, their religion, and their traditions? What values did they inculcate and seek to disseminate? How did their education and career influence their perception of national interests and their understanding of threats? What did they hope to achieve as leaders and how did they seek to accomplish their goals? In what ways and to what extent were they able to overcome constraints and shape the evolution of international history? What made them effective leaders? And to what extent were they truly agents of change?

The authors are experts in their field. They are writing in this series for the general reader. They have been asked to look at the forest, not the trees, to extrapolate important insights from complex circumstances, and to make bold generalizations. The aim here is to make readers think about big issues and important developments; the aim here is to make readers wrestle with the perplexing and enduring question of human agency in history.

In this first book in the series, Robert McMahon does a superb job assessing the influence of Dean G. Acheson, the U.S. secretary of state who did so much to shape the Cold War foreign policy of the United States. McMahon deftly looks at Acheson's upbringing and personality and shows how family and mentors shaped his thinking. Examining the influence of Justices Louis Brandeis, Oliver Wendell Holmes, and Felix Frankfurter, McMahon stresses that they taught Acheson lessons of law, politics, and life that the secretary of state never forgot. His aim was to employ U.S. power to serve a purpose: to fashion an international environment in which the American way of life could prosper and individual freedom could survive.

In McMahon's view, Acheson mattered. He cultivated a special relationship with his boss, President Harry S. Truman, ably reached out to legislators, and smartly sought allies abroad who shared American values. He helped build durable multilateral institutions, promoted Franco-German reconciliation, and nurtured European unity while he sought to balance the growth of Soviet power and contain the spread of communism in the third world. Acheson certainly erred at times and could not overcome his self-conceit, but he fashioned institutions and policies that endured for decades. Here was a man who made a difference, and McMahon brilliantly explains why that was the case.

ACKNOWLEDGMENTS

I am indebted to the remarkably efficient, friendly, and helpful professional archivists at the Harry S. Truman Presidential Library, in Independence, Missouri, and the Manuscript and Archives Division at Yale University's Sterling Memorial Library, in New Haven, Connecticut. Those two magnificent facilities hold Acheson's voluminous papers, public and private, which have been indispensable to this study. I also thank the archival specialists at National Archives II in College Park, Maryland; the Library of Congress, in Washington, D.C.; and the John F. Kennedy Presidential Library, in Boston, Massachusetts, for their assistance.

For generously sharing with me some important documents from their own research, I thank Mark Rice and Frank Costigliola. Melvyn Leffler and Thomas Schwartz each provided me with incisive comments and helpful suggestions on an earlier version of this manuscript. I am extremely grateful to both of them. Mel Leffler, who invited me to write this book for the "Shapers of International History" series, has been critical to the project since its inception. His support, encouragement, and astute advice have helped me enormously, as have his warm friendship and the stellar example set by his own scholarship.

Ohio State University, where I have taught since 2005, has provided me with a lively and supportive intellectual environment that any author would envy. I am especially grateful to Rick Herrmann, director of the Mershon Center for International Security Studies, and my colleague and good friend

Peter Hahn, the current chair of the History Department. Peter's predecessor as History Department chair, Ken Andrien, has also been wonderfully supportive since my arrival in Columbus. So, too, have been many of my Ohio State graduate students and faculty colleagues, who have probably heard more about Dean Acheson over the past few years than they ever needed to know. I am grateful to them all.

This book is dedicated to my wife, loving companion, and best friend of over thirty years now. More than anyone, Alison supported and encouraged me in the writing of this book–through good times and trying times–in countless and immeasurable ways. Her passion, balance, sense of humor, and infectious enthusiasm–which managed even to extend to the subject of this biography– helped ease the sometimes arduous burden of research and writing. I can never thank her enough.

INTRODUCTION

From World War II through the early Cold War years, the United States solidified its status as the world's dominant power, assuming a position of virtually unparalleled global supremacy. Not since the heyday of the Roman Empire two millennia earlier had any nation wielded a comparable degree of power, prestige, and influence. It has become customary to label the international order that obtained from the mid-1940s to the late 1980s as a bipolar system whose defining feature was the fierce rivalry between the United States and the Soviet Union, both as nation-states and as social systems. Yet, in truth, the Soviet Union was never a genuine rival to American hegemony. It never came close to matching the totality of America's multifarious strengths—which stretched from the military, nuclear, and economic realms to encompass the realms of culture, diplomacy, intellectual life, education, and politics.

Plainly, structural forces facilitated the American ascendancy. They constituted the indispensable preconditions for the erection, during the 1940s, of an American world order. That order, already firmly entrenched by mid-century, has remained the most fundamental fact of international life ever since. But the role of individual historical actors in its emergence should not be slighted. Structures do not make policy choices; flesh and blood human beings do—with all their frailties, limitations, and foibles. It was individual American policymakers who quite self-consciously labored to put in place an international system that reflected what they saw as the basic needs, interests, and values

1

of their own country. They shaped the system's contours; determined its particularities; harnessed the resources necessary to sustain it; fought to win acceptance of its legitimacy—with domestic and international audiences alike; identified the most likely impediments and threats to that order; and designed specific strategies to remove the impediments and counter the threats.

In those endeavors, no single individual proved more consequential than the subject of the present biography: Dean Acheson. A New Englander of modest family circumstance, Acheson was educated at some of the nation's most prestigious schools before embarking on what became a highly successful legal career. In 1941, months before U.S. entry into World War II, he joined the State Department as an assistant secretary of state. In that capacity, Acheson engaged in a number of important postwar planning exercises, including the establishment, at Bretton Woods, of what became the essential institutions that would govern the capitalist world's economic and financial system for the next several decades.

From the war years through the early postwar era, Acheson participated actively in, and helped craft, nearly all of the key initiatives that gave birth to an American-led world order—an order that has proved remarkably durable. During an unusually critical and highly fluid historical moment, Acheson succeeded in placing an indelible personal stamp not just on U.S. foreign policy but on the international system writ large. In the apt, if characteristically immodest, title of his memoir, Acheson was truly "present at the creation." As President Harry S. Truman's undersecretary of state, between 1945 and 1947, he exerted a major influence on such pivotal matters as postwar reconstruction, occupation policies toward Germany and Japan, the formulation and enunciation of the Truman Doctrine and Marshall Plan, and early nuclear weapons policy. Then, as the nation's fiftieth secretary of state, during Truman's second term in office (1949–1953), he led the efforts to establish and strengthen NATO, rearm Germany, foster European integration, intervene in Korea and Indochina, implement a global containment strategy designed to thwart Soviet expansion, and adjust to the twin challenges of collapsing empires and burgeoning third world nationalism. During the latter period, the patrician, self-assured Acheson also became a target for Senator Joseph McCarthy and other partisan critics of Truman's foreign policy, some of whom viciously attacked him–however risibly–for his alleged "softness" on communism. The attacks helped turn him into a symbol of the presumably lax, out-of-touch, Anglophilic establishment, making him in the process the most controversial secretary of state of the twentieth century.

Upon leaving high office in January 1953, Acheson returned to his law practice. Yet he managed to keep himself involved more deeply in foreign affairs as a private citizen than had any previous ex–secretary of state. During the Dwight D. Eisenhower presidency, Acheson's became one of the most powerful and articulate voices of the Democratic opposition. When the Democrats returned to the White House, first under John F. Kennedy and then under Lyndon B. Johnson, he became a respected elder statesman, often brought into the executive mansion and State Department as an informal adviser and consultant. He participated in highly secret policy deliberations during some of the great Cold War crises of the 1960s, including those over Berlin, the emplacement of Soviet nuclear missiles in Cuba, French challenges to American leadership, and the war in Vietnam. Once again, his role was significant, his involvement consequential. Three years before he succumbed to a stroke, in 1971, Acheson took the lead role in a climactic meeting between Johnson and a distinguished group of former high-level officials that led directly to LBJ's decision to open negotiations with North Vietnam and to place a ceiling on U.S. troop levels.

This compact biography examines, as will others in this series, the life and diplomatic career of one of the "Shapers of International History." Following a chapter that explores the formative influences on Acheson's worldview, values, and habits of thought, I devote a chapter to his service as assistant and undersecretary of state from 1941 to 1947. The next three chapters cover Acheson's years as secretary of state, concentrating on those issues and events with which he was most preoccupied: especially European and NATO challenges, U.S.-Soviet relations, the Korean War, U.S. rearmament and defense programs, overall Cold War strategy, and involvement in Japan, Southeast Asia, and the Middle East. The final chapter examines Acheson's continuing role as a foreign policy thinker, strategist, consultant, insider, and public intellectual during the final eighteen years of his life. A brief conclusion offers some broad reflections on Acheson's significance.

This book, though based mainly on primary sources, has benefited greatly from the rich secondary literature on U.S. foreign policy during the World War II and Cold War years, the broader international history of that period, and twentieth-century American political, legal, and constitutional history. References in the notes, for the sake of space, are chiefly confined to primary sources and to those secondary works from which I have drawn quotes, vignettes, or interpretive lines of argument. I have chosen, for the most part, to avoid any direct arguments with the extant historiography in the text and in the notes. Those ongoing debates, however, have certainly influenced and colored all of the major interpretive themes I develop herein.

1

YEARS OF PREPARATION

A PRIVILEGED YOUTH

Belying his subsequent image and appearance, Dean Acheson was not born into the American aristocracy. With his impeccably tailored clothes, distinctive mustache, regal bearing, and trademark erudition, this product of America's most exclusive private schools doubtless struck many, throughout his adult life, as one who was "to the manor born." Yet he was, in fact, no scion of an archetypal Eastern Establishment, ruling elite family—not in terms of familial pedigree or status, certainly not in terms of wealth, not even in *Americanness.* Quite to the contrary, he was the first child of a middle-class couple who had recently emigrated from Canada. The Achesons lived a comfortable, secure, and respectable existence in Middletown, Connecticut, where Dean was born on April 11, 1893, in the rectory of Holy Trinity Episcopal Church. But compared to the Rockefellers, Roosevelts, or Harrimans, theirs were decidedly modest circumstances.

Edward Campion Acheson, Dean's father, was very much a self-made man. The son of a Scots-Irish professional soldier who had fought in the Crimean War, he was born in southern England, where his father was garrisoned at the time. After the death of his Anglo-Irish mother, originally from County Cork, and his father's subsequent remarriage, Edward ran away to London at the age of fourteen. Two years later, he immigrated by himself to Canada, where he managed to put himself through school at the University of Toronto. During his school years, he also served as a member of the Queen's Own Rifles, a militia regiment, and gained national recognition, along with a citation for bravery, during a skirmish against rebellious Indians, in 1885, at the battle of Cut Knife Creek in Saskatchewan. Shortly thereafter, he chose the ministry over a military career and enrolled in Wycliffe Theological Seminary in Toronto. Edward Acheson met Dean's mother at Toronto's All Saints Church. They wed in 1892, shortly after his ordination as an Episcopalian minister and just one year before their first child's birth.

Eleanor Gooderham hailed from a wealthier and more socially prominent family. In 1832, her grandfather left Norfolk, England, where he had been a mill owner, for Canada; he quickly proceeded to establish a prosperous mill in Toronto. Her father, George Gooderham, turned to whisky distilling and banking, from whence he earned sufficient income to educate his daughter in England and, subsequently, to ensure that her marriage to a struggling prelate would not condemn Eleanor to a life of poverty. A strong-willed, stylish woman with a marked British accent, the cosmopolitan Mrs. Acheson became "the social arbiter of Middletown," in the words of one family friend.[1]

Graced with a loving, supportive, and secure family environment, Dean Gooderham Acheson enjoyed a carefree, Huckleberry Finn–like boyhood. "The Golden Age of childhood can be quite accurately fixed in time and place," he wrote in *Morning and Noon*, a charming memoir of his early years. "It reached its apex in the last decade of the nineteenth century and the first few years of the twentieth, before the plunge into a motor age and city life swept away the freedom of children and dogs, put them both on leashes and made them the organized prisoners of an adult world." He located "the Athens of this golden age," as he tongue-in-cheek dubbed it, in the fertile Connecticut River Valley of central Connecticut–his own aptly named home of Middletown.[2]

Acheson grew up there with his dog, his pony, a pony cart, and a fun-loving group of ball-playing friends. An open, three-acre field behind the rectory in which the young Dean lived formed, in his recollection, "an Elysian Field where heroes met for converse, council, and the game of heroes," and in which many a battle of the Spanish-American and Boer wars were reenacted. "Our life in our valley was wholly unorganized, wholly free," he recollected warmly. "Nothing presented a visible hazard to children. No one was run over.

No one was kidnaped. No one had teeth straightened. No one worried about children, except occasionally my mother, when she saw us riding on the back step of the ice wagon and believed, fleetingly, that one of the great blocks of Pamecha Pond ice would fall on us. But none ever did."[3]

If those reminiscences reflect the irresistible inclination of accomplished people to idealize and sentimentalize their childhoods, they also betray Dean Acheson's lifelong tendency to place himself, his experiences, and the outlook of his social class at the very epicenter of the world—much as he similarly situated his nation and its Anglo-Saxon heritage. One cannot help but marvel, nonetheless, at the reconstruction of so simple and yet idyllic a childhood in small-town, turn-of-the-century New England. Vacations took the Achesons to the Long Island Sound and the wilds of central Maine, where Dean's father taught his three children fly-fishing, camping, and a respect for nature and the rugged outdoors life. Mr. Acheson's "wild Ulster streak," as Dean termed it, together with his gift for colorful storytelling, enlivened many a campfire.

At home, the prelate effected an air of "Olympian detachment" from the day-to-day responsibilities of child-rearing, tasks shared by Mrs. Acheson and her Canadian governess. Dean, his brother, and his sister were for a time, in fact, the only American citizens in a household that also included Cazzie, their Irish-born cook. The Achesons solemnly celebrated Queen Victoria's birthday each year: his father ran the Union Jack up the rectory flagpole and allowed the children to sip diluted claret while they all toasted "The Queen." The odd ceremony suggests that for all the commonalities Dean's upbringing might have shared with small-town family life across the United States, the Achesons were hardly the typical American family of that era.

A socially liberal cleric whose sermons frequently touched on issues such as the rights of labor and the need for workmen's compensation, Edward Acheson imparted to Dean both a concern for those less fortunate than him and a strong ethical code. "No conviction could have been deeper than his in a code of conduct," his son later recollected, "based on perceptions of what was decent and civilized for man inextricably caught up in social relationships." The pastor, whose parishioners included Middletown's gentry, insisted in the fashion of the day that his eldest son be properly educated at an elite boarding school. At age nine, consequently, Dean was packed off to Hamlet Lodge, at nearby Pomfret, close enough to Middletown to permit weekend family visits. "After the golden age," he lamented, "life lost this pristine, unorganized, amoral freedom. . . . School life was organized from the wakening bell to the policed silence which followed lights-out."[4]

Three years later, in 1905, he enrolled at Groton, the newly established academy in northern Massachusetts that, under the austere, iron-hand guidance of Rector Endicott Peabody, aimed to educate the sons of America's upper classes along the lines of an English "public" school. Franklin D. Roosevelt was a recent graduate, and W. Averell Harriman, whose railroad baron father commanded one of the nation's great fortunes, was currently matriculating. "The transition from the wild freedom of my boyhood to the organized discipline of adolescence at boarding school was not a change for the happier," Acheson later confessed. "To adapt oneself to so sudden and considerable a change required what is now called a 'well-adjusted' personality. Mine apparently was not. At first, through surprise, ignorance, and awkwardness, later on and increasingly through wilfulness, I bucked the Establishment and the system. One who does this fights the odds. The result was predictable, painful, and clear." Revealingly, Acheson never even mentions Groton by name in *Morning and Noon*; he skips over his six years there entirely while elliptically alluding to them as "unhappy ones."[5] "At Groton, I didn't happen to feel like conforming," he recalled elsewhere. "And to my surprise and astonishment, I discovered not only that an independent judgment might be the right one, but that a man was actually alive and breathing once he had made it."[6]

Rector Peabody initially despaired of ever turning Acheson into a Groton man and sent home a string of less-than-adulatory report cards, which frequently highlighted Dean's immaturity and rebelliousness. Acheson graduated last in his class of twenty-four, earning an uninspiring average grade of 68 on his final report card. Yet Groton clearly influenced and shaped him in important ways. Arriving as a somewhat thin, frail adolescent who suffered his share of taunts and bullying from upperclassmen, especially since his clothes, manners, and family income failed to measure up to the Groton norm, Acheson developed an inner toughness at the legendary boarding school. Although never athletically gifted, he wound up rowing crew in his last year. Despite his distaste for Headmaster Peabody and his pieties, moreover, Acheson embraced and internalized the rector's emphasis on the ethic of public service. Tellingly, he later sent his own son, David, to Groton.[7]

Immediately following his graduation from Groton, Acheson used family connections to obtain a temporary summer job working on the Canadian Grand Trunk Pacific Railway, a transcontinental line then being built westward across Canada's northern reaches. By his own testimony, it turned into "one of the most important few months of my life." That was largely because of the freedom, independence, and test of incipient manhood that hard labor under primitive conditions offered him. Acheson especially relished the camaraderie and hard-earned sense of belonging that he gained from close association with a colorful cast of rough-hewn workers, many of immigrant or mixed ethnic stock. After the "suffocating disciplines and arbitrary values" of boarding school, Acheson found his months with simple, illiterate, extroverted, and frequently hot-tempered men to be a liberating experience. "They had restored to me a priceless possession," he subsequently wrote, "joy in life. Never again was I to lose it or doubt it."[8]

Acheson entered Yale University in the fall of 1911. He was one of about three hundred freshmen in that year's class, nearly three-fourths of whom had attended prep schools. Whatever insecurities might have lingered from his difficult years at Groton largely expunged by his invigorating work adventure on the Canadian frontier, Acheson, by then a handsome, self-possessed, six foot two, found Yale's social environment far more appealing. Indeed, his sense of humor, insouciance, and joie de vivre proved an ideal fit at a college where social grace and zest for extracurricular activities conferred substantially more status and plaudits than scholarship.

"What I remember best about Dean was his ebullience, his bright subtle wit," recalled Joseph Walker III, his Yale roommate and closest friend. "He was the wittiest one in our group. I don't remember seeing Dean study, although he must have. He was always ready for a good time, for a new experience."[9] Actually, he probably did not do much studying, since his grades rarely rose above the level of "gentleman's Cs" during his four years of matriculation. Two influential English professors did inspire him to hone his already impressive writing skills. For the most part, though, Acheson saw his studies as largely "meaningless" and invested far more energy in what became a lively social life. He joined a number of the clubs that stood at the apex of Yale's undergraduate life: including the Grill Room Grizzlies, the Turtles, the Hogans, and the Mohicans. Delta Kappa Epsilon, one of Yale's most elegant and social fraternities, also counted Acheson as an active brother (as it would George W. Bush during his years as a partying "Deke" at Yale during the 1960s).

Acheson also rowed freshman crew, his one athletic pursuit. He had been personally recruited by Harriman, then a junior and coach of the first-year squad. That summer he accompanied Harriman to England, ostensibly to study the Oxford rowers' technique. Just as important, the visit afforded Acheson an opportunity to soak up some of the English culture, style, and tradition that he found so enthralling as well as an excuse to participate in his share of partying. A stint, in his sophomore year, as coach of the freshman crew team was cut short when Acheson was relieved of his responsibilities following a disappointing loss to Princeton. Yet the setback hardly dented his budding self-assurance.[10]

In his junior year Acheson became one of just fifteen students tapped for the eminent senior secret society, Scroll and Key, second only to the legendary Skull and Bones in prestige. That achievement stood, in many respects, as the pinnacle of his undergraduate career; "for Acheson," observe journalists Walter Isaacson and Evan Thomas, "it was the culmination of his journey from miserable Groton outcast to worldly and popular college blade."[11] Decades later one of his classmates recalled, "Dean moved in a fast circle and seemed to have a great deal more money than he actually had."[12] According to Archibald MacLeish, the most accomplished scholar-athlete of the class of 1915 and later (but not then) an intimate friend of Acheson's: "He was the typical son of an Episcopal bishop—gay, graceful, gallant—he was also socially snobby with the qualities of arrogance and superciliousness. Dean led a charming social existence at Yale."[13]

Acheson and his circle of those years resembled "the last of the Victorians," in the apt description of historian John Lamberton Harper, "a generation who had lived too long and too well under the pre-1914 pax universalis to imagine a better time or place. Though they could convince themselves intellectually of the passing of the nineteenth century—of which their undergraduate life had been a kind of Indian summer—they were never able to accept its demise emotionally, and it remained fixed in their imaginations as the best of all possible worlds."[14]

A PASSION FOR THE LAW

Acheson's decision to apply to Harvard Law School appears less an act of deep conviction in choice of profession than a post-graduation drifting toward a respectable career–a career, not coincidentally, favored by several of his closest friends. Yet a dramatic transformation in the Yale bon vivant soon took place. At Harvard, which he entered in the fall of 1915, Acheson discovered that genuine intellectual achievement, in contradistinction to his experiences at Groton and Yale, offered the surest route to social respect and acceptance. Somewhat to his own surprise, he found that exhilarating. "Training in the law was an intellectual awakening for him," notes biographer David S. McLellan. "It not only afforded an intellectual challenge hitherto missing, but more importantly it provided him with a socially sanctioned mode of excelling and of achieving personal distinction which was destined to become a crucial goal in his life."[15] As Acheson himself later phrased it, "This was a tremendous discovery–The Discovery of the power of thought."[16]

In his second year Acheson took a class with the young, dynamic Professor Felix Frankfurter, the man destined to be his earliest, and most important, mentor and later an intimate, lifelong friend. A Jewish refugee from Austria who had gained renown as a brilliant assistant litigant to Henry Stimson during the latter's tenure as the U.S. attorney for the southern district of New York, Frankfurter overflowed with energy, ideas, reformist zeal, and intellectual firepower. The charismatic law professor, a pioneer in the field of sociological jurisprudence, was impressed by the youthful Acheson's combination of raw intelligence, social grace, and nimble wit. The once-mediocre Groton-Yale student soon became Frankfurter's favorite protégé; under his wing, Acheson flourished. He shared many of his mentor's liberal, political passions and adopted his pragmatic approach to the law, "learning that you need not make up your mind in advance, that there is no set solution to a problem, and that decisions are the result of analyzing the facts, of tussling and grappling with them."[17] Elected to the board of the prestigious *Harvard Law Review* at the end of his second year, Acheson ranked fifth in his class upon graduation in June 1918.

With war then raging in Europe, he enrolled in the Naval Auxiliary Reserve, only to be discharged in December following the armistice that brought the conflict to an end. Following his brief military sojourn, Acheson returned to Cambridge for postgraduate legal studies. Having become intrigued with the connection between the law and socioeconomic issues, he wrote a 140-page manuscript on labor that he then tried to get published by Harvard University Press. The law school graduate also began searching for possible employment opportunities as a legal counsel within the labor movement.

Acheson had a wife to support by then, and a child on the way, making a steady source of income imperative. In May 1917 he had wed the tall and elegant Alice Stanley, a Wellesley art student from a prominent Detroit family; his sister had introduced her to him three years earlier. All of Acheson's job-hunting efforts were suddenly put on hold when Supreme Court Associate Justice Louis D. Brandeis asked his friend Frankfurter if the latter had a student he could recommend as a law clerk. Frankfurter immediately recommended his star pupil, and Acheson jumped at the opportunity.[18]

In September 1919 Acheson arrived in Washington, D.C., the city that he would call home for the next half century, to take up his new responsibilities. His clerkship with the eminent Brandeis, the very personification of early twentieth-century liberalism, proved a crucial influence on the ambitious young lawyer. The first Jewish justice on the Supreme Court, appointed by President Woodrow Wilson just three years earlier, Brandeis was a stern taskmaster who held his twenty-six-year-old law clerk to the highest standards. "Brandeis possessed an almost stultifying sense of perfection," Acheson later marveled.[19] Given responsibility for researching and writing the first draft of the justice's opinions, he adopted the same meticulous habits of thought and logic in argumentation as his mentor. Brandeis taught Acheson to be guided always by the essential facts of the case at hand. During his two years as a Supreme Court clerk, consequently, Acheson became, like his mentor, both a confirmed empiricist and a pragmatist.

Acheson developed the deepest admiration not only for the rigor and precision of Brandeis's approach to the law but also for the judge's core values and for the way he conducted himself personally and professionally. He saw in Brandeis a man of the highest principles, one who lived his life with integrity, discipline, simplicity, and a commitment to the eternal verities.[20] Acheson formed his own incipient code of conduct in those years, a code that owed much to the powerful example of the towering Brandeis—and to that of his own father, who had by then risen to become the Episcopal Bishop of Connecticut. As Frankfurter later observed, Acheson grew convinced that "a code makes a man meaningful and organic; a whole man, a living civilized and free being. Otherwise one is a flaccid and vacillating creature."[21] The young law clerk placed integrity, loyalty, and allegiance to the truth at the very top of his hierarchy of values.

Acheson also learned from Brandeis that the law could not be divorced from questions of social justice. The Harvard Law School graduate came to share his mentor's fear of unregulated social conflict, much as he came to prize order and rationality. The justice's disdain for universal schemes aimed at the improvement of humankind and the perfection of society also made a lifelong impression on Acheson. He perceptively identified Brandeis less as the idealistic social visionary of popular legend than as a firmly grounded pragmatist devoted to incremental progress. In a letter to Frankfurter, in November 1920, Acheson reflected on an attribute he particularly admired about Brandeis. "It seems to me greater to be able with full knowledge of the facts to put a lifetime of the same energy and courage into gaining an inch, or even into preventing a loss, which other people put into a vision of world salvation," he ruminated.[22] Acheson's essential outlook on life, his core values, and his habits of thought were all stamped in fundamental ways under Brandeis's demanding but warm tutelage. Two decades later he called the judge "one of the greatest and most revered figures of our time" and described him as a man who had an enormous effect on all who were fortunate enough to begin their careers under his "guiding hand."[23]

During his two-year stint with Brandeis, Acheson also came into regular contact with the other Supreme Court justices, none of whom made a stronger impression or exerted a more profound impact than Oliver Wendell Holmes Jr. When Acheson first met him, the stately Holmes was seventy-six years old. A thrice-wounded Civil War veteran who had known Ralph Waldo Emerson and William and Henry James, Holmes doubtless struck the young law clerk as a figure from another era. Yet from the moment of his initial encounter with the distinguished justice, Acheson fell under Holmes's spell—succumbing, he later conceded, to a classic case of hero-worshipping. There was "about Mr. Justice Holmes a grandeur which I have experienced in only one other person," he recalled in a 1956 speech to the American Law Institute, "and that is General George Marshall. When those two men . . . entered a room, you had a feeling that a presence came in; when they left, you had a feeling that a light was turned out."

The Olympian Supreme Court member and the impressionable law clerk formed an odd bond. Acheson delighted in Holmes's "vast sense of the joy and eagerness and beauty of life."[24] The aged justice, for his part, found the company of a smart, deferential, and eager-to-learn law graduate a half century his junior to be refreshing. Holmes invited "Brandeis' lad, Atchison," as he once referred to him in a private letter, to his home frequently for wide-ranging discussions. Those usually left Acheson awed, and inspired, by the sweep of the grand old man's intellect.[25] The father of legal realism, as contemporary scholars typically salute him, Holmes helped solidify many of the lessons Acheson had imbibed from Brandeis about the imperative need for factual precision and for a pragmatic, experience-based approach to the law. Acheson would quote freely from Holmes's famous opinions and clever aphorisms throughout his life. He identified him to numerous friends and acquaintances as a personal hero and, on numerous occasions, as "the 'greatest' man I have known."[26]

Holmes's dictum that "General propositions do not decide concrete cases" became a particular favorite of Acheson's. Acheson frequently cited it as a signpost of his own legal—and, later, diplomatic and political—philosophy. "It seems to me profitless to be for or against things in broad categories depending either on the persons who advocate them or upon general principles of a great and sweeping nature," he confided in a 1937 letter. "It is much more satisfying to me to consider specific proposals from the point of view of whether they are practicable methods of dealing with immediate problems."[27] The echoes of Holmes—as well as Brandeis and Frankfurter—in that statement of foundational principles could hardly have been clearer.

It is difficult to imagine a young person of ambition having found mentors any more eminent, influential, or well placed than Acheson's golden trio of Frankfurter, Brandeis, and Holmes. Under their guidance, his own budding sense of destiny, nurtured from childhood by his parents, deepened substantially. A mere six years after graduating from Yale, Acheson now stood poised to make his mark. The Acheson of those years already exuded a striking self-confidence, a trait that distinguished him even from peers who had enjoyed more privileged backgrounds. That aura of self-assurance sometimes crossed over into arrogance, haughtiness, and a condescending sense of superiority; those too constituted elements of his developing style and demeanor.

As his final year with Brandeis drew to a close, Acheson faced a professional crossroads. He weighed a number of employment options, including an offer to teach at the University of Michigan Law School and a position as a labor lawyer with the United Mine Workers at the union's Springfield, Illinois, offices. Brandeis pushed Acheson to "get himself hitched up to some job with labor folk," suggesting to Frankfurter that such a post might enable his able assistant to contribute essays on labor issues to the *New Republic*, the liberal weekly that Brandeis himself often wrote for.[28] Acheson was evidently reluctant to relocate to the Midwest—"What are these places like?" he queried a friend. "I mean are they dominated by sparkplug manufacturers and oily Baptists?" He instead followed up on a representation made on his behalf by Yale friend Norman Hapgood with the new Washington law firm, Covington and Burling.[29] Its senior partners, doubtless impressed by the Brandeis imprimatur, offered Acheson a position helping to prepare an international claim brought by Norway and scheduled to be argued before the World Court at The Hague. This proved still another remarkably fortuitous break for Acheson. He joined the firm in 1922, helped win the Norwegian case in a spectacular debut, and just four years later, at the age of thirty-two, became a partner. Acheson specialized in corporate law and handled a number of cases that involved the federal government, a developing specialization of Covington and Burling. The firm rapidly established itself as one of Washington's most prestigious, and Acheson's reputation rose along with that of the firm.

By the late 1920s and early 1930s, Acheson had gained widespread recognition as one of the capital's most astute and accomplished attorneys, a reputation abetted by his consummate skill in handling appeals before both the U.S. District Court of Appeals and the Supreme Court. He managed to win approximately 20 percent of his Supreme Court appeals, a batting average that compared favorably with those of the very best appellate lawyers. In 1931, despite a losing argument before the Supreme Court in a difficult water rights case, both Holmes and Brandeis were so impressed by their protégé's performance that they personally complimented him—an exceptionally rare gesture from the exacting Brandeis and one that Acheson found especially touching.[30] As Frankfurter recalled in a 1960 interview, "Dean was a hot-house product in the best sense of the word. Everything conspired to enhance his reputation and position in Washington in those early years. He and his wife were a socially attractive couple. Both had poise and brains; both were charming and exciting people."[31]

The Achesons cultivated a wide circle of friends in those years, mingling regularly with people from the worlds of law, government, politics, and the arts. They prospered financially as well and lived quite comfortably. In 1922 the Achesons bought a small, mid-nineteenth-century house in Georgetown, the not yet fashionable section of Washington that still contained a sizable African-American population. Two years later they purchased a rambling farmhouse in Sandy Spring, Maryland, less than twenty miles outside Washington, where they would frequently retreat on weekends with their three children in tow. The rather primitive, unheated, 1795-built farmhouse, tagged "Harewood," helped Acheson recapture some of the rural charm of his own happy childhood in Middletown. Between the children, Alice's painting, Dean's flourishing legal career, gardening and horseback riding at Harewood, and an exceptionally active social life in Washington, theirs would have appeared to friends and casual acquaintances alike as a quite full and satisfying life.

Yet for a lawyer in a firm whose founding partners included a former Maryland congressman and an ex–Bull Moose Party insurgent, and who counted the politically engaged Frankfurter and Brandeis as role models, politics beckoned. With his residence in Maryland as a base, Acheson joined and became active in the Democratic Party of Montgomery County, attending local meetings and participating in county political campaigns. In 1928 Acheson actively supported the presidential campaign of New York governor Al Smith, the Democratic nominee. His enthusiasm for Smith and contempt for what he ridiculed as eight years of Republican torpor impelled Acheson to "begin an education in public speaking" on the candidate's behalf throughout

Montgomery County. After the disappointment of Smith's loss, he continued to dip his toe in political waters. In 1930 he made a number of trips to New Jersey to campaign for senatorial hopeful Dwight Morrow, a progressive Republican and personal friend of one of Acheson's law partners.[32]

Following a firsthand exposure to the rough-and-tumble politicking at the Democrats' 1932 national nominating convention in Chicago, Acheson vigorously supported nominee Franklin D. Roosevelt as a member of the Maryland State Democratic Campaign Advisory Committee. In his own recollection, he "took an energetic hand in a rough local campaign–organized meetings, made speeches, met with the Democratic Advisory Committee, and . . . took over the writing of political tracts." After Roosevelt's electoral triumph, and with senior partner J. Harry Covington's blessing and support, Acheson was invited to attend meetings at the White House aimed at drafting the incoming administration's legislative program. "Thus," he later wrote, "does one get drawn closer and closer to the flypaper of taking part in Government."[33]

THE "FLYPAPER" OF GOVERNMENT SERVICE

The well-connected Acheson vied openly for a high-level position in the Roosevelt administration. "The adventure for which I yearned," he recollected years later, "was to be Solicitor General of the United States."[34] That post, the number two position in the Justice Department, would have placed Acheson in charge of all of the government's appellate litigation and given him the responsibility for arguing the most important cases presented by the Justice Department before the Supreme Court. For a skilled appellate lawyer, it seemed the ideal government position. As fate would have it, President Roosevelt initially offered the post to Felix Frankfurter, who turned it down because of his recent acceptance of a prestigious visiting professorship at Oxford University. Frankfurter in turn recommended his former student to Roosevelt. The president almost certainly would have given Acheson the nod if not for the adamant opposition of Attorney General Homer Cummings, still evidently nursing a grievance against Acheson's father for the Episcopalian bishop's refusal to give the oft-married Cummings's latest matrimonial venture his ecclesiastical blessing. Acheson described his disappointment, in what up to that point in his life was a rare personal setback, as devastating–"a crushing blow."[35]

A very different opportunity soon emerged. In a classic case of the "old boy" network in operation, two of Acheson's friends, each a senior official in the outgoing Herbert Hoover administration's Treasury Department, invited him to join them for lunch with William Woodin, Roosevelt's appointee to be the new treasury secretary. They had praised businessman Woodin to him in advance as "a man after our own hearts." Then, following a luncheon he described as "gay, uninhibited," Acheson almost immediately received a phone call from Woodin offering him the position of undersecretary of the Treasury. The strong backing of Acheson's personal friend and fishing partner Lewis W. Douglas, FDR's budget director, doubtless influenced Woodin's choice as well. Acheson's inexperience in government and lack of training and expertise in monetary and fiscal issues might have given him pause in considering so important a subcabinet post. They did not. Supremely confident, Acheson breezily responded to a senator who asked about his previous financial experience: "None at all." Anxious to undertake a new "adventure," the forty-year-old Acheson was sworn in as the Treasury Department's second highest ranking officer on May 19, 1933.[36]

From the first, he found himself caught in the tangled thicket of New Deal monetary policy. The position became especially nettlesome when a serious illness forced Woodin to seek medical treatment in New York, thus leaving Acheson as the acting secretary of the Treasury within his very first month of government service. As such, Acheson was drawn ever more deeply into complex policy deliberations during an exceptionally tumultuous period. He represented the Treasury at the president's weekly cabinet meetings, where he typically took the seat to Roosevelt's immediate left. Initially, Acheson's relationship with FDR went well; their common Groton schooling helped, as did the close friendship each shared with Felix Frankfurter. But Acheson's proper style inevitably clashed with that of the freewheeling president who thought nothing of summoning senior officials to early morning meetings in his bedroom, during which young grandchildren frequently ran wild. Such meetings offended Acheson's sense of propriety; he found Roosevelt "condescending" and, moreover, his manner of dealing with subordinates as "patronizing and humiliating."[37]

Sharp differences over the legal scope of presidential authority with regard to a controversial government gold-purchase plan further beclouded his relationship with the president and led to Acheson's forced resignation a mere six months after his appointment. The contretemps stemmed from FDR's determination to stimulate a rise in prices as a means to increase productivity and thereby help lift the nation out of the Depression. Some of his top financial experts recommended that the president could advance that goal by depreciating the value of the dollar. That, in turn, meant increasing the price of gold. But Congress had fixed the price of gold by law at $20.67 an ounce, and Acheson, still very much the correct lawyer, fretted that it would violate existing statutes if the president authorized the purchase of gold at a higher price. In August 1933 Attorney General Cummings and other senior officials supported Roosevelt's decision to pay a higher price for gold, but Acheson adamantly refused to go along with the scheme, citing the absence of an explicit legal authorization. He insisted, with more than a touch of self-righteousness, "I would not violate the law." What he saw as a principled stand led to "a searing row" with a president who soon made it clear to his acting secretary of the Treasury that "anyone who could not accept his decisions could get out but could not stay and oppose them." Roosevelt's anger with Acheson had by then become palpable. In mid-November, recognizing that he would soon be dismissed, Acheson tendered a gracious and dignified letter of resignation to the president.[38]

Acheson's first stint in government, however abbreviated and inglorious, left a lasting imprint. Although Acheson appears never to have doubted that his position on the legally dubious gold-buying plan was both principled and correct, he subsequently came to recognize that a more pragmatic and adaptive response to the chief executive's political needs at the time might have been warranted.[39] Indeed, he became acutely aware in the aftermath of this episode that one of the most fundamental challenges for a public official lay in discerning the proper balance between principle and pragmatism—between holding fast to one's personal code of honor and accommodating to every extent possible the needs and priorities of one's boss. Clearly, Acheson relished his government service and found the aura of power and public responsibility that it conferred to be invigorating. As much as he might have enjoyed the fight with FDR for the opportunity it afforded to reaffirm his honor and the bedrock principles by which he lived, Acheson regretted the falling out—and, particularly, the distancing from the center of power that resulted. "The heady experience of being in on big political decisions was like getting used to French cuisine," Frankfurter quipped years later. "Once Dean had dined on such rare meat it was painful to return to the hardtack of the law."[40] At the time, Acheson confessed to a friend that while it was "strangely quiet and peaceful to be practicing the law again," it "also seems somewhat dull."[41] It hardly exaggerates to see the years following his dismissal from the Treasury Department as constituting a gradual, step-by-step movement back into FDR's good graces. Tellingly, he entitles the chapter of his memoir dealing with this period, "The Road Back."

Acheson's return to the practice of law as a senior partner at the firm now known as Covington, Burling, Rublee, Acheson, and Shorb was seamless. His resignation from the Roosevelt administration over the question of governmental currency manipulation actually enhanced his status in the business and financial communities as a person of "sound" judgment. During the mid- and late 1930s, Acheson handled a wide array of cases; his reputation as one of Washington's top attorneys at one of its premier law firms seemed secure. He also took on some new public service responsibilities during this period. In 1937 he was named a trustee of the Brookings Institution, one of the nation's leading think tanks, and that same year was elected as a member of the Yale Corporation, the university's powerful governing board.

Acheson also began to mend fences with FDR. He rejected an invitation from two friends to join a "Democrats for Landon" movement during the 1936 presidential campaign. Instead, he wrote a letter to the *Baltimore Sun*, proclaiming his opposition to Republican nominee Alfred Landon and unqualified support for the Democratic ticket. Although he never developed much personal affection for Roosevelt and described to a friend his support for a president whose "recklessness in finance" could one day "ruin us" as decidedly "unenthusiastic," Acheson increasingly came to respect many of Roosevelt's New Deal initiatives. On several occasions, he even criticized the Supreme Court's actions in declaring some important New Deal laws unconstitutional, charging the court with violating the dictates of judicial restraint.[42]

When FDR nominated Frankfurter for a seat on the Supreme Court early in 1939, his old law professor asked Acheson to represent him at the congressional oversight hearings. Following Frankfurter's bravura performance before the Senate Judiciary Committee, the professor insisted that Acheson accompany him on a spontaneous trip to the White House to see the president. As a Roosevelt intimate, frequent visitor, and virtual one-man recruiting agency for the New Deal bureaucracy, Frankfurter gained immediate entry. A relaxed, convivial meeting, marked with much laughter, ensued. Acheson's insubordination as acting treasury secretary now evidently forgiven, Roosevelt phoned several weeks later to offer him a judgeship on the U.S. Court of Appeals in Washington. The still very ambitious young lawyer politely declined, believing that at forty-five he was "too young for a life sentence to such a sedentary confinement." He also passed on an offer FDR made the next day, during a private White House chat, to become an assistant attorney general with responsibility in the area of civil rights. Even if unwilling at this juncture to accept the president's gracious overtures, Acheson must have felt great satisfaction in knowing that he had regained FDR's trust. His vigorous support of the administration's foreign policy as the shadows of war descended on Europe made that redemption complete.[43]

The German-Soviet invasion of Poland on September 1, 1939, led to the outbreak of war—and sparked Dean Acheson's transformation, virtually overnight, into a high-profile public figure. "Our world for the second time in my lifetime," Acheson later lamented, "was blown apart."[44] He quickly aligned himself with the Committee to Defend America by Aiding the Allies, a group that set itself in firm opposition to the America First Committee, which was seeking to prevent the United States from being dragged into war under any circumstances. Almost immediately, Acheson emerged as a leading spokesman. On November 28, 1939, he gave a stirring public address at an annual dinner at Yale University, a hotbed of isolationist sentiment, in which he laid out his own developing perspective on the global crisis with clarity, bluntness, and passion. In his remarks, Acheson emphasized the magnitude of the stakes for the United States in the ongoing struggles in Europe and Asia, displaying a remarkable prescience. "I think it is clear that with a nation, as with a boxer, one of the greatest assurances of safety is to add reach to power," he declared. To achieve that essential goal, Acheson insisted that the United States needed to develop "a navy and air force adequate to secure us in both oceans simultaneously and with striking power sufficient to reach to the other side of one of them." Such enhanced power was necessary both to guarantee American security and, assuming that the old economic and political order could not be revived, to assume a lead role in forging a new one.

Above all, he called for the United States to develop a "realistic policy." For him, that meant a policy that recognized that "our vital interests do not permit us to be indifferent to the outcome of the present war in Europe—and, may I add, to the present war in Asia." A realistic policy must derive not from "emotional or even moral or ideological sympathy" with those nations that were victims of aggression but rather from a clearheaded analysis of the disastrous consequences for the United States of a victory by the Soviet-German and Japanese aggressors. He spelled those out with chilling precision: "Our internment on this continent and such portion of the one to the south as we can physically control. Here, surrounded by armed and hostile camps, we will have to conduct our economy as best we can and attempt to preserve the security and dignity of human life and the freedom of the human spirit."

Acheson repeated Holmes's famous aphorism that "the judgment of nature upon error is death." In yet another echo of that consummate realist—the man whose thinking remained probably the most powerful intellectual influence on him—Acheson argued that the United States must balance risk against gain. The gain from providing aid to the allies, in his view, far outweighed any risks such a policy might entail. "We are in the most enviable position," Acheson averred, "of having other people who must of necessity fight the forces which are hostile to us. We can see to it that those conscripts of necessity have the weapons and supplies with which to fight." Plainly, the United States would be courting disaster if it failed to recognize and adapt to the grave peril to its security and its way of life posed by the actions of powers hostile to the nation's vital interests. Acheson thus recommended a threefold program of action. First, build sufficient air and naval power to guarantee the nation's security; second, "recognize that the further destruction of world order threatens our most vital interests and use and support the peoples who must fight those from whom the offense cometh"; and, third, be willing to assume some responsibility for the reconstruction of "a world of order" so as "to avoid having forced upon us the limitations of a world collapsing about our ears." The economic attributes of any such order were indispensable building blocks, in his view; they included open trade links, nondiscrimination, and the encouragement of the free flow of capital and goods.[45]

It is difficult to explain with any degree of precision how so sophisticated and full blown a strategic vision emerged at this juncture from a man who had no direct prior experience with the worlds of diplomacy or military affairs. Acheson's extensive private papers, unfortunately, offer surprisingly few clues to his evolving foreign policy views. Discussion of the German-Japanese threat and its implications for U.S. security was, of course, a staple within the elite Washington circles that Acheson inhabited at this time. He could not have avoided exposure to and involvement in such debates. Acheson's well developed habits of thought, moreover, especially his reverence for Holmesian realism, would have predisposed him to appraise the German-Japanese challenge through a risk-benefit matrix. Additionally, his close relationship and daily contact with Frankfurter, a vociferous opponent of Nazism and a man whose family had suffered personally from the brutality of Hitler's minions, probably sensitized Acheson early to the unique threat that the Third Reich posed to the values of Western civilization he so treasured. Whatever the exact mix of reasons, Acheson developed an analysis of the role of power and geopolitics in world affairs during this period that would guide his thinking not just during this crisis but throughout the remainder of his life.[46]

Years later Acheson reflected on the complex dilemmas that the Nazi regime's brutal internal policies posed for Americans unaccustomed to seeing connections between domestic repression and a state's external behavior. In an off-the-record speech at the National War College, he remarked that Americans have typically taken the attitude "that the internal affairs of a nation, particularly our own, are no concern of other people." So when Hitler's "inexcusable persecution of the Jews" became common knowledge, many Americans were "profoundly disturbed." They also grew disturbed about "the suppression of every sort of liberty in Germany, and the creation of the police state." Yet many thought that while Germany's internal policies were wrong, and they deeply resented them, those remained matters strictly internal to Germany—not matters of direct concern to the United States. Belatedly, he reflected, Americans learned some crucial lessons: "There are internal developments which inevitably affect the people outside of the country concerned. There are internal developments which lead inevitably to an aggressive foreign adventure." Unfortunately, he conceded, "It took years to see that."[47]

He saw it much earlier than most. On June 4, 1940, just before France's capitulation to the German invaders, Acheson delivered a second major foreign policy speech, this one before the International Ladies Garment Workers' Union in New York's Carnegie Hall. Once again, he railed that the threat posed to vital U.S. interests by German aggression must be recognized and countered. "Those who would doom you paint with blood upon half the earth," he thundered. "Theirs is a fighting faith, to which they bring unswerving purpose and competence, courage and cruelty, ruthlessness and power. They can be met only with greater power and steadfastness." He urged his audience not to be lulled into complacency by the foolish arguments that "the dictators have no quarrel with America" and that "they could not reach us if they would." Such naiveté had brought calamitous results in Austria, Czechoslovakia, Belgium, Holland, France, and Great Britain. "We are faced with elemental, unmoral, ruthless power," he insisted. "In dealing with it, we can be wrong only once. Remember, I beseech you, that the judgment of nature upon error is death." He then proceeded to underscore some of the possible consequences of a German conquest of Europe. Those included German control over the remnants of the British and French battle fleets and the huge British merchant fleet that together would enable Germany to become the globe's dominant naval power; the likelihood of German penetration of South or Central America and the concomitant establishment of military bases there; and the internal danger posed by those within the United States who sympathized with German efficiency or who preferred appeasement to confrontation.

For all those reasons, "the defeat of the western democracies would be a disaster striking at the very foundation of American security and the freedom of the American people," he said emphatically. "That defeat can and must be prevented." Acheson called for a gargantuan mobilization effort that he admitted would cost billions of dollars and require enormous sacrifice on the part of all Americans. He then closed with a stirring call to arms: "To shrink from this decision, to be satisfied with anything short of it, is to risk the error upon which the judgment is death, the death of hundreds of thousands of our men, the death of everything which life in America holds for us."[48]

The Carnegie Hall speech garnered considerable public attention. By then, Acheson had become one of the most visible and articulate of the private citizens who were rallying the public to meet the threat posed by Axis aggression. Throughout this period he stayed in close touch with top Roosevelt administration officials, including key White House adviser Harry Hopkins. Following the fall of France and the onset of the Battle of Britain, Acheson took an even more active role. Responding to what he saw as the administration's unfortunate hesitance to provide aid to Britain at its hour of most dire need, Acheson and fellow lawyer and friend Benjamin V. Cohen drafted a brief that asserted the president's legal authority to transfer World War I–vintage destroyers to the British, with or without congressional authorization. British prime minister Winston S. Churchill had, in the previous month, requested the transfer of "fifty or sixty of your oldest destroyers," but the administration had dragged its feet in responding for fear of arousing congressional opposition. On August 11, 1940, the brief, signed by Acheson and a number of other top lawyers whom he helped recruit for the purpose, was published in full on the editorial page of the *New York Times.* The position staked out there—that the president's constitutional power in the realm of foreign affairs allowed the bypassing of Congress on a matter of demonstrable national security interest—quickly received a legal stamp of approval from Attorney General Robert H. Jackson.

Acheson's legal opinion proved exceptionally helpful to Roosevelt, who had been seeking a way to respond positively to Churchill's plea without igniting a firestorm within Congress. It paved the way for the important Destroyers-for-Bases deal of September 3, 1940. His initiative on this crucial matter also enabled Acheson to redeem himself fully in the president's eyes; he was now using the law to justify executive action rather than, as in the earlier flap over the gold-buying plan, using the law to hamstring presidential initiative.[49] "The danger to [our institutions] seems not in resolving legal doubts in accordance with national interest," he remarked to Wall Street lawyer and fly-fishing buddy John J. McCloy, "but in refusing to act when action is imperative."[50]

Acheson restated his firm position on the critical issue of whether or not to aid Great Britain in a national radio program, broadcast on October 6. Pitted against two strong isolationist senators who displayed rabid anti-British biases, Acheson more than held his own. Characteristically, he framed the issue with crystal clarity and proceeded to defend his position with logic and passion. Describing the American people as having luxuriated for too long in "irresponsible security," Acheson said that they had now awakened in shock "to find ourselves the object of a hostile alliance which is making the greatest play in history to control all Europe and Asia and Africa and which makes no secret of its ambitions in this hemisphere." Americans had owed their security in the past, he stressed, to the existence of the British Navy and its benign control of the Atlantic. Now, Hitler's military machine was threatening to extinguish that crucial line of defense. "Not even the greatest stretch of my imagination, or yours," Acheson asserted, "could picture the incalculable disaster which the loss of that fleet could mean to us." Not to aid Britain when confronting "the greatest danger which we have ever faced in our entire national life" would amount to "mad folly." In response to the standard isolationist plea for avoiding entanglement with Britain and its empire, Acheson laid bare what he saw as the core issue: "that a German victory in this war would be a terrific disaster for the United States and that a British victory in this war would mean security for the United States." Closing with a paraphrase of his favorite Holmes quote, Acheson reminded his listeners across the country that "the judgment of nature upon error in this case is death."[51] To an erstwhile critic who misunderstood Acheson's argument, he restated it a few days later as succinctly as he could: "When a bully has said in no uncertain terms that our turn is next it is the height of folly for us not to help those who are fighting him now."[52]

The prodigal son was now moving ever closer into FDR's inner circle. That same month Acheson was summoned to the White House to partake in a discussion of the president's election campaign. FDR's bid for an unprecedented third term of office had hit some snags and Acheson was struck by the pessimism he heard being expressed among the president and his aides. When Roosevelt asked for his opinion, Acheson, with trademark bravado, proposed that the Democrats take the offensive against a Republican Party that, in the past, "had let us drift to the very brink of disaster with assurances that recovery was just around the corner." He insisted on the need to link the great opportunities the New Deal had opened up for ordinary Americans with the current threat to American freedom posed by the Axis powers. Impressed, Roosevelt asked Acheson to put his thoughts on paper and to present a memorandum by the next evening to Harry Hopkins.[53]

Whether his call for a more vigorous, go-on-the-offense approach made any difference in the tenor of the final weeks of the 1940 presidential campaign cannot be determined. What was abundantly clear by then, however, was that the young lawyer who had once crossed swords with FDR over a matter of principle had more than earned his way back into the fold. The president referred to Acheson privately at that time as "without question the ablest lawyer in Washington."[54] At the end of the year, following Roosevelt's third great electoral success, Secretary of State Cordell Hull, at Roosevelt's insistence, invited Acheson to join the State Department as the assistant secretary of state for economic affairs. Why remain, as Hull put it, on the fringes of power? Acheson wrestled with the offer. "It was an insane decision," he recollected, "for a supposedly responsible professional man, dependent on his earnings, with a wife and three children at their most expensive age. And I knew nothing of the Department of State, its internal and interdepartmental feuds and frustrations."

Yet the call of public service proved too strong to resist for a man as patriotic, ambitious, and self-confident about his abilities as Acheson was. He saw the world "moving toward a cataclysm," and he later described himself as "too conscious of this, too restless even to want to escape the current." Consequently, on February 1, 1941, accompanied by his wife and Justice Frankfurter, among others, he was sworn into office at the Connecticut Avenue apartment of Justice Brandeis—the very apartment where he had spent so much time decades earlier as a neophyte lawyer in training. Brandeis personally administered the oath of office to his former law clerk, with the proud Frankfurter—Acheson's first and most important professional and intellectual mentor and now his closest personal friend—looking on. It was a solemn, yet joyous, occasion. And it must have been a highly emotional and deeply gratifying moment for all three: America's two most famous and accomplished Jews of that era and the High Anglican whose intellectual potential both recognized long ago and had done so much to encourage, nurture, and sculpt.[55]

2

FROM WORLD WAR TO COLD WAR:
CLIMBING THE RUNGS OF POWER

STATE DEPARTMENT APPRENTICESHIP

Having made the leap from high-profile citizen-activist to government official, Acheson naturally craved a role commensurate with his ambition, energy, and ability. Leading newspapers praised his appointment. The *Washington Post*, lauding Acheson as "one of this city's outstanding attorneys," called him "especially well qualified," while the *New York Times* hailed Acheson as "eminently fitted for the post to which the President has named him" by way of "personality . . . intellect and integrity." Yet the responsibilities of the position that he formally assumed on February 2, 1941, were as modest as they were ambiguous, offering a rather limited field of action for a man of Acheson's activist proclivities. Although the assistant secretary of state for economic affairs was officially charged with responsibility for the "coordination of commercial and economic questions with questions of major policy," a not inconsiderable assignment, much of this coordinating responsibility, in reality, had been usurped by other State Department offices. Worse, the exigencies of war had reduced to "a bare minimum" his bureau's usual activities. At a time when the fate of the world seemed to be hanging in the balance, Acheson soon found his energies consumed with such diversions as trade agreements with Ecuador, Haiti, and the Dominican Republic, the negotiation of a treaty of commerce, navigation, and consular rights with India, and extended trade talks with

Iceland. The latter taught him "more about sheepskins than I wanted to know." The real action, as Acheson was keenly aware, was occurring elsewhere.[1]

Nor was the State Department itself the key player that Acheson thought it should have been in the Roosevelt administration's national security planning. It was presided over by Cordell Hull, a cautious, courtly, slow-speaking Tennessean whose single-minded devotion, ever since his appointment in 1933, had been to the elimination of tariffs and other trade restrictions so as to help forge a more economically integrated, less contentious, and more peaceful world. Those were worthy goals, to be sure, and goals that Acheson fully endorsed, as his public speeches and private comments of the past few years made abundantly clear. Like Hull, Acheson believed that unfettered commerce stood as a fundamental prerequisite for the stable world order and durable structure of peace that both considered essential. Yet the former congressman's fixation on the promotion of free trade, to the virtual exclusion of all other foreign policy priorities, rendered him peculiarly ill-equipped to deal with a world at war–a world in which issues of geopolitics, military strength, and strategic maneuvering had eclipsed matters of trade and tariffs. Hull and the department he led were woefully unprepared for that world, a fact that the perceptive Acheson quickly discerned. "The prewar State Department," he later observed acidly, "was closer to its nineteenth century predecessors in both what it did and how the work was done than to the department I was later to command." Acheson also complained that, "some brilliant exceptions" aside, the State Department of that period–indeed, the entire bureaucracy–remained ill suited to the essential task of assessing the capabilities and intentions of America's principal adversaries. "The position of the United States had undergone a drastic change," he recognized; regrettably, "the purposes and capabilities of the State Department had not."[2]

Acheson, of course, had not returned to government "to dream in a somnolent office," as he later put it.[3] Consequently, he looked for ways to insinuate himself into the ongoing policy battles about America's role in a world at war. He was convinced, as he had repeatedly emphasized in public addresses during the past year and a half, that the United States was already deeply and unavoidably enmeshed in both the European and Asian conflicts. He was equally certain that those struggles profoundly impinged upon America's vital interests. Recent developments—from the German conquest of France and much of Western Europe to the battle of Britain to Japan's increasing pressures on Southeast Asia—demanded forthright U.S. action in support of those interests before it became too late. Armed with those strong convictions, Acheson found that "the handiest entrance . . . to the field of action" was afforded by his supervision of the department's Division of Controls. When the new assistant secretary took office, that division was embroiled in an intense debate about whether, and how, to apply economic controls or sanctions against Japan in order to check its expansionist appetite. The key issue that soon emerged concerned the embargo, or drastic reduction, of petroleum exports to Tokyo—over and above the already embargoed aviation gasoline. "The aim was to limit Japanese military action in East and Southeast Asia; the danger, provoking Japan to seize or intimidate the Dutch East Indies—a great source of petroleum—or to move against us."[4] Acheson assumed a lead role in ensuring that an embargo policy with teeth placed the Japanese on the defensive. Indeed, his bureau interpreted FDR's loosely defined oil embargo directive of July 1941 in so firm and unambiguous a manner that Tokyo's military rulers came to see a clash with the United States as unavoidable.[5]

The Japanese attack on Pearl Harbor of December 7, 1941, caught Acheson completely by surprise, as it did most Americans—inside and outside of government. Having received the news while enjoying a relaxing Sunday afternoon at Harewood, Acheson rushed to the State Department, following accounts of the disaster on his car radio en route. From Acheson's perspective, Japan's attack and Germany's subsequent declaration of war on the United States at least had the welcome effect of unveiling America's mortal enemies and thus clarifying the nation's goals. "Our immediate military task was clear," he recollected in his memoir; "what should be our longer-range political aims and purposes, what were our major difficulties and dangers, remained shrouded in obscurity."

The State Department, to the frustration of this confirmed activist, seemed without direction at a crucial moment; if not technically leaderless, it seemed "adrift, carried hither and yon by the currents of war or pushed about by more purposeful craft." Never a member of Roosevelt's inner circle, Hull found his influence—along with that of the entire department he headed—even more circumscribed after U.S. entry into the war. Whereas the government overnight became a beehive of activity and energy, the State Department, in Acheson's biting depiction, "stood breathless and bewildered like an old lady at a busy intersection during rush hour."[6]

As assistant secretary of state for economic affairs, Acheson's responsibilities immediately expanded into the important, if murky, realm of economic warfare. Part of this portfolio—the task of procuring critical strategic resources for the war effort—drifted into the hands of more bureaucratically adept and well-placed actors outside the State Department, to Acheson's dismay. The bulk of his involvement in this sphere, as a result, was limited to the other side of the economic warfare coin: namely, the effort to curtail or cut off entirely the overland trade between Europe's neutral nations and the German enemy. The core problem posed by wartime neutrality, as during World War I, was that the neutrals were contributing to German strength by maintaining trade links. Determined to block German commerce with neutrals such as Sweden, Switzerland, Spain, and Portugal, Acheson pushed for a tougher U.S. stance—a policy with teeth. The challenge for the United States and Great Britain proved both delicate and complex. On the one hand, the German war machine could be weakened if it were deprived of the strategic resources and revenue derived from trade with the neutrals; on the other hand, the abrupt severance of trade with Germany, as Acheson advocated, might induce direct German aggression or occupation, or so the neutrals argued.

As was his wont, Acheson tended to downplay the risks. He viewed Germany as much less of a military threat to the neutrals than Sweden, Spain, and others averred. He dismissed their protests as mere rationalizations trotted out to cloak the selfish pursuit of economic benefits. Yet his strenuous efforts to apply pressure on Germany's neutral trading partners bore meager fruit; even Acheson himself conceded that, until the tide of battle had turned decisively in the second half of 1944, the results of his exertions proved marginal. The Swiss did not prohibit arms exports to Germany until October 1, 1944, and did not close one route until a month before the war's end. For its part, Francisco Franco's Spain refused to embargo the shipment of strategic materials to Germany until the waning days of the European conflict. Acheson thus learned an important lesson from this difficult episode about the ability of smaller nations to frustrate the designs of great powers.[7]

Economic relations with America's wartime allies constituted another policy arena in which Acheson assumed a lead role. Those proved nearly as contentious as the controversies surrounding neutral trade. A vigorous proponent as a private citizen of all aid to Britain short of direct U.S. cobelligerency, Acheson hailed as visionary FDR's enunciation, in December 1940, of the lend-lease idea. He was in government when the Lend-Lease Act was signed into law on March 11, 1941, stipulating that the United States would sell, lease, or lend any armaments or defense articles that the president considered necessary to any country whose defense he deemed vital to U.S. security. Hull delegated to Acheson the responsibility for negotiating a specific agreement with Britain to govern the transfer of American matériel. His opposite number on the British side was the eminent economist John Maynard Keynes, a brilliant if imperious man whom Acheson found as charming and urbane as he could be steely across the conference table. An intimate dinner at Frankfurter's apartment, shortly after Keynes's arrival in Washington, ensured that their personal relationship began on the right foot.

During their initial discussions, Acheson and Keynes reached a general agreement that the "excessive economic nationalism" of the prewar years and the "preposterous trade barriers" that resulted needed to be replaced with a system of free international trade. Yet the British representative presented Acheson with an initial draft agreement, on July 24, 1941, that called simply for the return after the war of all unused equipment of American origin. Since it required no obligations on Great Britain's part other than to accept graciously America's largesse, Acheson considered the proposal "wholly impossible." He presented Keynes four days later with an alternative draft, written jointly with Undersecretary of State Sumner Welles, that added a specific commitment to end all discrimination against one another's exports. Sensing a ploy to dismantle Britain's imperial preference trading system, Keynes rather intemperately voiced contempt for what he labeled "the lunatic proposals of Mr. Hull." In fact, Article VII was not just a product of Hull's singular passion for free trade. Rather, all components of the American policy elite, Acheson included, were agreed that the war must be followed by an end to discriminatory trade practices, a conviction that naturally extended to imperial preference. Fearing that its survival might cause "another acute economic depression," they sensed "grave dangers" to U.S. living standards and jobs if that system continued unchanged. All elements of the British government, meanwhile, believed that imperial preference could serve as a needed future bulwark given the desperate economic plight that their country would surely face after the war.

Acheson and Keynes, whose admiration and affection for each other grew during the course of these delicate negotiations, sought to compose those fundamental differences by stressing the significant areas of common ground between the two sides. Since each believed that world stability and international economic progress alike demanded a liberal, multilateral trading regime founded on the principles of free trade, such common ground was not difficult to identify. They reached a compromise agreement, accordingly, in December 1941, that made British movement toward nondiscriminatory trade contingent on liberal American tariff policies and domestic economic expansion. In February 1942 Prime Minister Churchill's firm opposition to any abandonment of imperial preference threatened to scuttle that compromise. It took a direct personal appeal from FDR to the British leader to salvage the hard-won agreement.[8]

Acheson's perseverance had paid off. Years later he complained that "the qualities which produce the dogged, unbeatable courage of the British, personified at the time in Winston Churchill, can appear in other settings as stubbornness bordering on stupidity."[9] Yet more than stubbornness or stupidity lay behind British reticence to abandon the hedge provided by their protected trading privileges within the empire. Keynes, no less than Churchill, recognized that the war was rapidly hastening Britain's economic decline and the corresponding ascendancy of the United States. Free trade invariably favors the larger, more efficient, and more productive trading state. By the middle of the twentieth century that was plainly the United States. Acheson and Keynes may have subscribed to the same basic economic principles—indeed, much evidence suggests that the British master economist served as somewhat of a tutor to the American lawyer on intricate economic matters—but each sensed that their nation's dramatically diverging financial fates demanded different policies.

Acheson was thrust into another portentous economic debate when, in January 1943, Hull tapped him to participate in negotiations with British,

Soviet, and Chinese diplomatic representatives about relief and rehabilitation planning for postwar Europe. This responsibility gave Acheson his second direct experience with the "boorishness" and "clumsy and difficult" style of Soviet diplomats. Earlier, he had helped facilitate the inaugural supply of lend-lease matériel to Moscow; the government of Joseph Stalin had become a recipient of U.S. lend-lease aid following the German invasion of June 1941 and an American ally of necessity in the war against Hitler that December. The Soviets insisted that all relief and rehabilitation efforts in Europe following the war should be funneled through an international relief organization, a position to which the Americans, the British, and the European governments in exile all acceded. Former foreign minister Maxim Litvinov, then serving as Stalin's ambassador to Washington, insisted that nothing should be done in any country "except with that country's consent and as it chose." Acheson's suggestion that relief efforts be "kept free from politics" clearly did not jibe with the Soviets' fierce determination to maintain a veto over any future foreign ventures within their own borders. "Nothing is free from politics," an amused Litvinov riposted.[10] Yet Acheson found that he could work with the wily old Bolshevik, much as he found earlier that he could work with the self-assured Keynes. When, in November 1943, the United Nations Relief and Rehabilitation Association (UNRRA) was inaugurated at a gala forty-four nation conference in Atlantic City, New Jersey, Acheson could take some justifiable pride in his own role as one of its midwives. UNRRA, moreover, served as the template for and precursor of the soon-to-be-launched United Nations.

During the war years, Acheson devoted considerable thought to the relationship between the world's economic structure and institutions and the overarching U.S. goal of a stable, peaceful, and prosperous international system. Those were intimately and inseparably connected, in his view. Well before most of his contemporaries, Hull's assistant secretary of state for economic affairs was worrying about and planning for the transition from a world at war to a postwar world sure to face gargantuan readjustment and recovery challenges. "We know that the only solution is one which provides more production everywhere for the needs of mankind which will not be denied, more employment, more trade, better living standards," he observed in a 1943 speech. "We know also that no nation can achieve this solution by isolating itself, that if any attempts to do so it not only injures itself but it imperils all others." Those long-held convictions remained central to Acheson's analysis of the proper role that the United States should assume in economic planning for the post–World War II era.

To avoid a repetition of the conflicts that wracked the interwar years, Acheson judged it imperative that the United States encourage through word and action the global expansion of production, employment, and consumption. If the United States failed to "join actively in the restoration of international trade," then the economic basis for a durable peace would erode. Such a failure would be calamitous: it would "destroy not only our markets and our customers but also our own economy and every chance of pursuing the course which we are all agreed is essential to an ordered and decent world." The Achesonian perspective held that enlightened self-interest, not some airy idealism, should guide all U.S. economic planning for the postwar years; and it held that well-conceived, collective actions by the world's main trading nations constituted the principal hope for building a liberal system of freer trade and increased production and consumption. "The process is all one process and we cannot block one artery without starting gangrene," he emphasized in a characteristically arresting analogy. The looming economic challenge of the postwar period required nothing less than decisive, concerted action. "We know that we cannot solve it by letting matters drift," he insisted. "We know that we cannot solve it by attempting to maintain here an isolated island of prosperity in a world of misery and depression."[11]

The next year Acheson played a direct role in helping forge some of the institutions he saw as essential to the achievement of those ends. He served as a member of the U.S. delegation that met at Bretton Woods, in New Hampshire's picturesque White Mountains, as part of an international conference assembled to help impart order and stability to the international monetary system. Although his personal involvement at that landmark conference remained at the margins, Acheson headed the State Department negotiating team and followed closely what he characterized as the "extraordinarily good" sessions that produced the International Monetary Fund, the International Bank for Reconstruction and Development (World Bank), and an innovative system of currency controls and convertibility. Testifying effectively before Senate committees on several occasions, he became even more centrally engaged in the administration's subsequent campaign to sell the Bretton Woods agreements on Capitol Hill. "We have created something," he proudly proclaimed to the Committee on Banking and Currency, "which goes the greatest possible distance toward creating an international monetary system in this world under which there can be international trade, under which trade can grow, and that is absolutely essential to bring any sort of order and peace to this world." Acheson proved himself an adept lobbyist, his efforts contributing to the Senate's decisive vote in favor of the new economic commitments on July 19, 1945.[12]

By then Acheson had moved to a new position in the State Department. Following the November 1944 elections, failing health had prompted Hull to resign, and Roosevelt, fresh from his latest electoral triumph, chose former U.S. Steel chief Edward R. Stettinius Jr. to replace him. Initially fearing that he was about to be sacked by the new secretary, a man whose abilities and style Acheson found wanting, he was instead assigned to the position of assistant secretary of state for congressional relations. In view of the pending need to facilitate the passage of a series of new and revised laws, treaties, and agreements, Acheson reasoned that this posting "could provide a strong position from which to influence policy." That proved a shrewd calculation. By early 1945 Acheson had become "chief lobbyist for State," as he later put it, in the process enhancing his visibility, and importance, within the administration. He assembled a crack staff, mastered the intricacies of the legislative process and backroom politicking, and even learned "to tramp the corridors of the Senate and House office buildings, carrying the gospel to converted and pagan alike."

Somewhat surprisingly, at least to those familiar with his rather patrician bearing and accustomed to his cutting private comments about the parochial interests and intellectual shortcomings of many elected representatives, Acheson seemed to relish the new job, accepting its small indignities with characteristic good humor and his ever-present sense of irony and rapier-like wit. He worked hard at cultivating support from congressional barons and made a special effort to win over such key figures as Senator Arthur Vandenberg, the powerful and vain Michigan Republican who proved himself susceptible to Acheson's calculated flattery. Vandenberg needed to be "placated," he reminded a top aide, in order for the administration to gain backing for its key legislative priorities. Against the common charge that he did not suffer fools gladly, Acheson offered the "anguishing hours" he spent in congressional offices during these months as at least a partial rebuttal. Success followed success, moreover, as Acheson and his staff helped build strong majorities behind the Bretton Woods agreements, the Trade Agreement Act, the UN Charter, and other key measures.[13]

On April 12, 1945, the day after Acheson celebrated his fifty-second birthday, Roosevelt succumbed to a massive cerebral hemorrhage while visiting Warm Springs, Georgia. FDR's sudden death shocked Acheson—even though he had seen firsthand the president's increasing frailty while briefing him for the Yalta Conference that February. Coming with a war still raging in Europe and the Pacific, it also shook up a government and people that had known no other president for more than a dozen years. "There was with millions of people practically a parent relationship in the psychological sense," he wrote his son David, "and the sudden shock of his death leaves people completely at sea."[14]

Although he had enjoyed little previous contact with new President Harry S. Truman, Acheson's initial impressions of the former Missouri senator were positive. He "has done an excellent job," Acheson wrote David after the new chief executive's first weeks in office. "He is straightforward, simple, decisive, entirely honest," he enthused. Acheson acknowledged that Truman's lack of experience placed limitations "upon his judgment and wisdom" but added hopefully, "I think that he will learn fast and inspire confidence."[15] Throughout the spring and early summer of 1945, Acheson became a regular visitor at the White House. His legislative lobbying responsibilities on such crucial matters as the new UN Charter brought him into close contact with Truman. The two men, despite their strikingly different backgrounds, developed a warm, mutually respectful relationship. Indeed, Acheson appreciated from the first Truman's modesty, directness, and dignified approach to the presidency; they stood in stark contrast to fellow Grotonian FDR's upper-class condescension, indirection, and breezy bonhomie.

Acheson, nevertheless, followed through with a personal commitment he had reached earlier to resign at war's end. Financial and family considerations prompted that decision. His State Department salary of $9,000 per year was a pittance compared to what he could earn by returning to his position as a senior partner at Covington and Burling. This was no small matter in view of Acheson's need to support a wife, three children (each in private school), two sprawling homes, domestic staff, and expensive tastes. In addition, his daughter Mary had recently been diagnosed with tuberculosis and had been moved to a sanitarium in upstate New York, a matter that weighed heavily on his mind. Weariness and frustration with his State Department superiors also influenced his thinking. Acheson had little respect for Secretary of State Stettinius, a man who had "gone far with comparatively little equipment" in his acid assessment, or Undersecretary Joseph Grew, "the Prince of Appeasers" who appeared to him "tired, worried, and very out-to-lunch."[16] Nor did Stettinius's resignation, on June 27, help much since it led to Truman's uninspired choice of James F. Byrnes as the new secretary of state. The news that the former South Carolina senator and Supreme Court justice would be his new boss, Acheson confided to his daughter Mary, "does not move me to any enthusiasm."[17] On August 8, just one day after Truman and Byrnes returned from the last of the great wartime conferences at Potsdam, he tendered his letter of resignation and left with his wife for a long-awaited vacation to upstate New York and Canada.

Three days later Byrnes phoned the vacationing Acheson at Saranac Lake, New York, with a request from Truman that he not only stay in the State Department but also assume the position of undersecretary of state, the number two job in the department. After a brief hesitation, Acheson accepted the offer on August 16, two days after Japan's surrender. An old-fashioned commitment to service, a value instilled in him long ago by Rector Peabody, doubtless factored into his acceptance. But, in the end, it was the exceptional opportunity to exercise real power at a crucial moment in history that made the undersecretary position irresistible. Power, as Henry Kissinger famously quipped decades later, is the ultimate aphrodisiac. "The frustrations were all that I expected them to be," Acheson reflected later, "but for reasons impossible to foresee at the time, the decision was one of the most fortunate of my life."[18]

BECOMING A COLD WARRIOR

The Acheson who began serving as undersecretary of state in August 1945, even before the completion of his confirmation hearings, had yet to form any fixed views about the Soviet Union. He certainly did not harbor the strongly anti-Soviet attitudes that such well-placed policymakers as Averell Harriman, America's wartime ambassador to Moscow, were putting forward at that very moment. In contradistinction to his old Yale rowing coach, Acheson subscribed, and was widely perceived as subscribing, to the Rooseveltian perspective: the view that postwar cooperation with the Kremlin was both possible and necessary; the conviction that Soviet-American understanding constituted one of the keys to the establishment of a postwar order of peace and security. In a radio address of February 24, 1945, Acheson described the results of the recently concluded Yalta Conference as "in complete harmony with American opinion," dismissing out of hand the accusations of critics that the Poles had been betrayed by FDR's concessions to Stalin. Tellingly, the *New York Times* heartily endorsed Acheson's appointment, calling him a proponent of Soviet-American cooperation, while I. F. Stone, a prominent left-wing journalist, noted approvingly in the *Nation* that Acheson was "friendly to the Soviet Union" and thus represented "by far the best choice for Under Secretary."[19] Such acclaim among liberals also derived from the fact that Acheson was then seen as one of them; his close ties to Frankfurter and long association with the recently deceased Brandeis served as key markers in that regard.

At a time when attitudes about the prospects for continued cooperation with the Soviet Union stood as a defining test of American liberalism, Acheson passed muster. Within a year, however, he had changed his views in dramatic fashion, not only joining the cold warriors but becoming one of the most articulate, persuasive, clear-headed, and forceful of their number. Acheson's conversion to reflexively anti-Soviet hard-liner forms a significant chapter of the broader story of the early Cold War and, in particular, of the Truman administration's abandonment of negotiations and gravitation to a policy of firmness and strength.

As World War II drew to a close, Acheson identified economic disorder and social unrest, not the possibility of Soviet aggression or opportunism, as the most likely sources of global instability. Therein, he believed, lay the principal obstacle to the forging of the new world order that, as early as 1940, he envisioned as the most fundamental task for postwar American statesmen. One of the most lucid and eloquent statements of his evolving outlook came during his testimony before the Senate Banking and Currency Committee, in June 1945, pursuant to the pending Bretton Woods agreements. "There is a situation in the world, very clearly illustrated in Europe, and also true in the Far East," he exclaimed, "which threatens the very foundations, the whole fabric of world organization which we have known in our lifetime and which our fathers and grandfathers knew." Decrying the wholesale breakdown of Europe's traditional transportation networks, industrial and financial systems, and institutional arrangements, he warned that Europe might turn in on itself, with dire consequences for an America that needed a prosperous and stable Europe to ensure its own economic health and physical safety. Not since the "Moslem conquests" of the seventh century, Acheson argued, had Europeans faced so profound a crisis. It was one in which "the whole fabric of social life might go to pieces unless the most energetic steps are taken on all fronts, and on all fronts at the same time." Acheson did not connect the Soviet Union in any manner whatsoever to these conditions; rather, it was the previous decade and a half of devastating global depression and war that bore responsibility for the prevailing situation of "unparalleled seriousness." In fact, he saw the Soviet Union as a victim of those same forces, not as an instigator of them. It is telling that, early in his tenure as undersecretary, he advocated an increase in UNRRA aid for the economic reconstruction of war-torn Russia.[20]

Acheson, it bears emphasizing, prized order above virtually all else. He feared that everything he held dear about the United States–its economic system, democratic institutions, social arrangements, core values–*required* order, both at home and abroad, to survive and flourish. Worried about the consequences for his own country of war-induced chaos plaguing huge swaths of Europe and Asia, Acheson devoted much of his formidable energy to the challenge of reconstruction and the related problem of reconstituting an international economic system based on free trade and currency convertibility. A thriving, depression-proof system of private enterprise at home, a sine qua non for Acheson, demanded nothing less. In comparison, the specter of the Soviet/communist threat that was already exercising Harriman, White House aide William D. Leahy, diplomat George F. Kennan, and others, did not alarm Acheson; he attributed their apprehension to a penchant for accepting exaggerated worst-case scenarios over prudent analysis. His sharp legal mind, sculpted by Frankfurter and Brandeis long ago to approach complex issues with a hard-boiled pragmatism and to be guided always by the weight of the available evidence, was still reserving judgment about the Soviet riddle. Instinctively, Acheson favored carrots over sticks; much like Roosevelt, he believed the development of trust and cooperation between Washington and Moscow to be an essential building block of a stable postwar order.

Such thinking also conditioned Acheson's initial approach to one of the thorniest issues that surfaced during his first weeks in the new job: What policy should be followed with regard to the uniquely destructive weapon that had so recently sealed Japan's fate? Acheson was not one of the select handful of high-level officials who had been informed in advance about the top-secret Manhattan Project. "The news of the atomic bomb is the most frightening yet," he wrote on the evening of the atomic blast over Hiroshima. "If we can't work out some sort of organization of great powers, we shall be gone geese for fair."[21] Truman called a cabinet meeting, for September 21, to consider the administration's options with regard to the atomic bomb "secret." With Byrnes traveling abroad (he was absent for 350 of his 562 days in office), Acheson was serving in what soon became the familiar capacity of acting secretary of state. Henry L. Stimson, the venerable, seventy-eight-year-old secretary of war, telephoned him in advance of the meeting in an effort to persuade Acheson of the wisdom of making a direct offer to the Soviets to share information about and ultimate control over the bomb. Stimson's case derived from the calculation that technical and scientific issues related to atomic energy could not long remain secret and that diplomatic benefits could accrue to the United States that would extend to the whole gamut of Soviet-American issues if it made an early, conciliatory gesture on this most sensitive of subjects.

Acheson responded favorably. His personal convictions about the cardinal importance of reaching some accommodation with Moscow predisposed him to accept the Stimson line. Ties of a personal nature probably played a role as well. Fellow Yale graduate Stimson, after all, had been Frankfurter's indispensable mentor, the man who helped launch the distinguished legal career of Acheson's own mentor and by then most intimate friend. A former secretary of war under President William Howard Taft and secretary of state under President Herbert Hoover, Stimson was a towering figure in American public life, one whose seemingly selfless devotion to duty for more than a generation made him an Achesonian favorite and role model. Additionally, in 1943 Acheson's daughter Mary had married William Bundy, whose father, Harvey, had been one of Stimson's closest wartime associates.

After Stimson made his case for atomic sharing before the president and his cabinet at the scheduled meeting, Acheson stepped forth to give the plan a ringing endorsement. The acting secretary of state exclaimed that there was "no alternative" to a policy of sharing atomic information with the Soviets, albeit on a quid pro quo basis, since he could not "conceive of a world in which we were hoarders of military secrets from our Allies, particularly this great ally" whose cooperation was essential for "the future peace of the world." Impressed with Acheson's presentation, Truman requested that he and Robert Patterson, who was slated to replace Stimson as secretary of war, each prepare separate memoranda for him on the issue. A few weeks later, in what resembled a well-crafted lawyer's brief, Acheson offered an eloquent reformulation of the Stimson position, emphasizing that it would be impossible to keep the well-known theory behind atomic weaponry shrouded in secrecy. The Soviet Union would soon gain the ability to make its own atomic bomb, he reasoned, regardless of what the United States did; hence a "policy of secrecy is both futile and dangerous." Consequently, Acheson echoed Stimson in arguing that the United States and Great Britain should approach the Soviets directly, offering a concrete plan for sharing scientific information and for establishing verifiable safeguards to protect against the future production of atomic weaponry by any country. Although he conceded that tensions with the Soviets were increasing, Acheson said, "I cannot see why the basic interests of the two nations should conflict." A failure to cooperate, further, would result in "an armed truce."[22]

Truman was sufficiently impressed with Acheson's memorandum that he asked him to help draft a presidential message to Congress on the subject of domestic and international control of atomic energy. The message that Truman transmitted on October 3, however, departed in significant ways from the Acheson-Stimson approach, both in tone and substance. The president chose not to refer to the inevitability of other powers achieving nuclear status, and in proposing international discussions, he mentioned only the United Kingdom and Canada, not the Soviet Union, as likely participants. Then, on October 27,

Truman publicly touted the atomic bomb as America's "sacred trust," a weapon too valuable to share with "a lawless world."[23] It was a sharp rebuke, whether intended or not, to the position Acheson was championing. He had suffered his first defeat since becoming undersecretary on a major policy question—though the issue would soon be reopened.

On November 14, 1945, Acheson delivered a speech at New York's Madison Square Garden that reveals much about his still largely sympathetic and accommodative approach to postwar Russia. Given before a raucous rally for the Soviet-American Friendship Society, featuring an overwhelmingly left-liberal, pro-Soviet crowd, Acheson's address stressed the need to understand Moscow's mammoth rebuilding requirements and legitimate security concerns. To put them in perspective, he suggested that an American would have to imagine what it would be like if Germany had invaded the United States, in the process destroying many of its northeastern industrial cities, ruining much of its agricultural heartland, and killing a third of the population. Such devastation naturally inclined Moscow to seek "friendly governments along her borders," a policy that Acheson described as "essential both for the security of the Soviet Union and the peace of the world." Having seemed to offer sanction to the developing Soviet sphere of influence in Eastern Europe, Acheson then shifted gears and began calling Moscow to account for its heavy-handed actions in that region. "We believe," he added pointedly, that the "adjustment of interests" between the Soviet Union and the peoples and nations along its borders "should take place short of the point where persuasion and firmness become coercion, where a knock on the door at night strikes terror into men and women."

Acheson's effort to present what he considered a balanced picture of Soviet behavior and the still solid prospects for U.S.-Soviet friendship aroused the ire of this openly pro-Soviet audience, leading to boos, catcalls, and his quick departure from the stage. Yet the moment also captures Acheson's determination to go to considerable lengths—as his remarkable analogy between the current Soviet plight and what a comparably devastated United States might look like—to evoke sympathy for the Soviet Union and to plead for understanding, cooperation, and mutual accommodation.[24]

Throughout the first half of 1946, Acheson clung to a Rooseveltian stance—despite the steadily mounting tensions between Washington and

Moscow over Eastern Europe, Germany, Iran, and other nettlesome issues. His remained a hopeful, if measured and watchful, outlook; Acheson occupied a kind of middle ground at that time between the hard-line, ideologically infused anticommunism of Navy Secretary James V. Forrestal and the soft-line views of Commerce Secretary Henry Wallace. When Kennan's "long telegram" from Moscow arrived in February 1946, bolstering the convictions and swelling the ranks of the hard-liners with its alarmist analysis of the Soviet rulers' insatiable appetite for expansion, Acheson refused to climb on board. He found Kennan's reasoning stretched, his rhetoric overblown. That spring, with a Cold War consensus building within the administration, Acheson kept his own counsel. He pressed the case with Byrnes for the negotiation of a European modus vivendi with the Soviets. As late as May 1946, he was still advocating the need for a broad European peace settlement that would leave the continent undivided.

At the same time, he was continuing to push for a policy of nuclear cooperation and sharing. In March Byrnes had given Acheson another crack at shaping the administration's atomic weapons policy. Since Moscow had, to Washington's surprise, endorsed the creation of a UN atomic energy commission, the secretary of state charged him with formulating a concrete U.S. proposal to take to the UN. Along with Tennessee Valley Authority head David Lilienthal, a fellow protégé of Frankfurter and Brandeis whom Acheson had personally selected as committee cochair, the undersecretary led a series of intensive discussions that resulted in the drafting of what became known as the Acheson-Lilienthal Plan. It called for the creation of an International Atomic Development Authority with broad powers for the ownership, licensing, and development of all nuclear materials of a potentially hazardous nature. At Acheson's insistence, the scheme eschewed intrusive inspection requirements that he knew the Russians would resent and oppose. His principal aim here, once again, was to foster bonds of trust between the United States and the Soviet Union in service of the broader goal of a stable and peaceful postwar order. "We must use [America's nuclear] advantage now," Acheson told a nationwide radio audience, "to promote international security and to carry out our policy of building a lasting peace through international agreement."[25] But Acheson was no woolly minded idealist; the proposal ensured that the United States would retain its atomic monopoly until the very final stages of any transfer of material to the proposed international agency.

Nonetheless, conservative critics blasted the Acheson-Lilienthal Plan as a foolish giveaway to an untrustworthy adversary. Truman guaranteed Soviet rejection of the overture—which probably would have occurred anyway—when he placed self-made millionaire and political operator Bernard Baruch in charge of its presentation to the UN. Baruch toughened the terms of the Acheson-Lilienthal Plan, against the undersecretary's vigorous protests, and Truman sided with him in the ensuing bureaucratic struggle rather than with Acheson. Staunch Soviet opposition to the Baruch Plan, from the first, rendered it stillborn at its mid-June unveiling. Plainly, Acheson had been dealt another policy defeat.[26] "One hope of our proposals was that the progress would be in cooperation for peaceful use, rather than in rivalry to achieve special advantages," he told a correspondent a year later. "That hope seems very small now."[27]

Not until the summer of 1946 did Acheson cease pressing for the development of conciliatory links with the Soviet Union and place himself foursquare in the cold warrior camp. The Turkish crisis of August 1946 was pivotal to his conversion; it removed for him the last shred of hope for a policy of conciliation, revealing a Soviet Union sufficiently opportunistic and aggressive to confirm the most negative prognostications of the hard-liners. The crisis broke when, on August 7, the Soviet Union sent a diplomatic note to Turkey, calling for a joint defense of the Dardanelles and Turkish Straits in order to guarantee the security of the Black Sea. The nervous Turks, who considered the démarche menacing, passed a copy of it on to Acheson as the acting secretary of state, as did the Soviets themselves. He judged it menacing as well. In response, he called for, and chaired, an August 14 meeting of senior national security officials, all of whom drew ominous conclusions about the wider implications of this Soviet probe. Not to be outdone by Forrestal and the other service chiefs, Acheson argued forcefully that Russian pressure on Turkey formed part of a larger global strategy aimed at gaining control not just over the strategic Dardanelles and Turkish Straits but also over Turkey itself, the whole Middle Eastern region, and even areas beyond. It was necessary to check the Soviet probe with a firm U.S. countermove, he and his senior defense associates agreed, even if a policy of strength increased the risk of war.

The next day Acheson stressed the gravity of the situation during a White House meeting. He took the lead at the meeting, telling Truman that the United States needed to call the Soviet bluff, even if doing so "might lead to armed conflict." The time "has come," Acheson exclaimed, "when we must decide that we shall resist by all means at our disposal any Soviet aggression." The president, eager by then for a showdown with an adversary he saw as increasingly recalcitrant, acted on his advisers' recommendation and immediately dispatched a naval task force to the region. Although the crisis ended as quickly as it had begun, Acheson's decision to join the anti-Soviet camp bore important, long-term consequences–for the evolution of U.S. Cold War strategy as well as for his own emerging role as a formulator of it.[28]

The reasons behind Acheson's rather sudden shift of views are difficult to pin down with precision; the available documentary record does not permit a definitive explanation. One can posit, of course, that Soviet pressure on the Turks was so heavy-handed that it settled for Acheson the issue of Moscow's intentions once and for all. As one who typically sifted through shards of evidence with care before leaping to larger conclusions, Acheson may well have seen the Turkish crisis as the proverbial last straw, rendering any further fence-straddling between a policy of conciliation and a policy of containment simply untenable–no longer in accord with the facts of the situation, as he might have phrased it. He had previously registered concern about Soviet behavior in Eastern Europe, in Iran, even in China, but had not seen those specific cases as part of a concerted strategy of expansion. Putting the Turkish case together with those earlier episodes of adventurism, Acheson for the first time now sensed a clear *pattern* of provocative behavior, one that met his lawyerly standards of evidence. A man of action by instinct and temperament, he immediately jumped into the policy fray with both feet, urging a vigorous U.S. counterstrategy and assuming as if by birthright a dominant role in its formulation and implementation.

Some cynics at the time, including the editors of *U.S. News and World Report*, attributed Acheson's newfound anti-Soviet fervor to careerist ambitions. Having been fired from his previous undersecretary post thirteen years earlier for falling out of step with a president, or so the logic went, he saw the winds blowing in an anti-Soviet direction and shifted course to avoid another humiliating dismissal.[29] That interpretation misses the mark, however, in important respects. For all his considerable ambition and his obvious fondness for power, Acheson always maintained a strong independence of judgment. He was not one to trim views to conform to prevailing sentiment and certainly not one to subscribe to, no less promulgate with passion, a position that he disagreed with.

What was almost certainly more germane to Acheson's adoption of an unequivocal Cold War outlook during the second half of 1946 was his penchant for thinking about world affairs in broad, geopolitical terms. It bears recalling that Acheson had grasped the profound implications for U.S. security of German and Japanese aggression well before U.S. entry into World War II–and much earlier than many top diplomatic and defense officials within the Roosevelt administration had. He drew connections at that time between the Axis challenge and the long-term physical safety, economic health, and domestic equilibrium of the United States that were unusually prescient. The Soviet challenge, at least from the Turk crisis onward, impressed him as eerily similar. Once again, an adversary had revealed itself as hostile to U.S. interests, values, and institutions and as willing to advance its expansionist program through militant–if not yet military–tactics. As the Axis challenge of 1940–1941 demanded strength, resolve, and watchfulness, so too did the Soviet threat of 1946–1947.

Acheson was fond, throughout his life, of quoting Holmes's famous dictum that "the judgment of nature upon error is death." By the summer of 1946 he must have found that warning especially apt as he grew convinced that greater risks inhered in a conciliatory policy than in a confrontational one. The Truman administration, in his judgment, simply could not afford to take any further chances with a Soviet Union poised to exploit existing vacuums of power and to capitalize ruthlessly on conditions of unprecedented social and economic disorder. The precipitous decline of the British empire, which Acheson had long viewed as an essential, stabilizing element of the prevailing world order, exacerbated the uncertainties and dangers of the immediate postwar situation. His Holmesean realism conditioned Acheson to appreciate international affairs in terms of underlying elements of power, manifest and latent, such as military strength, strategic location, war-making capability, and access to and control over base sites, resources, and industrial plants—an inclination strengthened by his extended wartime tutorial in the close relationship between resources and industrial-military power. Further, it conditioned him to aim always for a favorable balance of power, both short-term and long-term, and to accept some risks in its pursuit. U.S. security demanded a favorable balance of power; a prudent statesman could settle for nothing less.

Acheson's decision to lend his intelligence and energy to the burgeoning anti-Soviet consensus likely owed much, then, to earlier habits of thought about international affairs and about prospective dangers to U.S. security. Unlike many in Truman's inner circle, Acheson did not perceive the emergent Soviet threat as primarily ideological in character. To the extent that communist ideology offered the Soviet Union an additional means to extend its influence, it posed a serious, instrumental problem, to be sure, symbolized most trenchantly by the flourishing communist parties in postwar France, Italy, and elsewhere. He believed that the Kremlin tightly controlled all national communist parties, thereby granting the Soviets "an asset of . . . tremendous power."[30] But Acheson seems not to have been unduly concerned, as were others, about the threat communism might pose *to* or *within* American society. He was not plagued by self-doubts about the ability of American capitalism to compete successfully with the Soviet command-style economic model, and he did not worry especially about the ability of ordinary Americans to see through the false promises of a communist utopia. Rather, he concerned himself first and foremost with checking the power and potential power and reach of the Soviet Union. Acheson embraced, and helped calibrate, the developing strategy of containment because it struck him as the most prudent means for achieving that goal and hence for ensuring a global balance of power favorable to his own beloved United States.

"MET AT ARMAGEDDON"

Following the Turkish crisis, Acheson remained fixated on the eastern Mediterranean, the strategic region where a Soviet breakthrough appeared most likely. A raging civil war in Greece that pitted an unpopular, right-wing government against indigenous communists, supplied by Communist Yugoslavia, offered Moscow opportunities aplenty. On October 15, 1946,

Acheson insisted that U.S. policy should henceforth be one of unequivocal support for the Greek government–diplomatically, economically, and militarily. Prudence, once again, dictated that the United States do everything possible here to shore up a regime that, for all its shortcomings, remained solidly pro-Western. Acheson saw the Greek problem, as he had the earlier Turk crisis, in stark East-West terms.[31]

Secretary of State Byrnes's frequent absences from Washington while attending a series of UN and foreign ministers' meetings made Acheson an unusually powerful deputy. An ongoing power struggle and personality conflict between Byrnes and Truman, which came to a head in the fall of 1946, had the effect of further strengthening Acheson's position–once the dust had cleared. Truman had previously chastised Byrnes for his habit of conducting diplomacy as a one-man show, informing him of important decisions only after the fact. That the former senator harbored presidential ambitions of his own was an open secret in Washington and an affront to a chief executive who prized loyalty on the part of his appointees. When Commerce Secretary Henry Wallace gave an unapologetically pro-Soviet speech at New York's Madison Square Garden that September, an address that Truman had carelessly approved in advance, Byrnes felt undercut and demanded that either Truman discipline Wallace or he would act on an earlier tendered letter of resignation. Acheson returned from a vacation in the Canadian Rockies to find that "my worst forebodings about trouble between my chiefs seemed justified."[32] Truman fired the out-of-step Wallace at the end of September, and having secured a commitment in advance from former Army Chief of Staff George C. Marshall to take over the State Department, he accepted Byrnes's resignation less than two months later.

Acheson managed to retain Truman's support and affection throughout this rocky period. Unlike the presumptuous, freelancing Byrnes, Acheson always remained deferential and respectful to the president. After the disastrous Democratic defeat in the congressional elections of November 1946, a stinging personal blow to Truman, Acheson greeted the president on his return at Washington's Union Station; he was the lone government official to do so. Truman, who invited Acheson back to the White House for a consoling drink and a discussion of political strategy, long remembered the courtesy.[33]

On January 21, 1947, Marshall was sworn in as the new secretary of state. Walking back from the White House to their State Department offices, then still located across the street in the old State-War-Navy Building, he asked Acheson if he would stay on as undersecretary. Acheson responded affirmatively, though he indicated that "before too long I ought to get back to my profession if I'm to have one." When Marshall asked if six months would be too long, Acheson said no and together they set June 30 as his day of departure.[34]

Marshall's ascent proved a boon to Acheson, in both personal and policy terms. The general was, of course, a towering figure, one of the most widely respected and admired individuals of that era. He was a man of unquestioned personal integrity as well, if somewhat aloof and not given to easy sociability. Popularly regarded as the chief organizer of victory during the war, Marshall retained an extraordinarily favorable reputation with the general public—and with the president—even after the failure of his 1946 mediation mission in China. The former army chief of staff's assignment from Truman had been to help broker a settlement between the Chinese Communist and Nationalist factions so as to avert an outright civil war. Despite his strenuous efforts, it proved an impossible task and Marshall soon recognized it as such. Acheson, who had first worked with Marshall as his Washington liaison during the China mission, never spoke of the general with anything other than the deepest reverence. In his memoir, he compared his new boss's indispensability to that of George Washington's at Valley Forge. "It was, indeed, an act of God that made him chief adviser to the President and head of the State Department in the no less critical winter of 1947," he gushed.[35] In private correspondence, later in life, Acheson described Marshall as a personal hero who ranked second only to Oliver Wendell Holmes in his pantheon.[36]

It certainly did not hurt that Marshall delegated substantial responsibility to his undersecretary of state, making him a de facto chief of staff with the authority to settle any policy issues that did not require the secretary's direct involvement. In view of Marshall's frequent absences from Washington, Acheson was in charge of the State Department during the first half of 1947 more frequently than not. After a private dinner party at Acheson's Georgetown home, David Lilienthal wrote in his diary that Acheson "spent a good deal of time bubbling over with enthusiasm, rapture almost, about General Marshall.

. . . To work with [Marshall] is such a joy that he can hardly talk about anything else. It has made a new man of Dean and this is a good thing for the country right now."[37]

One of the areas that Acheson continued to monitor closely was the eastern Mediterranean, where conditions in Greece in particular were deteriorating at an alarming pace. Reports flooded into the State Department in early 1947 predicting an "imminent collapse" of the Greek government "due to mounting guerrilla activity, supplied and directed from the outside, economic chaos and impending British troop withdrawals." In Acheson's words, "All signs pointed to an impending move by the Communists to take over the country."[38] Then, on Friday, February 21, things suddenly went from bad to worse. On that date, the British ambassador, Lord Inverchapel, delivered two notes to the State Department indicating that British aid to both Greece and Turkey would end in six weeks and calling on the United States to assume the responsibility there that Britain could no longer afford. With Marshall out of town, Acheson sprung into action. He notified Marshall and Truman by telephone of the British notes, emphasizing the seriousness of the situation, and received their blessing to undertake a series of urgent policy studies examining U.S. options. In a memorandum to Marshall that same day, he offered his own preliminary assessment of the high stakes for which the United States was now contending. "The capitulation of Greece to Soviet domination through lack of adequate support from the U.S. and Great Britain," Acheson warned, "might eventually result in the loss of the whole Near and Middle East and Northern Africa."[39]

Working frantically through the weekend, Acheson and the State Department's Near Eastern experts prepared a series of background studies and policy recommendations for Marshall's consideration. On the morning of February 24, the secretary of state read the briefing material Acheson had provided and concurred fully with his deputy's appraisal of the crisis. Both men agreed that a sizable U.S. financial commitment to Greece and Turkey was essential in order to prevent demoralization and collapse on which the Soviet Union would inevitably capitalize. Later that day Marshall met with Truman, Secretary of War Patterson, and Secretary of the Navy Forrestal. All agreed about the need for immediate action and decided that Congress, now under the control of a Republican Party intent on cutting governmental expenditures, would need to approve the $400–500 million in aid that they thought necessary to prevent disaster. Following the White House decision, Acheson prepared a series of specific recommendations for congressional consideration. That same day he met journalist Louis Fisher for lunch. "The British are finished," he told Fisher. "They are through. And the trouble is that this hits us too soon, before we are ready for it. We are having a lot of trouble getting money out of Congress." Grimacing and throwing his hands in the air, according to the reporter's notes of their conversation, Acheson exclaimed, "If the Near East goes Communist, I very much fear for this country and for the world."[40]

On February 27 Acheson attended and made a crucial contribution to a climactic Oval Office meeting between Truman, his senior national security advisers, and all but one of the majority and minority leaders of the Senate and House. "I knew we were met at Armageddon," Acheson recalled in his memoir, vividly capturing his sense of the occasion's high drama and historic momentousness. Truman was seeking to persuade a budget-conscious Congress to accept the need for a totally new—and very costly—international obligation. After Marshall "flubbed his opening speech," at least in Acheson's impression, by offering a flat and uninspired summary of the problem, the undersecretary requested an opportunity to speak. "This was my crisis," he later wrote. "For a week I had nurtured it. These congressmen had no conception of what challenged them; it was my task to bring it home." Putting the weight of responsibility on his own shoulders, Acheson spoke with passion and forcefulness. Believing that the time for "measured appraisal" had passed, he instead presented an emotion-laden speech that highlighted the grave dangers that a Soviet breakthrough in the eastern Mediterranean posed to the future security of the United States. His own, oft-quoted recollection of his remarks runs as follows:

> In the past eighteen months, I said, Soviet pressure on the Straits, on Iran, and on northern Greece had brought the Balkans to the point where a highly possible Soviet breakthrough might open three continents to Soviet penetration. Like apples in a barrel infected by one rotten one, the corruption of Greece would infect Iran and all to the east. It would also carry infection to Africa through Asia Minor and Egypt, and to Europe through Italy and France, already threatened by the strongest domestic

Communist parties in Western Europe. The Soviet Union was playing one of the greatest gambles in history, at minimal cost. . . . We and we alone were in a position to break up the play.

It was, by any measure, an impressively chilling presentation. After a long silence followed Acheson's peroration, Senator Vandenberg said, "Mr. President, if you will say that to the Congress and the country, I will support you and I believe that most of its members will do the same."[41]

In the days that followed his timely intervention at that pivotal White House meeting, Acheson helped draft the speech that Truman would use to appeal to the whole Congress for an aid package of $250 million for Greece and $150 million for Turkey. Delivered on March 12, the Truman Doctrine, as it was soon dubbed, ranks among the most memorable and influential addresses in modern American history. In its essential outlines, it hewed closely to the rhetorical strategy whose effectiveness Acheson had demonstrated with his remarks to the Republican and Democratic leadership two weeks earlier. "At the present moment in world history," Truman declared, "nearly every nation must choose between alternative ways of life." After cataloguing the perfidies of the Soviet Union, though never directly naming it, Truman famously concluded with the exhortation, "It must be the policy of the United States to support free peoples who are resisting attempted subjugation by armed minorities or by outside pressure." Acheson saw this speech as couching a specific request in a broad, universal framework. "If FDR were alive today," he had remarked to a State Department colleague earlier, "I think I know what he'd do. He would make a statement of global policy but confine his request for money right now to Greece and Turkey."[42]

With Marshall attending the important Moscow foreign ministers' meeting, Acheson served as the administration's chief witness during public and closed congressional sessions on the Greek-Turkish Aid Act. He conceded the skeptics' charge that the current Greek government was less than fully democratic but stressed, "We do not have a choice between a perfect democracy and an imperfect democracy. The question is whether there shall be any democracy at all." A collapse in Greece, or in Turkey, which Acheson implied a congressional denial of aid would abet, would be "an unspeakable tragedy" whose consequences would be felt throughout Europe, the Middle East, and Asia. Only courageous and generous action by the United States could avert that calamity, Acheson said. Once again, he proved adept as a spokesman and lobbyist. Those efforts were crowned with success when the bill passed the House by a vote of 287 to 107 and the Senate by a vote of 67 to 23. On May 22 Truman signed it into law.[43]

Critics, especially on the Left, seized on the Truman Doctrine to complain about the administration's support for decidedly undemocratic governments in Greece and Turkey and about the hyperbolic language the president—and his undersecretary of state—used to mobilize congressional and public support behind that policy. Eleanor Roosevelt, the late-president's wife and the very embodiment of midcentury liberalism, spelled out those concerns in a personal letter to Truman. In drafting a response for the president's signature, Acheson vigorously countered her objections. He dismissed the notion that the United States should avoid "throwing our economic weight in at points which are of strategic importance but deficient in democracy" as self-defeating. "I would argue," his draft continued, "that if the Greek-Turkish land bridge between the continents is one point at which our democratic forces can stop the advance of Communism that has flowed steadily through the Baltic countries, Poland, Yugoslavia, Rumania, Bulgaria, to some extent Hungary, then this is the place to do it, regardless of whether or not the terrain is good." In a telling reflection of his now total conversion to cold warrior, Acheson catalogued the numerous concessions that the United States had made to Russia "that she might trust and not fear us," emphasizing that those concessions had led to nothing but disappointment and disheartenment. In closing, the Acheson draft stressed, "The American way of life cannot survive unless other peoples who want to adopt that pattern of life throughout the world can do so without fear and in the hope of success. If this is to be possible we cannot allow the forces of disintegration to go unchecked."[44]

His haunting fear about the consequences of disintegration prompted Acheson to call, in the midst of the Greek-Turkish crisis, for a much broader program of European reconstruction aid. Concerned that the United States "faced another looming and even more menacing crisis about to engulf all Europe," on March 5 he wrote Forrestal and Patterson to suggest that the

State-War-Navy Coordinating Committee, with the assistance of the Treasury Department, begin working on an overall European economic assistance program. "Prompt and effective aid for gravely threatened countries was essential to our own security," he noted.[45] The exceptionally harsh winter of 1946–1947 had exacerbated conditions of low productivity, financial distress, and social unrest that had been plaguing the Continent for the past year and a half. "Since the surrender of Germany," Acheson observed in his memoir, "the life of Europe as an organized industrial community had come well-nigh to a standstill and, with it, so had production and distribution of goods of every sort."[46] George Kennan's Policy Planning Staff assumed major responsibility for assessing the actual nature of prevailing conditions, pinpointing Europe's essential requirements, and proposing a specific plan and a strategy for carrying it out. Acheson oversaw that work but left the details to others. He agreed fully with Undersecretary of State for Economic Affairs William L. Clayton, who wrote him that "Europe is steadily deteriorating"; that the United States "grossly underestimated the destruction to the European economy by the war"; and that disaster loomed both for the peace and security of the world and for America's domestic economy if the current drift was not soon reversed.[47]

After securing Truman's advance approval, Acheson publicly sounded the tocsin about Europe's deepening economic crisis. The occasion and setting may have been unusual for a major foreign policy pronouncement—a fill-in speech for the president before the Delta Council in Cleveland, Mississippi—but Acheson ensured that his remarks would receive widespread media coverage by alerting the press in advance to the import of his upcoming May 8 address. In a part of the still rigidly segregated South that would soon gain national and international notoriety as a center of violent resistance to the black freedom struggle, Acheson talked to his audience of white businessmen and farmers about the connections between Europe's economic distress and America's needs. After describing in vivid language the current economic plight of Europe, battered by the physical wreckage of the war, the wholesale disruption of prewar trading patterns, and the devastating impact of the past winter, he identified the Continent's burgeoning foreign exchange and deficit problems as a threat to America's own economic interests as a trading nation dependent on foreign purchasers and markets. The United States, he said, "must push ahead with the reconstruction of those two great workshops of Europe and Asia–Germany and Japan–upon which the ultimate recovery of the two continents so largely depends." It must use its own economic and financial resources to facilitate European economic recovery not primarily on humanitarian grounds–"there is no charity involved in this," he assured his listeners–but "chiefly as a matter of national self-interest." Acheson emphasized that point several times in the speech; he believed firmly that appeals to self-interest always worked better than appeals focused on the needs of others. But he seamlessly combined the two motivating forces in his stirring concluding remarks. Support for European recovery "is necessary if we are to preserve our own freedoms and our own democratic institutions," Acheson proclaimed. "It is necessary for our national security. And it is our duty and our privilege as human beings."[48]

That address set the stage for the much more famous speech Marshall delivered as a Harvard University commencement address, on June 5, 1947, laying the foundation for the European recovery program that would bear his name. In the intervening month, Acheson participated in all the major planning meetings that struggled to refine the nature of the offer the administration was preparing to make. He also worked assiduously to ensure that Europe would pay close attention to the speech, meeting in advance with three prominent British correspondents–even telling them that he wanted British foreign minister Ernest Bevin, in particular, to be immediately apprised of its contents and significance.

Acheson saw the Marshall Plan as an essential element in the forging of a global power balance favorable to the United States. In conjunction with the Truman Doctrine, which signaled Washington's determination to check, with force if necessary, any further extension of Soviet power and influence into the Eurasian heartland, the European recovery program formed a cornerstone of the Cold War strategic vision that Acheson did much to formulate and implement. He later reflected that it aimed for "the creation of half a world without destroying the whole." Elaborating, Acheson emphasized that the Cold War stemmed essentially from basic changes in the nature and location of world power. The European-dominated "One World" that he often extolled as the epitome of a functioning, stable international order had been predicated upon Western control over the third world and had been held together by

British economic and military hegemony. Yet World War II, much to Acheson's dismay and regret, had shattered that world order irrevocably; nostalgia—and the romantic side of this consummate realist sometimes overflowed with longing for the old Pax Britainica—could not restore it. Instead, Acheson found it necessary to adapt to a radically different geopolitical environment that featured two competing centers of power. The ensuing clash that came to be called the Cold War was, in his assessment, less a struggle to control the world as a whole and more a struggle to shape "an environment—and a spacious environment—within the world in which free nations may exist and prosper."[49] In that effort, the recovery and reconstruction of Western Europe and the blunting of the appeal of indigenous communist parties played an absolutely indispensable role.

What Acheson sometimes referred to as a drive to create "a political economy of freedom" lay behind the key policy initiatives of the early Truman administration. The long-term prosperity and security of the United States, he was convinced, required American predominance within an economically revitalized Western Europe and eastern Mediterranean, much as it required a revitalized, pro-American Japan, reliable access to key raw material–producing areas, an international regime of free trade and currency convertibility, and U.S. military preeminence. Taken together, those ingredients would best ensure the reconstituted world order most suitable to U.S. needs and values. The key to early Cold War foreign policy, as Acheson often remarked, was "to foster an environment in which our national life and individual freedom can survive and prosper."[50] To achieve that, as he told a private audience of State Department employees on June 4, just one day before Marshall's Harvard address, the United States had to "combat the great disintegrating forces" currently plaguing Europe. Doing so, he explained, required "a desire to give up the immediate benefit in order to get the long run benefit."[51]

When Marshall delivered his epochal speech, Acheson was already in his final weeks of government service. During that time he helped groom his successor, Robert A. Lovett, a former assistant secretary of war and fellow Yale alumnus, to take over the responsibilities of undersecretary of state. On his last day Truman called him to the White House for what appeared a routine matter, and, to Acheson's great surprise, the president awarded him the

Medal of Merit during a short Rose Garden ceremony. A week later Truman wrote Acheson an affectionate personal letter, drawing on his own reading in the history of the American Civil War and admiration for Confederate general Robert E. Lee. "You have been an arm for me to lean upon," it read. "As Marse Robert said when Stonewall lost his left arm at Chancellorsville, 'General Jackson has lost his left arm, I have lost my right'—that's the way I feel when you leave State."[52]

3

CONSTRUCTING AN ATLANTIC COMMUNITY

RETURN TO "SEMIPRIVATE" LIFE

Exhausted from his six and a half years in the State Department, under self-described "war and near-war conditions," Acheson decompressed, in early summer 1947, during a long camping vacation in the Canadian Rockies with Alice and two of their close friends. On returning to Washington, he lost little time in resuming the comfortable role of highly paid senior partner at one of the capital's most prestigious and bustling law firms. Yet Acheson clearly missed the pulse, adrenaline, and high stakes of the policymaking realm; their sudden disappearance left a gaping void in his life. "Readjustment from public to private life involves something of the anguish and unhappiness of the drug addict in his 'withdrawal' period," he noted later. "Public life is not only a powerful stimulant but a habit-forming one."[1]

Although he enjoyed and found challenging the cases that awaited him, one of which involved another argument before the Supreme Court, working in the private sector simply could not compare with the excitement of public service. "There is no better or fuller life for a man of spirit," Acheson once explained in a private letter. "To everyone who has ever experienced it the return from public life to private life leaves one feeling flat and empty. Contented, interesting, busy–yes. But exhilarated–no. For one has left a life affording scope for the exercise of vital powers along lines of excellence."[2]

Acheson soon found an outlet for his excess energies–and a welcome opportunity to reconnect to ongoing debates about the great issues of the day– in the Citizens' Committee for the Marshall Plan (CCMP). Formed in the fall of 1947, at the initiative of Clark M. Eichelberger, director of the American Association for the United Nations, the committee aimed to win popular and congressional backing for the proposed European recovery program. The willingness of esteemed elder statesman Henry Stimson, a lifelong Republican, to serve as the group's honorary president gave it both instant prestige and impeccable bipartisan bona fides. Truman's former Secretary of War Robert Patterson agreed to serve as chairman of the executive committee–after receiving encouragement in the task from Undersecretary of State Robert Lovett. Acheson seemed a natural for the committee. Patterson avidly recruited his fellow ex-Truman administration principal, inviting him to the CCMP's founding meeting, held on October 30. Acheson proved an easy sell. Not only did he join, but he embraced the nongovernmental organization's mission with characteristic gusto and his inimitable take-charge style, quickly assuming major operational responsibility. Acheson also signed up as one of the committee's designated speakers, emerging as perhaps the group's most effective public spokesman-cum-lobbyist.

In many respects the Citizens' Committee for the Marshall Plan resembled– and was, in fact, partly modeled on–the prewar Committee to Defend America by Aiding the Allies. Acheson, whose lead role in the latter organization had done much to bolster his public profile (and facilitate his subsequent appointment to the State Department), certainly saw the two committees as comparable. Each, in his view, reflected the uniquely American penchant for using prominent, private citizens as unofficial lobbyists on behalf of important governmental policy initiatives. Each, moreover, dealt with what he considered issues of crucial import. Given the tepid public support for the Marshall Plan at the time of the committee's formation and the burgeoning congressional opposition to what some conservatives were disparaging as a giveaway program for lazy, undeserving foreigners, the CCMP faced an uphill struggle.[3]

Acheson did his part in that struggle. He gave numerous public speeches, off-the-record talks, and press interviews, as well as formal testimony before Congress, all in an effort to help advance the strongest possible case for legislative approval and full funding of the Truman administration's plan for European recovery. On October 14, 1947, two weeks before the committee was officially launched, he offered a preview of the basic rhetorical strategy he would employ over the next several months. As a featured participant in a national broadcast of the popular, New York–based radio program, *Town Meeting of the Air*, Acheson found himself debating a staunch opponent of the Marshall Plan. It proved a decidedly uneven contest. The articulate, knowledgeable, and self-possessed Acheson, a master of the parry and thrust of verbal combat, dispassionately shredded each of his forensic rival's points with laserlike precision. His core message—then and in all subsequent appearances on behalf of the CCMP—held that U.S. security needs made imperative the economic revival of Western Europe; American interests demanded nothing less than the assurance that Western Europe would soon regain its strength, allowing "free institutions" to "survive and flourish there." Without generous and immediate U.S. aid, Acheson insisted, rations of essential food and fuel would soon run out. Disaster—economic, social, and political—would inevitably follow: "hunger, cold, shut down factories and mines, hopelessness," and worse. His uncompromising conclusion followed in cool, logical progression, as in a careful attorney's brief. "We cannot afford not to give this essential aid," Acheson exclaimed.[4]

The CCMP's star orator repeated and elaborated on those themes during a strenuous, eleven-day speaking tour in late November and early December. Traveling by train, Acheson spoke before varied audiences in major cities throughout California, Oregon, Washington, and Minnesota. As in his landmark Mississippi address that May, which preceded and set the stage for Marshall's more famous June speech unveiling the U.S. aid offer destined to bear the general's name, Acheson shrewdly combined an appeal to America's traditional humanitarian impulses with an appeal to national self-interest. The precise mix of the two typically varied depending on the audience. When Joe Rauh of the liberal Americans for Democratic Action, for example, urged Acheson to "stress the humanitarian—rather than the anti-Communist—aspects of the aid program" to certain Minnesota audiences, the accommodating Acheson happily complied.[5] Still, he nearly always wove the two themes together. "We have a broad and deep humanitarian interest that those Western

Europeans do not starve," he reminded a Duluth gathering; "these people from whom our institutions and culture sprang, and from whom so many of us are descended." Then, without shifting gears, he stressed that "we have an even greater interest" in the plan because it was implicated with U.S. security. Economic failure in Western Europe would "sooner or later" lead to the region's "incorporation in the closed economic and political system of the Communists." Such a development, he warned, would grievously weaken U.S. security and well-being.[6]

In all of his statements in support of the Marshall Plan, Acheson emphasized the organic connection between European economic rehabilitation and the fundamental security needs of the United States. The European recovery program "is the very heart of our foreign policy," he proclaimed at one stop. It forms the "front line of American security," he declared at another. Adopting the standard language of realism, Acheson regularly described the Marshall Plan as "a soundly calculated risk" for the United States. An economic breakdown would lead to the rise of fascist or communist regimes throughout the region—"probably first fascism but ultimately communism," he predicted. In the absence of aid from Washington, desperate European states would look to Moscow for financial assistance; the Kremlin would, in turn, insist on ideological allegiance as its price for the needed aid. The result of such a dire progression of events? In his oft-repeated assessment, it would be nothing less than "a shift of power to Russia" that would constitute one of the most far-reaching, and ominous, such shifts in world history. The cost of the program, Acheson said, "would be insignificant if it succeeded in preventing that."[7]

Interestingly, these high-profile talks, widely reported in local and national media, rarely touched on what Acheson had for some time recognized as the intimately related question of Germany's future. Probably because he did not want to muddle, or needlessly complicate, the message, he steered clear of the tangled German question. On one occasion, however, during a closed meeting of the Portland, Oregon, Committee on Foreign Relations, a questioner specifically asked Acheson about the connection between Germany and the prospects for European recovery. Acheson responded with surprising frankness, encouraged perhaps by the absence of reporters. Recovery in Western Europe simply would not be possible without the simultaneous recovery of Germany, he explained matter-of-factly. "But German production must be controlled to prevent rearmament."[8] Those comments offer a revealing if brief glimpse into the former policymaker's thinking with regard to one of the most contentious and complex issues facing the Truman administration at that time. It was one he would be forced to confront, once more in an official capacity, much sooner than he, or anyone, could then have imagined.

In the course of his pro–Marshall Plan appearances, Acheson spoke with much more frequency—and with greater candor—about the Soviet Union. His remarks on that all-important subject, in fact, provide useful signposts to Acheson's evolving views about the nature and extent of Moscow's ambitions as well as important insights about the forces that he thought were shaping its international behavior. Although he was by then a confirmed cold warrior, the man behind the ideologically infused Truman Doctrine speech continued to downplay the role of ideological impulses in Stalinist foreign policy. "The Russians are primarily realists, not mere ideologists," he told the Commonwealth Club of San Francisco in a November 28, 1947, address. On that score, Acheson's judgments stand in stark contrast to those of some former colleagues in Truman's inner circle, such as Defense Secretary Forrestal, who were convinced that the ideological compunctions of Marxism-Leninism determined all of Moscow's actions. The undersecretary of state turned private citizen typically depicted the Soviet Union, instead, as a classic opportunist state: ever vigilant for chances to expand its influence and territorial reach, yet sufficiently realistic to withdraw when its probes met firm resistance or when it was faced with superior force combined with the resolve to use it.[9]

In a press interview just before his San Francisco speech, Acheson contended that the Soviets had grown confident, prior to Marshall's aid offer, "that within four years the sick countries of Western Europe would fall into their laps like rotten apples." They were still "frantically shaking trees in Italy and France," he observed, "hoping that some apples will fall." Effective implementation of the European recovery program, however, would almost certainly doom Soviet efforts to failure. Indeed, the "Russian hysteria" that greeted the plan's unveiling confirmed for him its essential wisdom.[10]

Two days later, in Portland, Acheson returned to the theme of Soviet pragmatism. "The Russians do not want real trouble with anyone at present," he asserted. "They have been genuinely surprised at the opportunities for expansion that have been presented to them, and at the success of their policy," Acheson observed. "Their goal was first to push toward the Dardanelles, and then into France and Italy, but they will not pursue this policy so vigorously as to cause war for the time being."[11] In late January 1948, in testimony before a House of Representatives committee examining the administration's European aid proposal, he presented a similar appraisal of Soviet leaders as fundamentally realists. If faced with a union of healthy European nations, which is what he insisted a vigorous Marshall Plan would do much to establish, the Soviet Union would most likely "accept the fact of stability in Western Europe and adjust to it." The Kremlin's rulers would do so, in Acheson's judgment, much as they had previously identified, and seized upon, the opportunities offered by weakness and instability. Without an adequately funded recovery program, however, Europeans would soon be unable to purchase essential goods and supplies, and this would lead to "endless poverty and an unchecked opportunity for Russia to take advantage of their plight." The Soviets, in short, were sufficiently flexible and pragmatic to adjust to changed circumstances; ideology did not constitute a fixed, guiding star that left them impervious to changed circumstances and immune to outside pressure. And the Marshall Plan, he never tired of emphasizing, represented the most effective instrument at present to check Soviet ambitions and curtail Soviet gains.[12]

On April 3, 1948, Congress overwhelmingly ratified the Marshall Plan legislation, much to Acheson's delight. His work on its behalf doubtless played at least some small role in that happy result. It also did much more than simply provide him an outlet for his excess energies. The work kept the Covington and Burling senior partner in the public eye—and reminded Truman, if he needed reminding, that his former undersecretary of state remained a loyal personal ally and reliable friend of the administration. Robert Butler, the U.S. ambassador to Australia, who attended one of Acheson's Minnesota speeches, was so impressed that he wrote Truman in glowing tones about the power, clarity, and persuasiveness of his presentation. "It was masterful," Butler enthused. "What we need today is more Dean Achesons." Truman sent Acheson a copy of the Butler letter. "I thought you would appreciate what he had to say—I know I certainly do," he wrote.[13]

Acheson finds weekend relaxation by working in the garden at his farm, Harewood, in Sandy Spring, Maryland, summer 1949. Courtesy of the Harry S. Truman Library

On April 4, just one day after Congress signed off on the European recovery program, Truman called Acheson at his Maryland farmhouse to ask if he would consider an appointment to become chief administrator for the Economic Cooperation Administration (ECA). Flattered by the offer to head the governmental agency that would be implementing the program he considered so crucial, Acheson nonetheless demurred. In a remarkable display of sage political advice and astute analysis, he told Truman that nominating him would constitute a great mistake. Acheson was perceived as too political a person, too partisan a Democrat. He advised Truman that a nonpolitical and nonpartisan figure could more easily garner needed congressional support from Republicans. The rather bumptious and egotistical Senator Arthur Vandenberg, in Acheson's view, seemed certain to be a key person in any effort to shake loose the necessary funds from Congress, and the Michigan Republican, whom Acheson had previously tried—with mixed success—to court, would likely oppose the former undersecretary's nomination and prefer a moderate Republican businessman such as Paul Hoffman. Acheson suggested to the president that he phone Vandenberg and inform him that he was thinking of putting Acheson's name forward to head the ECA. Vandenberg would complain, Acheson predicted, and indicate a strong preference for Hoffman. Imagining the scenario destined to play out almost exactly as he forecast, Acheson said that Hoffman was a good man and Truman would be well advised to accept him. Acheson reasoned that if Truman nominated Hoffman after having received the powerful Michigan legislator's stamp of approval, the appointment would then "irrevocably commit Vandenberg to the support of an adequately financed program." In the unlikely event that the senator found him acceptable, Acheson quickly added, "I would do it."[14]

Acheson thus remained on the fringes of power as a tumultuous period in U.S.-Soviet relations unfolded. He privately expressed dismay and alarm at the increasing heavy-handedness of Soviet policy, from the Czech coup of February 1948 to the blockade four months later of land routes into West Berlin. Acheson applauded the "determined opposition" of the United States and its Western allies to "all these Russian sorties." He remained convinced, as he declaimed in one public address, that while there was no simple formula for exorcising the dangers posed by Soviet adventurism "steady nerves and determined purpose" would eventually lead to the "free and secure international life" that Americans craved. When Great Britain, France, and the Benelux nations formed the Brussels mutual security pact that March, Acheson heartily commended the initiative. He fully supported as well the Truman administration's decisions to launch the so-called Berlin airlift and to begin exploring modalities for a broader cross-Atlantic security alliance with the Brussels Pact nations and Canada.[15]

Like most political observers at the time, Acheson expected that President Truman, despite his laudable foreign policy, would go down to defeat in the November 1948 presidential election. Ever the loyal Democrat, Acheson nonetheless stayed up most of election night at the home of his law partner and friend Gerhard Gesell, listening to the voting returns on radio. "By dawn," according to one account, "he was overjoyed and quite drunk." At Washington's Union Station, where he and Gesell needed to catch an 8:00 a.m. train to New York for a meeting with a client, Acheson "announced solemnly, 'I'm going to do something I've never done. I'm going to have a highball for breakfast.' Together, they toasted the President."[16]

Shortly after the election, Truman considered a small number of men, including W. Averell Harriman, to replace the retiring Marshall as secretary of state. Truman displayed little hesitancy, though, in selecting Acheson, his first choice and a man for whom he had the utmost respect and affection. The often-insecure Truman was sure he could work closely once again with his former undersecretary of state and was confident that Acheson would never upstage him or betray his trust—as Byrnes had. In late November the president summoned Acheson for a private meeting at Blair House, the stately Pennsylvania Avenue home where Truman was residing while the White House received much-needed renovations. The president wasted little time. "I want you to come back and be Secretary of State," he said. "Will you?" The offer, in Acheson's telling, left him "utterly speechless." The next day, after gaining Alice's consent, he formally accepted. At Truman's request, they kept the news secret for six weeks, leaving official Washington in the dark about this most important appointment and allowing false rumors and misleading speculation to spread. Then, on January 7, 1949, the president broke the silence, announcing that Dean Acheson would become his fourth secretary of state.[17]

BACK TO FOGGY BOTTOM

On January 21, 1949, Acheson officially assumed the reins of power at the State Department. That he was replacing and moving into the old office of the Olympian George Marshall, a man the new secretary not only respected deeply but whom he looked up to as a genuine national hero, made ascending to the head spot at Foggy Bottom an especially meaningful honor—and challenge—for

Acheson. When Marshall wrote Acheson in a warm personal letter that he was "very much gratified and reassured" to hear of his appointment and that he considered his former deputy "more than eminently qualified to do what must be done," the new secretary of state was nearly overcome with emotion. In a handwritten reply, for which Acheson begged the general's forgiveness, he offered a heartfelt tribute to a man he admired more than anyone. "Greatness," he wrote, "has to do with grandeur and with completeness of character." Only twice in his life, Acheson wrote—in what for him was an extremely rare display of adulation—had he been close to "greatness in a man. . . . Once with Justice Holmes and once with you." He closed by referring to the eighteen months he had worked with Marshall as "a great honor." "I shall . . . take comfort in thinking from time to time that if what I am doing is what you would have done," he added, "then it meets the highest and surest test I know how to apply."[18]

Cold War tensions between the United States and the Soviet Union had deepened appreciably during the final year and a half of Marshall's tenure. Conditions in much of the world, Acheson observed, offered little basis for optimism. Europe, in his assessment, provided the single exception to that general rule. "Four years of increasingly purposeful effort had brought the beginnings of recovery in Western Europe," he remarked subsequently, "but at the same time had intensified Soviet control of Eastern Europe and produced dangerous action farther west, of which the most ominous was the blockade of Berlin."[19]

Two high-stakes European issues demanded his immediate attention: the not-yet-finalized North Atlantic pact and the conjoined problem of Germany's tangled future. Since at least the beginning of the year, the German problem had progressively deteriorated. On January 27, just six days after Acheson took the oath of office, the recently established National Security Council (NSC) met to consider what Secretary of the Army Kenneth C. Royall described as a near-crisis situation. Royall reported that France was obstructing any movement toward the establishment of a West German state, as agreed upon by the United States, Great Britain, and France during the London talks of June 1948. He recommended an early meeting between Acheson and the French and British foreign ministers to resolve the current deadlock; until it was resolved, Royall urged, the North Atlantic Treaty (NAT) negotiations should be suspended.

Acheson found himself at a distinct disadvantage at this early stage of his tenure. In office less than a week, his boxes barely unpacked, he could hardly be as well versed on the particulars of so complex an issue as Germany as those who had been dealing with it for a long time, some virtually on a daily basis. Nonetheless, he reflexively took strong exception to the army secretary's proposal. Acheson considered the North Atlantic pact essential to his vision of European recovery and Western security; he had no desire, consequently, to postpone its completion any longer than absolutely necessary. So he played for time. Opining that he personally saw no alternative to proceeding with a semi-independent West German government, the new secretary of state proposed that the German dilemma be discussed more thoroughly later–after further study–and asked the director of State's Policy Planning Staff, Soviet and German expert George F. Kennan, to travel to Germany, carefully assess current conditions, and make policy recommendations at a subsequent NSC meeting.[20]

With the German question effectively put on hold, Acheson could turn his full attention to the outstanding issues requiring common assent before the North Atlantic pact could be concluded. Marshall and Lovett had carefully nurtured negotiations leading toward a European–North American security agreement ever since the so-called Washington exploratory talks had commenced that past July. The talks had proceeded inexorably, if methodically, toward an agreed vision of the kind of mutual defense pact that would best meet individual nations' security needs on both sides of the Atlantic. The negotiations had advanced sufficiently far, in fact, that the treaty most likely would have been completed well before Acheson became secretary of state if not for the intrusion of the 1948 presidential election campaign. The uncertainty of Truman's status through the summer and early autumn of that year–indeed, the widespread belief in informed political circles in America and abroad that New York governor Thomas Dewey would crush the unpopular Truman and then appoint John Foster Dulles as his secretary of state–complicated the diplomatic talks. Any effort to render into final form so historically momentous a treaty while occupancy of the White House for the next four years remained up in the air would have been both premature and impolitic.

When Acheson reentered government service in the wake of Truman's upset electoral triumph, he quickly brought himself up to speed on the issues still under debate. In a statement released to the press on January 26, the State Department's new chief succinctly summarized the core reasons, as he saw them, for the proposed pact. The fundamental goal of the treaty, he explained, was to deter aggression by providing "unmistakable proof of the joint determination of the participating nations to resist armed attack from any country." The North Atlantic Treaty was to be "a collective arrangement within the framework of the United Nations Charter." Although the NAT negotiations had been spurred, in fact, by the widespread belief that arrangements other than the UN would be necessary to secure the peace, Acheson deliberately–if disingenuously–depicted the two as fully compatible. The North Atlantic pact, in this construction, merely aided and complemented the UN's commitment to preserving the peace through collective security. This spin constituted a shrewd political move in view of growing popular and congressional concern that the North Atlantic grouping represented a deliberate bypassing–even an undercutting–of the UN. Those concerns needed to be met head-on, Acheson understood, if unequivocal congressional support was to be secured–a sine qua non for the treaty's success.[21]

Woodrow Wilson's failure, in 1919–1920, to gain Senate ratification of the Versailles Peace Treaty, it bears emphasizing, ranked among the defining political events of Acheson's young adult years. That treaty's covenant, drafted personally by Wilson, had aimed to establish the principles and mechanisms for implementing the new League of Nations' collective security commitment. When Acheson first arrived in Washington to take up his clerkship with Justice Brandeis, it was late September 1919. His introduction to the city he would call home for the remainder of his life coincided, within a matter of days, with the debilitating stroke Wilson suffered in Pueblo, Colorado, in the midst of a strenuous Western speaking tour. The president's incapacity strengthened the hands of the treaty's senatorial opponents, much to the neophyte lawyer's dismay. "In Congress wolves tore at the carcass of the Covenant and howled for the blood of the Administration," Acheson later recalled poignantly. "In the circle in which we moved depression and bewilderment deepened." At the center of that circle stood Brandeis. The very embodiment of early twentieth century liberalism, the Kentuckian was a fierce supporter of Wilson and the League as well as Acheson's earliest guiding light. The justice "wouldn't even talk about the treaty fight," Acheson remembered decades afterward, "giving the impression that things were so much worse than could be imagined as to be beyond discussion. We went on with our work and our lives, as I imagine people did in Rome in the fifth century with the defenses of the frontiers crumbling." Support for the League of Nations remained an article of faith among liberals of that era, and beyond. Acheson characterized belief in the League as one liberals "held with passion, first as a fighting faith for battle, and after battle as love of a lost cause."[22]

Not surprisingly, given his vivid recollection of the Versailles treaty debacle, the new secretary of state was determined that he and the president he now served avoid Wilson's missteps. Acheson thus made it a point to stress in every public and private utterance during this critical period that any U.S. commitment to the envisioned Atlantic pact would be "strictly in accordance with our constitutional processes." Congress, in other words, would retain its war-making powers; the executive branch had no intention whatsoever, he insisted, of impinging on the prerogatives of the legislative branch. No latter-day Henry Cabot Lodge would emerge, if Acheson had anything to do with it, to hack away at the essence of *this* treaty. He would not repeat his former idol Wilson's monumental political misjudgment that the give-and-take of White House–Capitol Hill negotiations required by the Constitution before any treaty became law could simply be brushed off as one would deal with an annoying gnat.

Acheson also placed great weight here, and in all subsequent explanations of the pact's rationale, on the positive psychological benefits he was certain it would spur throughout the West, especially across Western Europe. In conjunction with its line-in-the-sand pledge that the NAT partners would resist Soviet-backed aggression, the alliance's anticipated effect of fostering confidence in the future among leaders and ordinary citizens of Western Europe formed for him a crucial element of its value. The key to global peace and stability, in this formulation, thus lay in the NAT states' collective determination to make it "absolutely clear in advance that any armed attack affecting our national security would be met with overwhelming force."

Acheson's earliest public statements affirming the importance of the proposed treaty also touched on what would become a pet theme: that common values and traditions had forged natural bonds among the peoples of what he termed "the North Atlantic community." It was a constructed community, to be sure, if one adopts the parlance of today's social scientists, for it existed at that time only in the minds of those who were consciously striving to bring it into being, as was Acheson, through their words, actions, and sheer force of will. "The peoples of the North Atlantic have a common heritage and civilization," Acheson proclaimed solemnly. "We North Atlantic peoples share a common faith in fundamental human rights, in the dignity and worth of the human person, in the principles of democracy, personal freedom, and political liberty." The common heritage and values of the governments and citizens of the North Atlantic region, in this formulation, thus made the proposed alliance a natural, organic, even inevitable development.[23]

The soaring rhetoric could only partially camouflage the flawed logic and shaky history that lurked underneath Acheson's flights of fantasy. Were Italy and Germany, to take the most obvious problem with this conceptualization, part of this "North Atlantic community"? If so, how could their recent war of aggression, comparable action for which Acheson's projected community of like-minded North Atlantic peoples were now resolved immediately to counter, be explained? Simply as an aberration? Surely, one presumes, the secretary of state would not—*could* not—attribute such aberrant behavior to some fundamental flaw embedded within the very same peace-loving North Atlantic community that he was seeking now to differentiate from what he depicted as the innately aggression-prone Soviet state. Acheson, it will be recalled, had expressed privately his conviction that Germany (or at least its western portion) needed to be brought into the treaty area at the earliest practicable moment. But how could the very same Germany whose Third Reich had ruthlessly carried out the organized mass murder of perhaps six million Jews and hundreds of thousands of non-Jews—an atrocity that stands as the most flagrant, brutal, and almost unfathomable crime against humanity in the annals of human history—be appropriated now into the fraternity of liberal, peaceful, human rights–tolerant states that were to form the NAT's core?

And what about Italy? Surely, its ugly fascist interlude, its militaristic expansionism under Benito Mussolini's reign, and the bombastic Mussolini's embrace of and alliance with Hitler does grave violence to any notion of a uniquely virtuous North Atlantic community. So, to a lesser extent, would the inclusion of Portugal in the projected alliance, a country Acheson hoped to recruit largely because of its control over the strategically located Azores Islands. Yet Portugal, under the heavy-handed rule of dictator Antonio Salazar, could not meet any reasonable person's definition of a liberal state that promoted democratic freedoms and respected individual liberties and human rights. Even France, with its sorry recent history of collaboration with the Nazi occupiers and its less-than-heroic efforts to save the lives of its own Jewish citizens from persecution and death in Hitler's horrific concentration camps offered an uneasy match for Acheson's imagined North Atlantic community of tolerant, open, plural, freedom-loving states.

Acheson was much too smart, savvy, and historically conscious to have been unaware of the stark contradictions between his stirring words and the more sober, underlying reality of the corner of the globe he held up for veneration. One must conjecture, consequently, that he was engaging here in a quite conscious act of historical construction. He was seeking to create, as it were, a useful fiction: the fiction of a like-minded group of North American and European countries, moving bravely to forge a collective self-defense pact against future aggressors. The pact would build on centuries of common heritage and tradition and be fastened by a shared commitment to democracy, peace, and individual rights. The idealism of Acheson's mythical conceptualization of "North Atlantic peoples" certainly made for a more comfortable, and comforting, image than that of a simple alliance of convenience forged to meet a common foe. The language of realism, although ever-present in Acheson's public and private musings about the European–North American security pact he was striving to bring to fruition, was thus frequently subordinated to Wilsonian notions of spiritual bonds and hallowed cross-Atlantic traditions.

The final stage of the Washington talks offered Acheson his first major opportunity to tackle a complex negotiating process as his nation's principal representative. Although the most junior in tenure of all the European and Canadian diplomats who were his interlocutors, Acheson emerged quickly as the central player in the talks. This was partly because, of course, Washington was indispensable to any viable transatlantic defense pact. But it also derived from Acheson's sheer strength of intellect, command of the issues, and mastery of the fine art of diplomacy. By successfully finessing a range of thorny, last-minute problems while opportunistically seizing on unexpected openings to effect a dramatic expansion of the alliance's geographic reach, Acheson earned accolades and respect on both sides of the Atlantic. Acheson was a "tough-minded" diplomat who excelled in "the give-and-take of hard bargaining, which he enlivened with his sallies or illumined with his quick grasp of the issues," observed Dutch foreign minister Dirk U. Stikker. "We Europeans were never in any doubt as to Acheson's stewardship of America's interest," the Dutch statesman added. "But he rose above many of his contemporaries in his ability to combine this stewardship with a full understanding of the nature and conduct of an alliance."[24] By mid-March Acheson had skillfully navigated the path toward an agreed final version of the treaty, one he felt confident would win overwhelming support on Capitol Hill.

Among the nettlesome issues that he helped resolve during this last stage of the Washington talks, an especially sensitive one concerned possible expansion of the treaty's membership beyond the original seven nations. Those were Great Britain, France, Belgium, the Netherlands, and Luxembourg (the original Brussels Pact signatories) plus the United States and Canada. Italy, despite a tenuous geographic claim to North Atlantic status and an all-too-real status as a member of the Axis coalition that precipitated the last war, wanted in. France championed Italy's case for its own—largely anti-German—reasons. Acheson, for his part, saw few advantages and more than a few disadvantages in inviting Italy to become a charter member of the about-to-be-formed club. He was much more interested in stretching the membership into Europe's northern reaches than in embracing its southern Mediterranean flank. Acheson saw substantial potential value in persuading one or more of the Scandinavian countries to join. He thought that a firm, treaty-based commitment to the anti-Soviet cause by at least one of them could help drive a wedge between Sweden, a neutralist nation of long-standing, and the other states in the region. That would, in turn, serve to derail a worrisome recent movement toward some form of Scandinavian neutrality pact. The prospect of a neutralized, nonaligned Scandinavia, on the Soviet Union's doorstep, rattled Acheson; he worked assiduously, as a result, to discourage its consummation—and the NAT played an instrumental role in those efforts. Additionally, he and the administration's leading defense officials believed that the Scandinavian countries constituted major geopolitical assets to the anti-Soviet coalition that the United States was laboring to bring into being. Their value derived not just from their proximity to the Soviet Union and window to the North Sea, but from certain strategically located overseas territories that they controlled—none more important than Denmark's Greenland.

In mid-February Acheson urged his European and Canadian colleagues to consider extending a formal invitation to Norway to become a signatory to the pact. His proposal immediately met objections, especially from the French. Ambassador Henri Bonnet insisted that if Norway was to be asked to join then his government believed Italy should be invited as well. Further complicating matters, the French diplomat made clear that Paris considered it imperative that any North Atlantic defense arrangements encompass not just metropolitan France but its North African possessions as well, a position that Acheson immediately tried to discourage. Any effort to extend the treaty area beyond Europe, the new secretary of state pointed out, would likely spark serious reservations from within the U.S. Congress. Reminding Bonnet that the proposed treaty marked a historic departure for the United States from its long tradition of avoiding "entangling" alliances, he cautioned that French insistence on either of these two recent requests—membership for Italy or the inclusion of French overseas territories—might impel the Congress to balk, placing the whole treaty in jeopardy.[25]

On February 25 Acheson cabled Jefferson Caffrey, the U.S. ambassador in Paris, to complain that Bonnet's impolitic presentation of France's self-interested, last-minute demands amounted to an "extraordinary exhibition" of obstructionism. In view of current Soviet pressure on Norway and Oslo's corresponding interest in linking itself to the about-to-be-completed treaty, Acheson thought a rebuff at this juncture could be "catastrophic." Earlier that day, during a formal session with the representatives of the projected NAT states, Acheson laid into the French envoy. "I stated that Bonnet appeared ready, in order to get Italy in, to run extreme risks over Norway," he recorded, "risks to which she was not entitled to subject all of us and that if [the] French gov[ernmen]t insisted on this position I would not take responsibility for [the] consequences." Acheson urged Caffrey to see Foreign Minister Robert

Schuman promptly in the hopes of impressing upon the French government the critical importance of resolving this impasse and extending an invitation to Norway forthwith.[26]

In a private meeting with Truman three days later, Acheson informed the president of France's deplorable effort to link the Norwegian and Italian cases. After gaining the president's assent to stand firm on the question of Norway's admission, he advised his boss to keep an open mind on the Italian question. Although Acheson and Truman both harbored major reservations about adding Mediterranean Italy to a pact long advertised as an exclusively North Atlantic grouping, the secretary of state argued that larger concerns—especially the need to win France's trust and to help ease its deep-seated security fears so as to solidify the emerging Western bloc—might warrant an American-brokered compromise down the line. Truman, as he usually did, deferred to the judgment of his most trusted foreign policy hand.[27]

Following the Oval Office tête-à-tête, Acheson met with the two key members of the Senate Foreign Relations Committee: the Democratic chair, Senator Tom Connally of Texas, and the ranking Republican member, Senator Arthur Vandenberg of Michigan. Acheson, correctly, saw them as the pivotal figures in his campaign, already well under way, to sell this treaty to Congress— even if he privately considered them "two prima donnas." When he gained assurances that they, like Truman, could live with an accord that extended security coverage at least to Algeria, he pocketed the concession. Acheson intended to wait for the opportune moment to put it on the table.[28]

That moment occurred on March 1, at a climactic meeting of the NAT negotiators at the State Department. Tension mounted during that session to the point where it threatened to explode. British ambassador Sir Oliver Franks, while conceding that there might legitimately be differences between Britain and France regarding their respective assessments of Italy's strategic value, complained that this was a very late date for his French counterpart to be laying down conditions for his country's acceptance of a treaty under discussion now for over seven months. "Although it might be a defect of national temperament on his part," Franks noted in a remark dripping with sarcasm, he found it difficult "to reach an agreed solution if, using the natural metaphor, a pistol was put at his head." The French representative responded in kind. Bonnet said "his natural reaction was the same, when he was engaged in a negotiation and had the impression of talking to a wall." The French ambassador added that "he was sorry if his views were interpreted as conditions because they certainly had not been intended as such"; he was merely trying to ensure that any final treaty gain sufficient support from the French public.

In an impressive display of coolness and tact, Acheson chose to ignore the heated exchange that was now becoming quite personal and instead took the high road. He even went so far as to compliment the French representative, expressing his delight in learning that Bonnet was *not* insisting on an invitation to Italy as a precondition for France joining the NAT. Acheson then appeared to digress, noting that he had come into the discussions "at a relatively late date" and had been surprised to learn that conversations with leading U.S. senators were still at a preliminary stage. The responsibility had thus fallen on his shoulders to explain patiently to Senate leaders the complexity and sensitivity of a number of issues, including the Algeria question. They had gradually, as a result of those private talks, come to see the folding of Algeria into the treaty area in a different light. Now, he was happy to report, the U.S. government was agreeable to the inclusion in the treaty of "the Algerian Departments of France." There was "nothing Machiavellian," he hastened to interject, in the U.S. approach. Evidently stunned by this most welcome news, Bonnet profusely thanked Acheson "for the effort he was making to have the French position understood in the Senate."

Without missing a beat, Acheson then turned quickly to the issue of Norway's inclusion. Claiming somewhat presumptively that the matter now appeared settled, he asked for the assent of the assembled ambassadors for a formal offer to Norway to join the NAT discussions. After receiving unanimous support for that motion, Acheson next made a case for the additional inclusion of Denmark, describing the tiny nation as "one of the most critical countries." But he was careful not to call for a vote on the Danish case, probably because the question of Italian membership remained up in the air. Acheson had privately decided that it would be best, at this delicate stage, regardless of his own views about Italy's suitability, not to rule out the possibility of a compromise. Still, he did not yet have a green light to offer one. Accordingly, he told his European and Canadian colleagues of his concern that the pact might encounter more difficulty with the Senate "if a larger Mediterranean factor was involved," while assuring them that Italy's possible inclusion remained a matter of active debate within the Truman administration. He promised to report shortly on the results of that debate.[29]

The next day Acheson broached the Italian question with Truman. During their private conversation, he gained the president's definite, if less-than-enthusiastic, support for bringing Rome into the Atlantic alliance as an original member. The short meeting, in which Acheson presented Truman with two different State Department working papers, one making the case for Italy's inclusion, the other the case against, offers a richly instructive illustration both of Acheson's governing pragmatism and of his diplomatic modus operandi. He emphasized to Truman that "the real issue" at the present time did not simply hinge on the merits of the Italian case but concerned the probable impact that a rejection of Italy's bid would have on France's attitude toward and future connection with the emerging Western bloc. Because France was "so emphatically in favor of Italian participation," a rebuff could drive a wedge between it and the other NAT member-states. Consequently, Acheson said, the administration should "probably" accept Italian inclusion. If it did not, an open split among the Western powers could occur, with serious consequences for the image of Western unity.[30]

From the outset, the secretary of state had approached the negotiations surrounding the historically momentous transatlantic security pact without any fixed, unalterable views about process or about the treaty's ultimate geographic contours. Thus Acheson remained open to creative, workable solutions to the problems, and opportunities, that surfaced as the talks moved from generalities to specifics. Latter-day analysts of the early Cold War ofttimes assume that the consummation of this pact simply represented the logical and inevitable unfolding of a containment strategy first initiated in mid-1947 with the Truman Doctrine and Marshall Plan. According to what has almost become the conventional wisdom, the early politico-economic scaffolding of that strategy moved naturally to encompass a military-security arm in the wake of the Czech coup, Brussels Pact, and Berlin crisis. As the preceding analysis suggests, however, the birth of the North Atlantic Treaty Organization was never so simple and straightforward a development, never quite so predetermined.

Right up to the final Acheson-facilitated negotiating breakthroughs, ample opportunities existed for failure—or, nearly as worrisome to him, an open split among the Western partners that could have provided plentiful grist for the Kremlin's propaganda mill. Such a split, he was keenly aware, could easily have undermined the very goal of Western solidarity that the pact had been designed to promote.

Acheson's feel for the art of the possible, and his ability to remain focused on the big picture, even when sudden, unanticipated tactical shifts became necessary, stood him in good stead in these often-tense talks. Those skills had been honed during his years of experience in the world of corporate law, where meeting the fundamental needs of high-powered clients was a sine qua non, the knack for finding common ground between two contending parties imperative. Top corporate lawyers invariably seek to settle legal battles out of court; it is a time-honored axiom of the legal profession that allowing a case to go to trial not only increases expenses for both parties but invites uncontrollable risks. Acheson, like any accomplished attorney, preferred always to minimize potential risks while maximizing likely gains.

That habit of thinking, not surprisingly, guided his approach to diplomacy as well. During the NAT negotiations, and throughout his years as secretary of state, Acheson always worked to limit and control the risks that inevitably inhere in any diplomatic bargaining. In this particular case, he grasped from the first that a successful treaty meant building support and consensus, and that in turn meant conducting three-tiered negotiations: with America's prospective Atlantic pact partners, with the president, and with key congressional representatives. That he managed to succeed at all three levels, while keeping each of the negotiating partners apprised of what was happening at the other level, testifies to an unusual ability to carry complex discussions to a satisfactory conclusion—a conclusion fully consonant with the goals he aimed to meet. Senior Canadian diplomat Escott Reid later observed, in a complaint tinged with grudging admiration, that Acheson frequently used the presumed limitations imposed by the Senate Foreign Relations Committee—the proverbial "tough guy in the back room"—so as to strengthen his own bargaining power in the intergovernmental negotiations. The technique proved effective in this case since Washington's prospective partners were reluctant to risk a congressional veto over the treaty's final form.[31] Acheson's overarching strategy, its bears note, also involved fostering a positive atmosphere for subsequent negotiations aimed at reaching a concerted U.S.-British-French position on the German problem. If a transatlantic security pact had been finalized in a way that rendered a common Western position on Germany less likely, then the NAT achievement could have been a mere transitory blip in the context of a broader Cold War setback. No one was more attuned to those linkages than Acheson.

Following the Algerian and Italian concessions, each of which contributed to building the good faith with France that Acheson considered essential for an acceptable German resolution to be hammered out down the road, Acheson moved swiftly to put the other pieces of the NAT puzzle in place. On March 7, despite continuing British skepticism, he led his European and Canadian colleagues to a collective position of full support for Italian membership. Having broadened the geographic expanse of the pact with the Norwegian and Italian invitations, the secretary of state then pressed for adding Denmark, Iceland, and Portugal to the pact. That proposition, too, brooked almost no dissent. Connally and Vandenberg, kept fully briefed by Acheson, made clear that they would not oppose the broadened membership and suggested only minor modifications in the language of the NAT charter. By March 15 the negotiators had reached agreement on the treaty's final form.[32]

Three days later Acheson went public, citing former Secretary of State Henry Stimson's adage that the understanding and support of the American people could be achieved only through full discussion "on the basis of complete information." Such understanding and support, Stimson always insisted, were essential to the success of any policy. In that spirit, Acheson delivered a nationwide radio address designed to explain the meaning and significance of this fundamental break with more than a century and a half of national tradition. Not since the French alliance of 1778, after all, had the United States entered into an entangling alliance with a foreign power or powers. Cutting right to the heart of the matter, Acheson said that the American people would want to know the answers to three principal questions: "How did it come about and why is it necessary? What are its terms? Will it accomplish its purpose?" The fundamental goals of the treaty, he emphasized throughout the speech, were peace and security. "If peace and security can be achieved in the North

Atlantic area, we shall have gone a long way to assure peace and security in other areas as well." Those objectives depended to a large extent on the promise, embedded in the proposed treaty, to meet aggression promptly by means of collective defense. But peace and security depended as well, Acheson stressed, on a psychological element. "In the most practical terms," he asserted, "true international peace and security require a firm belief by the peoples of the world that they will not be subjected to unprovoked attack, to coercion and intimidation, to interference in their own affairs." In other words, the North Atlantic Treaty aimed to deter aggression through its commitment to prompt and effective collective self-defense measures, thereby discouraging military adventurism *before* it occurred while erecting a military-psychological shield behind which the nations of the North Atlantic region could return to ordinary, productive activity.

"We have learned our history lesson from two world wars in less than half a century," Acheson continued. "That experience has taught us that the control of Europe by a single aggressive unfriendly power would constitute an intolerable threat to the national security of the United States." Recent history also taught that "if free nations do not stand together they will fall one by one." Acheson wove those lessons into a didactic narrative about the cardinal importance of standing up to aggression, meeting any threats to the peace through collective action, and ensuring the maintenance of a European balance of power favorable to "the free nations." As in his earlier public statements on the NAT negotiations, Acheson labored to depict an idealized Atlantic community. He held that the treaty's "ethical essence" emanated from a common commitment among its member-states to democracy, human rights, and liberal values. In a rhetorical flourish that elided over countless inconvenient historical events and forces—not least among them two global conflicts precipitated as much from within, as outside, that very same peace-loving Atlantic community—Acheson declared the North Atlantic pact to be "the product of at least three hundred and fifty years of history, perhaps more." A community linked by "common institutions and moral and ethical beliefs," in this construction, had connected Western Europe to North America centuries earlier and then spread across the European continent. The resulting "western civilization," as he termed it, prominently featured an "ingrained spirit of restraint and tolerance"; that spirit stood in dramatic contradistinction to "the Communist belief that coercion by force is a proper method of hastening the inevitable."[33]

Acheson's idealized community thus arose from much more than a simple fear of Soviet power and disdain for communist ideology; in his construction, it sprouted naturally from shared values, history, and traditions. The speech was a tour de force by a master rhetorician, offering a seamless–if historically shaky–rationale for a security pact that represented a radically new departure for the United States. His president could not have been more pleased. After listening to Acheson's exposition over a radio station from Key West, his favorite vacation spot, Truman cabled his "hearty congratulations" for the secretary of state's "clear, lucid, and forceful" explanation of the treaty's basic principles.[34]

On April 4 the foreign ministers of the twelve founding states assembled in Washington for the formal treaty-signing ceremonies. Each minister was allotted five minutes to speak, and Acheson used his time to deliver a "Lincolnesque" speech, replete with Biblical language and striking imagery. Among the chief purposes in the "minds and hearts" of the treaty's drafters, he mused, was "to set down realities for the guidance of men, whether well or ill disposed." "For those who set their feet upon the path of aggression," he proclaimed solemnly, "it is a warning that if it must needs be that offenses come, then woe unto them by whom the offense cometh." Once more Acheson insisted that the treaty merely formalized an underlying reality: what he termed "the unity of belief, of spirit, of interest of the community of nations represented here." That unity, he asserted, derived from common "moral and spiritual values" and was "the product of many centuries of common thought and of the blood of many simple and brave men and women."[35] Acheson did not mention the Soviet Union, nor did he need to do so. Everyone understood that the North Atlantic Treaty sprang from a common determination to check Soviet expansion. His primary goal, as reflected in his public and private remarks over the past several months, was to assert the existence of a North Atlantic community rooted in common values, history, and tradition. It stood as a natural community, in his rendering, and it was a community now committed formally to resist any form of aggression against any of its members by common action so as to protect its kind of life. In his concluding remarks, President Truman picked up on those themes, emphasizing that the North Atlantic Treaty was "a neighborly act" undertaken by the voluntary association of countries that, for all their differences, shared common values, were committed to peace, and had decided freely to enter into a pact of "mutual self-protection."[36]

TACKLING THE GERMAN PROBLEM

In the warm afterglow of the Atlantic pact ceremonies, Acheson moved swiftly to tackle the other outstanding Cold War question: Germany's future. Seeking to capitalize on the positive momentum the completed treaty had generated among the Western allies, he invited British foreign minister Bevin and French foreign minister Robert Schuman to remain in Washington for a few days so that they could jointly review allied policy toward Germany. From the earliest weeks of his tenure, Acheson had grasped that a successful North Atlantic Treaty constituted an essential precondition for any Anglo-French-American breakthrough on the troubled German front. On February 14, 1949, in a revealing exchange with Connally and Vandenberg, Acheson had pointed out that the great value of the proposed treaty derived not just from its promise to deter future aggression but also from its inducement to France to take a more tolerant approach to the inexorable recrudescence of German power. He expressed doubt that, in the absence of a transatlantic pact, "the French would ever be reconciled to the inevitable diminution of direct allied control over Germany and the progressive reduction of occupation troops." The consummation of such a pact, Acheson told the senators, "would give France a greater sense of security against Germany as well as the Soviet Union and should materially help with the realistic consideration of the problem of Germany."[37] Well before the treaty was finalized, in short, Acheson saw it as inseparably intertwined with the critical issue of Franco-German relations.

On that score, the secretary of state found himself at odds with more than a few of the administration's other senior diplomatic and defense officials. Some, such as Army Secretary Royall, had advocated using the NAT negotiations as a club to force the French to reverse their policy of delay and obstruction in Germany. Acheson, of course, took a completely different tack. His sympathetic handling of several French-imposed stumbling blocks during the final stages of the NAT talks made clear that he preferred to win French cooperation through compromise and understanding rather than through heavy-handed pressure.

Yet the precise stance that the Truman administration should take toward Germany was far from resolved in the spring of 1949. As Acheson was steering the North Atlantic Treaty to harbor, George F. Kennan was leading a group of State and Defense Department experts that was conducting a comprehensive reassessment of German policy. The secretary of state and his policy-planning director agreed on much. They both appreciated Germany's indispensability to the economic and political revival of Western Europe, a goal that each considered essential if a favorable balance of power vis-à-vis the Soviet Union was to be maintained. Acheson and Kennan agreed as well that Germany needed to be integrated into the broader Western European community. They each recognized that, as Kennan phrased it, "There is no solution to the German problem in terms of Germany; there is only a solution in terms of Europe."[38] Acheson placed greater weight than did Kennan, however, on the need to harness Germany's latent power for the emerging Western bloc—not only to ensure the success of the European recovery program but to add solidity to the military alliance that the Atlantic treaty aimed to put in place. He was also much more willing than Kennan to entertain the prospect of a permanently divided Germany, particularly if the western occupation zones—which contained two-thirds of occupied Germany's territory, three-fourths of its population, and the lion's share of its industrial infrastructure and most valuable natural resources—could be tied closely to the emerging Western sphere. The London accords of June 1948, which called for the French occupation zone to be combined with the already merged U.S. and British zones, held out the prospect of exactly such an outcome: an independent West German state integrated into Western Europe. Yet, in the months that followed the London Council of Foreign Ministers (CFM) meetings, fears of a militarily revived Germany had led the French to block progress on a trizonal accord, thereby postponing the promised termination of the military occupation regime. Those delaying tactics produced a worrisome diplomatic stalemate among the allies; they also fostered political restiveness among West Germans desperate to regain some form of sovereignty.

By the time of the Acheson-Bevin-Schuman meetings, Kennan had long been arguing for a German policy that eschewed any permanent division of the country based on current Western and Soviet occupation zones. He saw wisdom, instead, in a U.S. policy aimed at forging a unified Germany in the heart of a unified Europe. The policy-planning chief feared that a permanent division of Germany into pro-American and pro-Soviet spheres would severely undercut prospects for peace and security in postwar Europe and hence needed to be averted. Although the two men had yet to clash openly over their competing inclinations, Acheson already sensed potentially unacceptable risks in any negotiated four-power compromise that might sanction a unified Germany. The specter of a fully independent Germany, unmoored to the West, constituted one of his worst geostrategic nightmares. A revivified, democratic, firmly anticommunist Germany, conversely, offered the key to a European– and global–power balance favorable to the United States. If the pursuit of that objective made a territorial split unavoidable and consigned Germany's eastern regions to the Soviet sphere, it was a price Acheson was prepared to pay. France, in Acheson's calculation, posed nearly as great an obstacle to that end as did the Soviet Union; he felt certain that its leaders would accede to the end of the occupation regime and the formation of an independent German Federal Republic only if their deep-rooted security fears about resurgent German power could be put to rest.[39]

In three days of intensive, and surprisingly amicable, talks with Bevin and Schuman, Acheson helped build a consensus behind the policy direction he believed most consistent with that fundamental objective. Since the French foreign minister saw the recently concluded North Atlantic Treaty as providing a sufficient security guarantee against German–as well as Russian–aggression, he conceded early in the talks that his government was now amenable to pressing ahead with full implementation of the London accords. Much to Acheson's relief, Schuman assured his interlocutors that France would no longer delay fusing its occupation zone with the Anglo-American zone, nor would it any longer obstruct movement toward the creation of a partially sovereign, federal republic in West Germany. Those important concessions enabled the three diplomats to speedily compose their differences not only on the critical issues surrounding the phasing out of the allied military occupation but also on a host of other vexing matters, from reparations to the nature of the newly drafted German constitution (or "Basic Law") to control over the Ruhr to state boundaries.

Despite wide differences in background, temperament, and style, the three men quickly established an excellent rapport. Acheson and Bevin, the burly, quick-tempered, and occasionally gruff ex–union leader whose formal education had ended in grade school, made an unusual pair. Yet they developed strong affection for each other and a good working relationship. "Ernest Bevin was as honorable and loyal a colleague as one could wish," Acheson later wrote in an admiring tribute. The more reserved and formal Schuman never operated on the easy first-name basis that "Ernie" and "Dean" enjoyed. Nonetheless, Acheson held him in the highest regard. He once praised Schuman as a "gallant and gentle and great man," placing him among the truly visionary French statesmen of the twentieth century. The trust and mutual respect that all three of these Western foreign ministers displayed toward each other, during this initial tripartite negotiation and subsequently, made possible many of the key accomplishments of Acheson's tenure.[40]

On April 7 the threesome met with Truman to discuss what Bevin proudly referred to as the "complete accord" they had reached on a common German policy during their "highly successful and gratifying series of meetings." It was "remarkable," the British foreign minister quipped, that in a matter of days he and his French and American colleagues had reached agreement "after years of no agreement." Schuman and Acheson heartily concurred, and Truman, for his part, expressed his happiness in receiving news so good that he called it "the best thing that had been done in his administration."[41] The next day Acheson transmitted a memorandum to the president that illuminated the momentous nature of the just concluded tripartite accords. "I am convinced that the success of these negotiations on German affairs has been greatly facilitated by the conclusion of the North Atlantic Treaty," he emphasized. "Without it, I doubt that we could have come to a successful conclusion of these Agreements at this time."[42]

The successful three-way discussions were almost certainly hastened, as they were made more urgent, by Stalin's recent public remark about the need for renewed four-power talks on the German question. On April 11 Soviet diplomat Jacob Malik made Stalin's offhanded comment more concrete when he told Philip C. Jessup, the U.S. deputy representative at the UN, that Moscow was prepared to lift the Berlin blockade. In return, the Soviet government wanted Western economic countermeasures against Soviet-controlled eastern Germany ended and, most significantly and controversially, insisted that the Council of Foreign Ministers be reconvened for another round of negotiations on Germany's future. The Soviet offer impaled the Western powers on the horns of a painful dilemma. If they were to dismiss summarily Stalin's overture, the Kremlin could then pin responsibility for the division of Germany on the United States, Great Britain, and France. If they acceded to the Soviet offer and reopened formal discussions, however, the recently concluded tripartite agreements could be put in jeopardy, especially if the Soviets might genuinely be willing to countenance unification. A complex question thus loomed: Would the likely gains associated with the establishment of a sovereign, unified Germany, along with mutual Western and Soviet troop withdrawals, outweigh the prospective risks? Acheson thought not. He remained exceedingly wary, as a result, of the prospect of further East-West negotiations.

By the same token, Acheson was determined not to leave the Western allies vulnerable to the charge of having *caused* Germany's partition. The secretary of state considered it essential, accordingly, that they accept the Soviet offer for another CFM round of talks. His British and French counterparts agreed. Over the next month Acheson helped coordinate and preside over an elaborate series of policy debates within the State Department and at the highest levels of the national security bureaucracy in preparation for those talks. He wanted all possible scenarios examined. And they were—in exhaustive detail. Acheson may have made up his mind on the German issue, however, well before the studies were formally vetted, the various position papers dissected. Unlike Kennan, whose meticulously drafted "Plan A" made a strong case for a unified Germany, Acheson saw grave, uncontrollable risks in such an outcome. He worried that a reunited Germany, untethered to the West, could either drift over time into the Soviet sphere of influence or, nearly as frightening, emerge as an unaligned, balance wheel in European diplomacy and East-West relations. Either scenario, from Acheson's perspective, was wholly unacceptable to the United States.[43]

On May 18 Truman presided over an NSC meeting that served as the culmination of those deliberations on German policy. Acheson dominated the discussion. He lined up with the Joint Chiefs of Staff and the civilian policy analysts in the Defense Department who also identified substantial risks in Kennan's Plan A and who adamantly opposed any premature consideration of troop withdrawals. Acheson, who could as usual count on the president's firm support, recommended that the United States not "abandon the advantages" it now held in West Germany. Rather, he proposed that the allies go forward with the establishment of the planned federal republic in the Western occupation zones and agree to unification only "on the basis of consolidating the Eastern zone into ours." The latter was of course more a posture than a serious negotiating position, as Acheson well appreciated, since it was one the Soviets were sure to dismiss out of hand. What Acheson wanted to accomplish at the Paris meeting, essentially, was "to probe the Soviet attitude" while shifting the burden of responsibility to the Soviets for what now looked to be the inevitable division of Germany.[44]

The next day Acheson unveiled the administration's uncompromising negotiating stance before a closed meeting of the Senate Foreign Relations Committee. "What we are concerned with," he told the senators, "is the strengthening and recovery of Western Europe and the extension of that strength and recovery as far eastward as possible." To those committee members who hoped for a more conciliatory U.S. policy, Acheson responded that his State Department experts had found no "sugar" to offer the Russians in Paris. To those who worried about a prolongation of the Cold War, Acheson responded that America's adversary simply could not be trusted; the proper policy for the United States, at this juncture, was to shore up Western economic and military strength—not to search fruitlessly for ways to bridge Soviet-American differences. "The most dangerous thing in the world that we can do," he remarked, "is to again enter into any agreement which depends for its execution upon Russian cooperation and Russian good will." The secretary of state's toughness shone through during the extended give-and-take with committee members of both parties.[45] Following the session, Vandenberg wrote in his diary, "One thing is sure—if there ever was any suspicion about his being pro-Russian it is all different now. As a matter of fact he is so *totally* anti-Soviet and is going to be so completely tough that I really doubt whether there is any chance *at all* for a Paris agreement."[46]

On May 23, 1949, the much-anticipated meeting of the Council of Foreign Ministers opened at Paris's ornate Palais Rose. It closed four weeks later, in predictable stalemate. Although the sessions were courteous, businesslike, and surprisingly free of polemics, they revealed nary a hint of common ground between the Soviets and the Western allies. Acheson recognized, from the very first week, that Moscow simply would not run any risks in central Europe. The "fundamental determination" of the Soviets, he informed Truman by cable, was "not to be drawn into any agreement in regard to Germany which would involve a weakening in any respect of their absolute unilateral control over Eastern Germany and [the] Eastern sector of Berlin." Months later he told the Senate Foreign Relations Committee, in a closed session, that he had become "absolutely convinced" at Paris "that the Russians will not take one single solitary step of any sort which weakened [their] control in any way over Germany." Indeed, what most struck–and gratified–America's senior diplomat was the extreme defensiveness of the Soviet negotiating stance. From a confident, offensive attitude in 1947, the Soviets had now retreated to a cautious, defensive strategy. That was a direct result, Acheson was convinced, of the successful Western initiatives that had marked the past two years. He also found significance in the Soviet disinclination to dissolve the CFM, despite the deep East-West divisions so evident in the talks. "They may be genuinely concerned," he surmised, about avoiding "real international isolation."[47]

Acheson and his party returned home on June 21, exhausted but pleased with their handiwork. They had challenged the Soviets to accept true independence for East Germany, along the lines of the allies' recent decisions regarding West Germany, only to receive the categorical rejection they had expected. Truman met the plane on its arrival in Washington, despite the early morning hour, greeting his secretary of state with a warm, "Well done!"[48]

In the days that followed the important, if inconclusive, Paris conference, Acheson implored the president and Congress to maintain the positive momentum in U.S. policy that he was certain had forced the Soviets to the defensive. "You either move forward or you move back," he said flatly.[49] Moving forward meant for him immediate action in ratifying the North Atlantic pact and enacting the Military Assistance Program (MAP). Both appeared necessary to further the economic, political, and military reinvigoration of Western Europe that Acheson continued to rank as the highest priority of U.S. foreign policy. "The most profound conviction that I got in this whole business is that the North Atlantic Treaty is the Rock of Gibraltar," he told the Senate Foreign Relations Committee in executive session, "and that the military assistance pact, or act, is absolutely vital."[50]

The latter, which called for $1.4 billion in military support to America's allies, approximately two-thirds of that sum earmarked for Europe, aimed to help close the sizable gap between Soviet military capabilities in Europe and the collective defense capacity of the Atlantic pact nations. The Soviet Union at that time maintained a formidable thirty divisions on the ground in Eastern Europe. "Facing them," Acheson pointed out in his memoir, stood just "three and a half American and two and a half British divisions scattered throughout Germany, performing occupation and police duty," coupled with France's "less than half a dozen ill-armed divisions" and perhaps another six divisions in the Benelux countries.[51] The Atlantic pact promised protection to its member-states, but the actual military capabilities it could draw on remained woefully inadequate to the task. Hence, the secretary of state saw the MAP as an indispensable step on the road to the West's military buildup. Enhancing the military strength and productive capacity of Washington's Atlantic partners ultimately enhanced "our own freedom and security," Acheson emphasized on Capitol Hill, whereas continued European weakness compromised U.S. security. "Western Europe is now an organism with a soft shell, and as such it invites attack from the predatory," he remarked. "It must develop a hard shell of adequate defense forces to discourage such an attack."[52] Unless the United States promptly began providing military assistance to its Western European allies, he pleaded during a closed Senate hearing, "then any planning becomes mere paper planning with no force underlying it. . . . It is just too dangerous to allow that situation of almost complete immobility of these minute forces that you now have."[53]

Acheson exulted when, on July 25, the Senate overwhelmingly ratified the North Atlantic Treaty. Just hours later Truman submitted the MAP legislation, formally requesting an unprecedented $1.4 billion in peacetime military assistance to America's allies. For the first time since the close of World War II, Acheson believed, events were moving decidedly in America's direction.

The ratification of the Atlantic pact capped a phenomenal six months of diplomatic activity and achievement for Truman and his head diplomat.

Arguably, no secretary of state before or since has accomplished more in his or her first half year on the job than did Dean Acheson between January and July 1949. The European recovery program was beginning to pick up steam; the transatlantic alliance had moved from dream to reality; French fears of a resurgent Germany had been partially assuaged; a new constitution, heralding an independent, federal republic, was being promulgated in West Germany; Soviet adventurism had seemingly been checked; and the critical MAP legislation was before Congress. Acheson had played a major role in each of those initiatives. He had every right to take enormous satisfaction, accordingly, in his early performance as the nation's chief foreign policy steward.

Yet major problems loomed on the horizon—some foreseeable, some much less so. Heated resistance to the MAP soon erupted within Congress, highlighting the serious problem caused by the imbalance between America's mounting defense commitments and the resources available to meet them. Vicious political partisanship reared its head during the MAP debates as well, as it did in the deepening controversy about the Truman administration's responsibility for the imminent demise of the Chiang Kai-shek regime in China, foreshadowing another daunting challenge. Other third world problems simmered just below the surface, from Southeast Asia to the Indian subcontinent to the Middle East—parts of the world well beyond Acheson's familiarity and expertise but each now inexorably being drawn into the Cold War struggle. And, perhaps most fatefully, in mid-summer 1949 the Soviets were planning to test their first atomic device. Acheson, temporarily buoyed by his spectacular debut as secretary of state, would soon find himself in the vortex of a frightfully powerful storm.

4

INTO THE CAULDRON

Acheson inherited enormous challenges in postwar Asia, challenges every bit as complex as those he faced in Europe. Yet he was, in nearly every way, much less prepared to meet them. As assistant and undersecretary of state between 1941 and 1947, he had dealt primarily with European matters and U.S.-Soviet relations. Eurocentric by background and experience, he had no firsthand exposure to any part of Asia. Acheson had never traveled to that vast continent, nor had he met more than a few of Asia's emerging leaders. Perhaps Dean Rusk, who served as his loyal and devoted assistant secretary, overstated the case when he observed that Acheson "did not give a damn about the brown, yellow, black, and red people in various parts of the world."[1] That perception, nonetheless, albeit harsh, captures the combination of disdain, condescension, and racial stereotyping with which Acheson often approached the non-Western world. Certainly the great complexities of a dynamic Asia undergoing nothing less than profound, revolutionary upheaval lay well outside his area of expertise–and zone of comfort.

FORGING A COHERENT ASIAN POLICY

Not surprisingly, Acheson's personal views–and policy inclinations–about Asian developments were still somewhat unformed when he assumed his new responsibilities. Japan stood as perhaps the single most important exception to that general rule, largely because it fit well within Acheson's wider assessment of the economic and strategic needs of the United States in the Cold War. It will be recalled that in his major speech to the Mississippi Delta Council, in May 1947, Acheson equated the economic recovery of Japan with that of Germany. The United States, he emphasized then, "must push ahead with the reconstruction of those two great workshops of Europe and Asia—Germany and Japan—upon which the ultimate recovery of the two continents so largely depends."[2] That declaration reflected his most deeply held conviction about postwar Asia: namely that Japan should be seen and treated as the Asian analogue to (West) Germany; it was a nation whose advanced industrial infrastructure, skilled workforce, and technological prowess made it both the indispensable engine of regional economic growth and a Cold War strategic asset of incalculable value. Acheson and other leading U.S. strategists, at least from 1947 forward, judged a stable, economically vibrant, pro-American Japan to be just as essential to overall U.S. policy objectives in postwar Asia as a stable, economically vibrant, pro-American Germany was to overall U.S. policy objectives in postwar Europe. It was the one nation in Asia, in Acheson's view, that could significantly affect the overall balance of world power. Consequently, when Acheson joined Truman's cabinet as secretary of state in January 1949 he was certain of at least one element of his approach to Asian affairs: the critical importance of ensuring that a stable, prosperous Japan was oriented firmly toward the West.[3]

The new secretary's policy preferences vis-à-vis the fast-moving events in revolutionary China were less fixed. On January 20, 1949, the same day that Acheson was sworn in as secretary of state, Nationalist Chinese leader Chiang Kai-shek resigned his presidency and turned over the nominal reins of power to Gen. Li Tsung-jen. The generalissimo's grip on power had become ever more tenuous during Acheson's one-and-a-half-year interlude in private life. "I arrived just in time to have him collapse on me," Acheson observed sardonically in his memoir.[4] "We passed, I coming in, Chiang going out," he quipped on another occasion.[5] Chiang fled the mainland for the island of Taiwan—or Formosa, as most Americans at the time called it—intent on creating a sanctuary for himself and his followers. The rout of the Nationalist armies by their Chinese Communist rivals was by then a fait accompli, recognized as irreversible by virtually all informed China watchers. "The disaster in the military operations is complete," Acheson proclaimed to a closed hearing of the Senate Foreign Relations Committee in March. "[T]he government and the army are completely disintegrated," he said. "There is no will to fight, there is no will to resist."[6]

The disintegration of Chiang's military forces and the ascendancy of the Chinese Communists neither shocked nor surprised Acheson. As Marshall's undersecretary of state, he had come to share fully his boss's assessment of Chiang as hopelessly inept and corrupt. Long before Acheson left that post,

Dean Acheson as secretary of state. Courtesy of the Harry S. Truman Library

he had adopted the conventional wisdom among State Department experts that Chiang's defeat and the ultimate triumph of Mao Tse-tung's communist movement were well nigh inevitable developments. No action taken by the United States could reverse Chiang's rapidly declining fortunes; that unfortunate state of affairs, Acheson and his State Department colleagues were convinced, stemmed not from any U.S. failing but from the generalissimo's own incompetence. Still, Acheson believed that even the establishment of a communist regime in China need not be a major strategic blow to the United States for two reasons: first, China's weakness meant that its international orientation would exert little impact on the overall balance of power; and, second, the force of Chinese nationalism would militate against any true or lasting politico-military alliance between Stalin and Mao.

On February 3, 1949, at the first NSC meeting of his tenure devoted to the China problem, Acheson recommended that all aid to Chiang and the Guomindang (GMD) immediately be suspended, with those resources being reallocated to areas of greater priority. Although that recommendation made eminent sense on foreign policy and fiscal grounds, political considerations gave Truman pause. Given the strong sentimental attachment to China on the part of the American people and the powerful pro-Chiang "China bloc," an early cutoff of funds could leave the administration vulnerable to charges of having abandoned a long-term American friend and ally. Vandenberg, still the stalwart champion of bipartisanship, alerted Truman to this peril and urged him, accordingly, not to suspend aid to the GMD abruptly. If the United States should "take *this* step at *this* fatefully inept moment," the Republican senator cautioned, "we shall never be able to shake off the charge that *we* are the ones who gave poor China the final push into disaster."[7] On February 7, as if to confirm Vandenberg's warning, fifty-one Republican members of Congress sent a letter to Truman, inquiring about the administration's plans to aid the noncommunist forces within China.

On February 24, at the president's behest, Acheson met with thirty of them. He used his formidable logical talents in a vain effort to persuade the legislative delegation that Chiang's was a lost cause and that the United States should adapt itself gradually and with appropriate prudence to the new Chinese political realities. During the course of the meeting, one lawmaker asked Acheson for his forecast about the likely course of events in China. The secretary of state remarked philosophically, "When a great tree falls in the forest one cannot see the extent of the damage until the dust settles."[8] Predictably, someone leaked that comment to the press. The next day newspapers across the country described Acheson's China policy, to his acute embarrassment, as waiting "until the dust settles." However awkward, the phrase did capture the essence of Acheson's position on China at this juncture. He sought to distance the United States from the remaining elements of the Nationalist regime as quickly as politically feasible while waiting to see what kind of a relationship might be established with their Communist successors. In classic realist vein, he thought it foolish to continue throwing away military aid on a lost cause. Doing so, moreover, would only solidify the support of the Chinese people for Mao and "perpetuate the delusion that China's interests lie with the USSR."[9]

On February 25 Senator Pat McCarran of Nevada, a Democratic maverick and outspoken critic of Truman's Asian policy, further complicated matters by introducing a bill that called for the provision of $1.5 billion in aid to the Nationalists and the authorization for U.S. military officers to direct Chinese Nationalist units in the field. The Senate Foreign Relations Committee summoned Acheson to offer the administration's response to McCarran's legislative initiative. Testifying on March 18, in executive session, Acheson presented a withering appraisal of the "gross incompetence" of Chiang's forces, stressing "the futility of further aid to China at this time, plus the grave danger that you would be helping the wrong person." Acknowledging that the United States had "experienced a very serious disaster," he labored to put matters in perspective. "I doubt very much whether China is a great strategic springboard for the Communists," Acheson stated. Quite to the contrary, he suggested that Moscow's support for a communist government there might "turn out to be a strategic morass." That estimate stemmed from his deep-set conviction that China, as an overwhelmingly agricultural country with comparatively few natural resources, and a society likely to be plagued indefinitely by political and economic instability, presented the Soviets with a problem as much as an asset. Acheson agreed with Vandenberg's wry depiction of current administration policy toward China as "wait, look, see." The secretary also unhappily concurred with the Michigan senator's summation of the political difficulties such an approach posed for the administration. "In order to justify that [policy] to countless zealous friends that China has in the United States," Vandenberg observed, "something has to be told to them, and at that point you find yourself on the horns of a dilemma, do you not?" Acheson replied, without equivocation or elaboration, "That is the difficulty, yes."[10]

That difficulty worsened throughout the spring and summer of 1949 as the Chinese Communist armies scored victory after victory and critics of Truman's Asian policy sharpened their knives. Dewey's surprise loss to Truman in the 1948 presidential election had stunned congressional Republicans. In its wake, they increasingly bridled at the Cold War bipartisanship championed by Vandenberg and other party leaders, viewing it as a politically self-defeating strategy. Asia, and especially China, were especially fertile ground for partisan attacks on Truman's foreign policy. Communist advances in Asia, at least on the surface, seemed to give the lie to the administration's public assertions of vigorous anticommunism—and thus provided a rich opportunity to opposition critics. In May Representative William Jenner, an acerbic Indiana Republican, charged on the floor of the House that "the Chinese Communist conquest of Asia was not made possible in China. It was engineered right here in Washington, by the top policymakers of this Government."[11] Acheson served as a lightning rod for Jenner and other partisan critics; they increasingly singled him out for vicious personal attacks. Senator Styles Bridges, a New Hampshire Republican, assailed Acheson for "what might be called sabotage of the valiant attempt of the Chinese Nationalists to keep at least part of China free." Senators McCarran and William F. Knowland (R.-Calif.) weighed in with equally harsh accusations of Truman's top diplomat, questioning both his competence and his loyalty. That June, twenty-two senators, including six Democrats, addressed a letter to Truman in which they asked the president to state unequivocally that the administration would not recognize a communist government in China.[12] That happened to be precisely the policy Acheson was considering adopting—after, of course, the dust had settled.

Ever the rationalist, Acheson foolishly thought he could silence his uninformed, politically motivated critics by overwhelming them with what he saw as the objective facts of the case. He chose an unusual vehicle for the task: the publication of more than a thousand pages of documentary evidence on the actual course of U.S.-Chinese relations over the previous five years. The issuance, on August 5, of the infamous China *White Paper* almost immediately backfired, offending and infuriating the administration's political foes rather than mollifying them. Acheson's oft-quoted letter of transmittal proved particularly inflammatory. In it, he blamed the Nationalists' defeat on their own "ineptitude" and loss of "the will to fight" and sought to absolve the United States of any responsibility for the outcome of the Chinese civil war. Nothing Washington could have done, Acheson concluded, short of the "colossal" intervention of U.S. armed forces, could have saved Chiang's regime. The communist victory was, in sum, "the product of internal Chinese forces."[13]

If Acheson believed that lashing Chiang with tough, scornful language would win favor with the generalissimo's China bloc friends or that trying to lift all blame for Chiang's defeat off the administration's shoulders would persuade those already convinced otherwise, he was sorely mistaken. Acheson was, in fact, just handing his enemies more ammunition to fire at him. China bloc supporters in Congress wasted little time in disparaging the *White Paper* as "a 1,054-page whitewash of a wishful, do-nothing policy which has succeeded only in placing Asia in danger of Soviet conquest."[14] Gen. Patrick Hurley, FDR's ambassador to China, issued a typical blast, lambasting the publication as "a smooth alibi for the pro-Communists in the State Department who had engineered the overthrow of our ally, the Nationalist Government of the Republic of China and aided in the Communist conquest of China."[15] The China bloc even went so far as to issue, on August 22, a formal rebuttal of its own, and one that matched the *White Paper* in length. The success of the opposition's campaign can be glimpsed in a public opinion poll that recorded angry opposition to the State Department publication among nearly two-thirds of those sampled who were familiar with the controversy.[16]

In his memoir, Acheson refers to the *White Paper* as "a plunge that ranks high among those that have caused me immediate, unexpected, and acute trouble." Yet there and elsewhere he refused to accept much personal responsibility for the ensuing political debacle. Acheson, instead, too neatly claimed that the paper's conclusions simply were "unpalatable to believers in American omnipotence, to whom every goal unattained is explicable only by incompetence or treason."[17] But much of the resulting brouhaha can be laid at his door. The secretary's usually sharp political antennae failed him in this case; he badly misread the gathering storm over China policy, underestimating the crucial role that emotion and partisanship can play in the foreign policy arena. The needlessly harsh language in his letter of transmittal just inflamed an already heated political environment. Not only did he insult Chiang in his statement, and by implication the Nationalist leader's American supporters, but Acheson also disparaged the soon-to-be-victorious Chinese Communists.

The secretary charged that the latter had "publicly announced their subservience to a foreign power, Russia." America's hope, he proclaimed, was that the Chinese people "will throw off the foreign yoke," implying clearly that the Chinese Communist revolution amounted to little more than a foreign imposition. Yet he himself held more sophisticated and nuanced views. Acheson also still clung to the belief that the United States could drive a wedge between Mao and his Soviet patrons while forging at least a correct and businesslike relationship with the former. That view was predicated on the notion that Mao's China would be capable of pursuing a foreign policy quite independent of Moscow. The simplistic, ideologically infused rhetoric of Acheson's letter of transmittal contradicted that insight, however, while undermining his wedge strategy. Perhaps the secretary's deep-seated anticommunism overwhelmed his trademark pragmatism in this instance, or perhaps his opportunistic side could not resist the temptation to throw some red meat to the conservatives, thinking he could somehow insulate policymaking from any accompanying public turmoil over China's fate. Whatever his motivations, the release of the *White Paper* was a foolishly counterproductive move, and, given that the Defense Department had argued strenuously against the need for such a public airing, a wholly unnecessary one.[18] Defense Secretary Louis Johnson, whose relationship with Acheson was already tense, warned wisely that he and Truman "should carefully consider whether the usefulness of this Paper . . . is greater than the [political] risks inherent in the disclosures that are made."[19]

On October 1, 1949, Mao Tse-tung triumphantly proclaimed the new People's Republic of China from Beijing's historic Gate of Heavenly Peace. The declaration, at one level, merely formalized an outcome that most informed observers, in the United States and elsewhere, had long anticipated. Yet, coming as it did just eight days after Truman announced to the American public that the Soviet Union had detonated its first atomic device, Mao's proclamation served to deepen public unease about the global situation–and about the course of U.S. foreign policy. Taken together, those developments transformed the Cold War in manifold ways. As Acheson recalled years later, "Collapse of the Nationalist regime in China and the Soviet explosion made it clear that changes in power relationships were imminent."[20]

CREATING SITUATIONS OF STRENGTH

Although the unsettling events of late summer and early fall 1949 were hardly unexpected, the Soviet entry into the atomic club, followed so closely by the proclamation of the People's Republic of China and its immediate recognition by Moscow, nonetheless caused great consternation in official Washington. On September 23 Truman announced to the American people that the United States now had unmistakable evidence that an atomic explosion had recently occurred in the Soviet Union. In a statement released to the press that same day, Acheson sought to downplay the significance of the Soviet nuclear blast, as had Truman. Echoing the president, he emphasized that "we have been fully aware that sooner or later this development would occur" and noted that "in our thinking it has [already] been taken into account." Acheson insisted, again echoing Truman, that since the Soviet Union's emergence as a nuclear power had been anticipated, and planned for, no alteration in U.S. policy would be required.[21] Hidden behind those soothing public words of reassurance lay churning anxiety at the highest level of Truman's national security bureaucracy. Acheson fully shared that anxiety: not because he believed the Kremlin could now challenge America's overwhelming strategic and military superiority in any meaningful way–he remained confident that it could not–but because the political and psychological ramifications of Moscow's technological achievement were likely to be far-reaching.

What made a nuclear Soviet Union so disturbing to Acheson was that, at the core of his Cold War statecraft, lay the conviction that America's atomic monopoly conferred upon it the freedom to run calculated risks vis-à-vis the Soviet Union without having to fear retaliation. That risk-taking was essential to the construction of what Acheson liked to call "situations of strength." Only the development of its own atomic capability, Acheson reasoned, would embolden

Moscow to counter American initiatives by courting risks of its own in pursuit of its own situations of strength. The Soviet atomic test of August 1949, consequently, prompted Truman, Acheson, and other top planners to begin a reexamination of the efficacy of current U.S. national security programs.[22]

As those deliberations gathered steam, Acheson briefly departed Washington for Paris and the latest round of negotiations over German policy with his French and British counterparts. For all the recent hoopla surrounding events in China, Acheson continued to view Western Europe as the main theater of the Cold War–and West Germany's integration into Western Europe as the administration's paramount foreign policy goal. Developments in Germany were moving at so rapid a pace in the summer and autumn of 1949 that Acheson believed they necessitated another set of face-to-face meetings with Bevin and Schuman. Consistent with the London accords of 1948 and the U.S.-U.K.-French agreements of April 1949, elections for the German lower house, or Bundestag, had been held on August 14. Then, on September 15, the Bundestag elected Konrad Adenauer, the former anti-Nazi mayor of Cologne, as the first chancellor of the Federal Republic of Germany. Six days later Adenauer and his chief ministers formally called on the freshly installed Allied High Commissioners at their headquarters in Petersberg, near the federal republic's new capital at Bonn. The ensuing ceremonies marked the official termination of the military government in West Germany and its replacement with the Allied High Commission.

The natural desire of the German people to regain full sovereignty as swiftly as possible almost immediately produced friction between the new Adenauer government and the allies over such ticklish matters as the continued Anglo-French dismantling of German industrial plants. During a meeting in Washington that September, Acheson delicately explained to Bevin and Schuman the American position that dismantling German steel plants and other industrial concerns worked at cross-purposes with the Marshall Plan's objective of fostering Germany's economic recovery for the greater good of Western Europe as a whole. Yet he acknowledged the political sensitivities involved in dealing with a former enemy state and foreswore any leadership role for the United States on these issues in view of its geographical remove. "The best chance and hope seems to us to be under French leadership," he said. "In the long run if there is to be an answer, there must be a solution of Franco-German troubles under French leadership."[23] In a subsequent personal message to Schuman, Acheson reiterated those themes. The key question for him came down to "whether Germany will in the future be a benefit or a curse to the free world," and French actions, he stated, would go a long way toward determining the answer. Acheson, accordingly, implored Schuman to recognize the crucial role that France could play in seizing the "rare opportunity" that now existed "to enlist the cooperation of the Germans with Western Europe." Soviet pressure was driving the Germans "into the arms of Western Europe," he argued. "Unless advantage is taken of this political opportunity, we may again face a Germany aligned with the Soviet Union or feeling itself able to ask for bids." French leadership and initiative on this crucial matter, he insisted, was essential.[24]

The Paris talks between Acheson, Schuman, and Bevin, held on November 9 and 10, largely accomplished their intended purpose of hammering out a concerted American-British-French approach to dismantling, reparations, and other nettlesome issues. Acheson cabled Truman that, although the compromises reached on the specific subject of dismantling "were slightly less than I had hoped," solid progress had been made during the talks on the broader goal of establishing conditions "for the integration of Germany into the framework of Western Europe."[25]

That all-important goal was advanced even further during Acheson's first meeting with Adenauer. At the urging of John J. McCloy, the new American high commissioner in Germany, Acheson flew from Paris to Frankfurt on November 11. It was the secretary's first trip to Germany since he accompanied his father there as a teenager. Forty years and two world wars later, he found himself in a very different Germany. On the afternoon of November 13, Acheson met with the seventy-three year old Adenauer at the chancellor's residence in Bonn and came away highly impressed. The feeling was mutual. "Dean Acheson made an excellent impression on me," Adenauer later wrote. "I found him most likeable from the very first day of our meeting."[26] The American secretary of state, for his part, was "struck by the imagination and wisdom of [Adenauer's] approach." He recalled approvingly that the chancellor's "great concern was to integrate Germany completely into Western Europe."

Adenauer's presentation was, in fact, carefully designed to win the American diplomat's favor. The German leader drew a sharp historical contrast between west and east Germans—to the distinct advantage of westerners like himself. While Prussian-dominated easterners were militaristic and leaned toward Russia, in Adenauer's rendering, westerners had been more influenced over the centuries by "Roman and Christian culture," which had "tied the West German closer to Western Europe." The aging Rhinelander pledged his wholehearted commitment to cooperation with France and his determination "to pursue this goal to the utmost of his ability."[27]

It was music to Acheson's ears. He had already found the ideal French partner in the Alsace-reared Schuman, who had grown up under German rule, actually served in the German army during World War I, and now preached the gospel of Franco-German reconciliation. "I think Schuman is one of the greatest strokes of luck that has come along for a long time," he told the Senate Foreign Relations Committee. In Adenauer, Acheson believed he had found the ideal German partner, one who shared his—and Schuman's—hope that a historic Franco-German rapprochement could lead to West Germany's integration into Western Europe. The Soviet threat made such a transformation imperative, in Acheson's assessment. "To me, one conclusion seemed plain beyond doubt," Acheson recalled thinking at the time. "Western Europe and the United States could not contain the Soviet Union and suppress Germany and Japan at the same time. Our best hope was to make these former enemies willing and strong supporters of a free-world structure. Germany should be welcomed into Western Europe, not kept in limbo outside, as had been the case after the war of 1914–18, relegated to maneuvering between the Soviet Union and the allies."[28]

Acheson returned home to face an equally urgent policy question: whether or not to proceed with the development of a thermonuclear bomb. On November 10 Truman had appointed him, Secretary of Defense Louis Johnson, and Atomic Energy Commissioner David Lilienthal to act as a special committee of the NSC for the purpose of advising Truman "whether and in what manner the United States should undertake the development and possible production of super atomic weapons [and] whether and when any publicity should be given this matter."[29] The "super" or hydrogen bomb, which could theoretically be created through a fusion process, would be a thousand times more powerful than the atomic bombs used against Japan in World War II. The military had been pushing hard for going forward with the H-bomb and the acerbic Johnson vigorously represented that position on the committee. Acheson's old friend Lilienthal, however, opposed both testing and production, largely for moral reasons: he considered the super's destructive power appalling and thought a U.S. decision to cross this latest ethical threshold would set in motion a spiraling arms race with the Soviets.

Acheson, who formed the critical swing vote on the committee, appears to have begun the deliberations with an open mind. He encouraged several State Department analysts to provide him with their unvarnished views. George Kennan, soon to depart his post as director of the Policy Planning Staff, embraced the Lilienthal position, presenting Acheson with a seventy-nine-page memorandum of characteristically eloquent, heartfelt prose that made the moral case against developing the H-bomb. As was his wont, the secretary showed little patience with arguments rooted solely in moral concerns. He found the position of Paul H. Nitze, a former Wall Street investment banker whom Acheson had tapped to be Kennan's replacement as policy planning chief, more realistic. For Acheson, as for Nitze, the critical issue came down to whether the Soviet Union was likely to develop an H-bomb—regardless of what decision the United States reached on the matter. Not Lilienthal, Kennan, or anyone else could provide him with plausible evidence that the Soviets would forgo development of a weapon that could alter the strategic balance. "How can you persuade a paranoid adversary," mused Acheson at one point, "to disarm 'by example'?" He gravitated inexorably to the military's position that the United States could not afford to forswear development and production of H-bombs. Doing so, Acheson feared, could permit the Soviets to create a superior nuclear arsenal that would enable them, in effect, to hold Western Europe hostage.[30]

On January 31, 1950, the NSC special committee met for its final session at the old Executive Office Building, across from the White House. Acheson chaired the meeting. Convinced that Truman would be served best by a unanimous committee vote, he persuaded Lilienthal to put aside his objections and join him and Johnson in a positive recommendation. Immediately following the session, the three walked to the White House for a scheduled meeting with the president. After presenting Truman with a memorandum containing the committee's recommendation to go forward with the H-bomb project, Acheson encouraged the president to hear Lilienthal's own summary of his main concerns. "Can the Russians do it?" asked Truman, before Lilienthal could even finish. When his atomic energy commissioner responded in the affirmative, Truman said, "In that case, we have no choice. We'll go ahead."[31]

For all the weightiness of the H-bomb commitment, Acheson considered the buildup of conventional forces even more important than the enhancement of America's nuclear capabilities. That contentious issue, entangled as it was with highly politicized defense spending and budgeting matters, opened perhaps the most significant breach between the views of Truman and Acheson. Convinced that a healthy economy required a balanced budget, and unwilling either to cut spending for his domestic programs or to raise taxes, Truman decided in mid-1949 that defense allocations must be cut in order to avert the budget deficits he dreaded. The president, consequently, set a $13.5 billion ceiling on defense expenditures for fiscal year 1950. The Joint Chiefs of Staff immediately protested the reductions that such a budgetary ceiling would force on crucial elements of the nation's military buildup. Defense Secretary Johnson, appointed by Truman largely to impose fiscal discipline on the national military establishment, backed the president. Acheson, for his part, quietly found common cause with the Joint Chiefs—especially in the wake of the successful Soviet atomic bomb test of August 1949.

Worried that a nuclear-armed Soviet Union could over time neutralize the woefully undermanned conventional forces of the North Atlantic Treaty Organization (NATO) and thus demoralize America's Western European allies, Acheson advocated a wholesale reexamination of U.S. national security policies in light of Moscow's newly acquired atomic capabilities. Truman endorsed Acheson's appeal and, in January 1950, a State-Defense Review Group commenced work on what would become a seminal Cold War document: National Security Council Paper 68. Nitze, Acheson's trusted associate and alter ego, chaired the group that began drafting NSC 68. Both he and his patron saw the exercise, above all, as an opportunity to persuade Truman that he was imposing a dangerously rigid fiscal straitjacket on the nation's defense posture at a time of great international uncertainty and peril.[32]

A preliminary study prepared by Nitze that February stressed that "recent Soviet moves reflect not only a mounting militancy but suggest a boldness that is essentially new—and borders on recklessness." He attributed the Kremlin's boldness to an increased confidence rooted in a series of favorable recent trends: "It has developed an A-bomb; it has achieved the prewar level of production and other solid economic successes; it has made progress in consolidating its control over the European satellites; and it has apparently effected an increase in the prestige of the Communist Party among the Russian people."[33] Acheson's thinking mirrored Nitze's. "We are on the defensive and the Soviets are apparently showing more self-confidence," he remarked in a discussion with top State Department aides. Acheson voiced the fear that "we would slip backward" if the West did not soon take some new initiative.[34] Soviet leaders appeared now to possess "a sense of confidence" that both men found worrisome. In a meeting with Congressman Christian Herter, who later became secretary of state, Acheson framed the problem with characteristic clarity and bluntness. "During the last six to nine months," he said, "there has been a trend against us which, if allowed to continue, would lead to a considerable deterioration in our position." He described the international situation as extremely grave, one in which the United States was confronted with an adversary, "intent on world domination," that had been extending its sphere of control while radically enhancing its military power and political influence.[35]

Former undersecretary of state Robert A. Lovett, who was currently serving at Acheson's invitation as a State Department consultant, echoed those fears. On March 16, he told a meeting of Nitze's State-Defense review group that Americans "must realize that we are now in a mortal conflict; that we are now in a war worse than any we have yet ever experienced." For Lovett, America's present course was not only insufficient to meet the mounting threat but actually placed American freedom in danger. "Anything we do short of an all-out effort is inexcusable," he stated bluntly.[36]

The sense of urgency so keenly felt by Acheson, Nitze, Lovett, and others was codified in NSC 68. That highly classified study, written in dire, apocalyptic prose, reached Truman's desk on April 14, 1950. U.S. citizens stood "in their deepest peril," it announced. "The issues that face us are momentous, involving the fulfillment or destruction not only of this Republic but of civilization itself. They are issues that will not await our deliberations." NSC 68 represented a shot across the fiscally conservative Truman's bow.[37] The national security reappraisal aimed to shake up complacent assumptions animating the president's cautious budgetary strategy and to force a relaxation of the Truman-imposed fiscal restraints that Acheson, Nitze, and the uniformed military considered detrimental to the nation's core security needs. But, much to Acheson's frustration, Truman showed no inclination to ratchet up defense spending—even after receiving NSC 68's grim warning. Quite to the contrary, as late as June 19, just six days before the outbreak of the Korean War, Truman's Budget Bureau was still calling for a balanced budget and the president was still refusing to budge from the $13.9 billion defense ceiling that he had earlier established for fiscal year 1951.[38]

ASIAN POLICY UNRAVELS; THE REPUBLICANS ATTACK

Although those internal deliberations about the adequacy of U.S. national security efforts remained shrouded in secrecy, a very public debate about those same efforts raged simultaneously—in the press and in the halls of Congress. Acheson found himself at the center of the public debate, as well as the one being conducted quietly within the executive branch, largely because he remained the perfect foil for conservative critics of the administration's Cold War policies. Not only was Acheson the most visible spokesman for and symbol of Truman's foreign policy, but his elegance of style and manner, aristocratic bearing, and intellectual arrogance—even his rakish mustache—combined to make him an irresistible target for right-wing populists. The latter looked suspiciously at the nation's traditional elites and bridled at what they considered the condescension of Ivy League–educated, Eastern Establishment types such as Acheson to those from the provinces. "I look at that fellow, I watch his smart-aleck manner and his British clothes and that New Dealism," sneered Republican Senator Hugh Butler of Nebraska, "and I want to shout, Get out, Get out."[39] The staunchly Republican *Chicago Tribune* rebuked Acheson as "another striped-pants" snob who betrayed both the peoples of Asia and "true Americanism" while serving "as a lackey of Wall Street bankers, British lords, and Communistic radicals from New York."[40]

Such vicious assaults on the secretary of state's competence, character, and patriotism became much more frequent in the early months of 1950. Before then, anti-Acheson invectives emanated mostly from the China bloc, a group that held the secretary personally liable for the Chiang Kai-shek regime's collapse. Senior Republican legislators, for the most part, held their fire; bipartisanship still breathed some life through the end of 1949. On January 10 and 11, however, the pillar of the GOP establishment—"Mr. Republican" himself—added a powerful, new voice to the partisan chorus of the China bloc critics. In a radio address, followed by a speech on the floor of the Senate, Robert A. Taft blasted Acheson and the State Department for deliberately sabotaging Chiang. America's China policy, the Ohio lawmaker charged, had "been guided by a left-wing group who obviously have wanted to get rid of Chiang and were willing at least to turn China over to the Communists for that purpose." He even went so far as to claim, however ludicrously, that bipartisanship "died when Dean Acheson became Secretary of State."[41]

Political opportunism and personal pique lay behind Taft's broadsides. At odds with Truman over domestic policy priorities, the veteran politician sought to weaken the president by exploiting the administration's demonstrated vulnerability on the emotional China question. He had weeks earlier called for a firm U.S. commitment to the defense of Taiwan. Taft then became irritated when he found out, through a leak, that Truman and Acheson had decided not to intervene if, as anticipated, Chinese Communist forces invaded Taiwan as the final act of the Chinese civil war. Acheson, still convinced that the corrupt Chiang did not deserve any additional U.S. support, argued forcefully—and successfully—against a military commitment to the rump government in exile that the generalissimo had established on Taiwan. In two climactic meetings at the end of December 1949, Acheson's position had prevailed over that of opponents in the Pentagon who saw Taiwan as a valuable, though not vital, complement to U.S. security interests in the Pacific that should be protected. The secretary of state insisted that backing a losing cause—with U.S. troops no less—represented the height of folly, and Truman concurred.[42] Taft thus seized on an already contentious issue, provocatively framing the Taiwan question as the latest demonstration of the Democratic Party's weakness toward communism. In so doing, he was tacitly encouraging more Republicans to take off their gloves and join him in a public thrashing of the Truman-Acheson foreign policy. His personal dislike of Acheson and his distaste for his fellow Yale Corporation member's "cool air of superiority" made such an attack especially satisfying to the self-righteous Taft.[43]

An inveterate believer in the efficacy of what today is termed public diplomacy, Acheson sought to blunt those criticisms by presenting the case for the administration's Asian policy openly, using the occasion of a major address before the National Press Club in Washington. Acheson's speech, delivered on January 12, laid out the basic calculus that informed his approach to postwar Asia in a manner both straightforward and sophisticated. He correctly identified nationalism as the dominant force sweeping the continent since the end of World War II. Asian nationalism, Acheson emphasized, combined "a revulsion against the acceptance of misery and poverty as the normal condition of life" with "a revulsion against foreign domination." With the recent posturing of Taft and other critics doubtless firmly in mind, he noted that any further U.S. intervention into China's affairs, including the dispute over Taiwan, would arouse "righteous anger" on the part of the Chinese people toward the United States and hence prove counterproductive to the American goal of a stable and peaceful Asia.

In the part of the speech destined to become most memorable—and controversial—Acheson declared that U.S. security interests in the Pacific could be demarcated by a defensive perimeter that ran from Alaska's Aleutian Islands to Japan and from the Ryukyus to the Philippines. The United States, he added, could not by itself guarantee the military security of other parts of the Asia-Pacific region. Nearly all available evidence indicates that Acheson was simply stating the obvious here—that U.S. security interests in Asia were limited rather than unlimited. He was certainly not seeking to draw attention to areas that the United States would not defend from external attack.[44] Nonetheless, he should have been more cautious with the signals he was sending. It is now clear that the absence of South Korea from this defense perimeter gained the notice of Joseph Stalin and North Korea's Kim Il Sung, among others, setting the stage for the most significant military challenge Acheson would face.[45]

The secretary of state's attempt to preempt partisan sniping through a forthright presentation of U.S. interests and policies in Asia also went awry.

In fact, the Press Club speech ignited a new round of attacks on him. Senator Bridges called for a vote of censure against the administration's foreign policy while Senator Knowland demanded Acheson's immediate resignation. Then, on January 25, with those latest blows still ringing, Acheson added a self-inflicted one. In a press conference, he responded to an anticipated question with a carefully prepared statement defending Alger Hiss, a former State Department official accused of espionage who had recently been convicted of perjury. The Hiss case had become a cause célèbre, and California congressman Richard M. Nixon had been catapulted to national prominence for holding up Hiss as a symbol of Democratic laxness toward communist-sympathizing, government insiders. Alger Hiss was an acquaintance, not a friend, of Acheson's; they had overlapped in the State Department but never worked together. Donald Hiss, Alger's brother, had previously served on Acheson's staff and had earned his respect and warm regard, a factor that most likely influenced Acheson's infamous comment: "I do not intend to turn my back on Alger Hiss."

Probably more to the point, though, the well-bred Hiss could not have possessed more impeccable credentials for a man of Acheson's class, background, and personal ties. He held a degree from Harvard Law School, where he had studied with Acheson's close friend Felix Frankfurter, and had clerked for Acheson's hero, Supreme Court Justice Oliver Wendell Holmes. How could such a person, he must have asked himself, have become a Soviet spy? Still, a more prudent official would have simply eschewed comment on so controversial and politically charged a case. That was exactly the course of action that Nitze and some other Acheson associates would have urged their boss to follow—had he allowed them to see him prior to his fateful press conference. The secretary of state instead followed his own counsel on this matter, choosing to stand on principle when most others in his position would have opted for the expedient "no comment." As he explained to David Lilienthal the next day, "After a while you get tired of the curs yipping, and have to have your say." The price he paid for that defiant declaration of personal honor was high.[46]

Responses to Acheson's statement about Hiss were immediate, overwhelmingly negative, and often venomous. He "couldn't have created more commotion by disrobing in public," observed *Newsweek* archly.[47] Nixon called Acheson's comments "disgusting"; Bridges asked if the secretary's support for

Hiss did not make Acheson himself a security risk; and Representative James C. David, a conservative Democrat, wondered, "How long can Americans be expected to show respect for Acheson when he hugs to his bosom those who have betrayed their country?"[48] On the Senate floor, Wisconsin Republican Joseph A. McCarthy interrupted colleague Karl Mundt's anti-Hiss diatribe to ask Mundt if he had heard the "fantastic statement" uttered by Acheson moments earlier. Was the secretary of state, McCarthy asked caustically, implying that "he will not turn his back on any other Communists in the State Department?"[49]

McCarthy's snide comment proved a mere prelude to the main event. On February 9 the junior senator from Wisconsin gave a blistering speech in Wheeling, West Virginia, in which he pushed the attacks on Acheson and the State Department to a new level of calumny. McCarthy claimed to be in possession of the names of 205 communists currently serving in the State Department. Acheson, "this pompous diplomat in striped pants," was presiding over a department filled with traitors and dupes, he charged. The numbers changed almost daily; they were nothing more than the figment of the unscrupulous McCarthy's vivid imagination. The ensuing sensation made clear, nonetheless, that the senator had found a resonant political issue. "The attack of the primitives," as Acheson contemptuously called the phenomenon soon labeled McCarthyism, had commenced. For its initiator, whose wild accusations overnight gained him headlines and power, Acheson always remained a prime target. The "elegant and alien Acheson," McCarthy declaimed, was "Russian as to heart, British as to manner"; he was a "pompous diplomat in striped pants with a phony British accent." McCarthy liked to mock Acheson by referring to him as "Red Dean" or "the Red Dean of Washington."[50]

Acheson's friends and family marveled at how he persevered in the midst of such vicious personal attacks. Doubtless the stiff upper lip tradition in which he was reared helped, as did the enormous self-confidence he still possessed. Truman's unswerving support was surely a balm as well. On March 29 the president proclaimed that Acheson would "go down in history as one of the great Secretaries of State" while denouncing McCarthy and his treacherous associates as Moscow's "greatest asset."[51] Other prominent citizens also rose to Acheson's defense. "You will come out of this period as the greatest Secretary of State this country has ever had," predicted ex–White House adviser Clark Clifford. "The statements of McCarthy and his ilk remind me of curs snapping at the heels of a thoroughbred."[52] Former Secretary of State and War Henry Stimson, the grand old man of the Republican Party's internationalist wing, penned a letter of support that the *New York Times* published, in which he vigorously rebutted McCarthy's accusations against the man who now occupied his old post.

In response to a separate, private letter of sympathy and support he received from Stimson, Acheson wrote, "I have tried not to let the present barrage of charges and innuendoes go below the surface or to deflect me from the main business at hand, but it is not possible to prevent altogether their having a depressing effect."[53] Following a relaxing and intimate lunch with Lilienthal, in January 1951, Acheson remarked to his old friend and colleague that "the talk that a fellow gets used to attacks is nonsense. . . . Criticism I don't really mind. That is to be expected. But what I can hardly endure is to have my personal life and my personal characteristics brought into public discussion."[54] Alice Acheson later speculated that the cumulative weight of the charges and innuendoes–what journalist Eric Sevareid called "the most uninhibited guerrilla attack in modern times" directed against any public official–probably took ten years off her husband's life.[55]

Acheson's habits and lifestyle changed little during the McCarthyite onslaught. Weather permitting, he still walked the mile and a half from his Georgetown home to his State Department office nearly every morning, accompanied by dear friend Frankfurter. Their friendship had deepened with age, and the two talked about virtually everything on their ritual walks to work, except for politics and foreign policy–or so they always claimed. In addition to the understanding and support of old friends, Acheson found solace in his exceptionally close family. Both of his daughters, Jane and Mary, were married by then, as was his son David. He saw them often and remained in touch by telephone regularly. Throughout his time as secretary of state, Acheson took especial delight in the young grandchildren that they had brought into his life. Like Marshall, Acheson eschewed late hours at the office and the round-the-clock work pace that has become the contemporary norm in official Washington. Instead, he returned home after nearly every workday for a quiet dinner with

Alice in their Georgetown home. Most evenings he found time to read for pleasure, long one of his favorite pursuits; history, biography, and literature particularly absorbed him. Always a highly social person, Acheson entertained much less during those years than he had in the past—one concession to his visibility and the demands on his time. He also avoided formal diplomatic functions and embassy receptions whenever he could in favor of a relaxed meal, intimate conversation, and good book at home.

There was another constant in his life during these trying times: the tranquility he found at his Maryland farm. He and Alice repaired to Sandy Spring nearly every Saturday, driving up typically in the early afternoon and staying through Sunday evening. The role of country squire suited his small-town origins and lifelong love of nature, and gave him a welcome respite from city life and from the oppressive heat of summertime Washington. Family members and friends often dropped by for visits, joining Acheson for informal meals and the ubiquitous cocktails he so heartily enjoyed. He also usually persuaded visitors to partake in some of the outdoor activities he relished: tennis, swimming, and gardening in the warm weather; skeet-shooting and horseback riding on occasion throughout the year; and vigorous walking, clearing brush, handiwork, and carpentry all year round. Carpentry became a particular passion during this period; Acheson took justifiable pride in the skills he developed as a furniture-maker. The concentration demanded by carpentry, he once commented, also helped relieve the stress of his official responsibilities.[56] That stress never ceased; it came with the job he had accepted. The personal attacks unleashed by McCarthy and his supporters, however, guaranteed that a high level of personal stress would be a constant presence in his life.

Even with the president's unwavering support, Acheson found it difficult to insulate policymaking from the swirl of controversy that now surrounded him. Such was particularly the case with regard to the tangled China question. Acheson's preferred policy course remained that decided upon in the fall of 1949: avoid intervention in Taiwan, wait until the dust of the civil war settled, and then salvage some kind of a relationship with Mao's regime, while remaining ever alert to opportunities for drawing Beijing away from Moscow. Yet events, domestic and international, conspired to render such a course of action impossible to attain.

Not least among the obstacles proved to be Mao's adamant opposition to any form of a normalized relationship with Washington, a factor that Acheson was slow to appreciate. Driven by a determination to remake China, a determination fueled by his fury at the Western imperialists who had for so long defiled China, and needing an external foe to help mobilize popular support for his grand revolutionary ambitions at home, Mao gravitated naturally toward the Soviet camp. He thus rejected all suggestions from underlings that Beijing offer an olive branch to Washington. Instead, the Chinese leader traveled to Moscow in December 1949 and, despite the chilly reception he received from a still wary Stalin, managed to negotiate a treaty of friendship with the Soviet Union. The Sino-Soviet treaty, announced on February 14, 1950, obligated each power to come to the aid of the other if attacked by a third party; it served as perhaps the most ominous symbol of a Cold War now firmly implanted on Asian soil.

In a press conference the next day, Acheson asserted that China would soon grow disillusioned with its new partner and the "meager" aid it would be able to provide. Those remarks amounted to wishful thinking—or, to be more accurate, an assessment premature by about a decade. On March 29 Acheson elaborated on his views during testimony, in executive session, before the Senate Foreign Relations Committee. He acknowledged that he expected Chinese Communist forces would soon seize Taiwan; they would be foolish not to, he added. The secretary, nonetheless, refused to rule out a future accommodation between the United States and revolutionary China. Even "if the devil himself runs China," Acheson remarked, "if he is an independent devil that is infinitely better than if he is a stooge of Moscow."[57] Yet the domestic political climate, combined with the emerging Moscow-Beijing axis, rendered such brave speculation essentially moot for the time being.

SOUTHEAST ASIA TO THE FORE

With the administration's China policy mired in intractable problems, Acheson had begun to concentrate more on Southeast Asia, an area where the prospects for bolstering anticommunist forces appeared much brighter. The stakes there, moreover, impressed him as even weightier. Developments in rapidly decolonizing Southeast Asia intersected, in fundamental ways, with the prospects for economic recovery and political stability in both Japan and Western Europe–the two areas that Acheson long considered most vital from the standpoint of U.S. security.

Acheson and other leading officials in the State and Defense departments were convinced that Japan needed access to the markets and raw materials of Southeast Asia for its industrial recovery. They feared that without the establishment of vigorous trading links to Southeast Asian countries either Japan's economic recovery would stall or it would revert to its prewar dependence on trade with China. The advent of a communist government in China made the latter prospect especially worrisome. U.S. experts feared that the development of close commercial ties with its Communist neighbor could lead Tokyo gradually to reach a political accommodation with Beijing. Acheson had long considered it vital for U.S. security, and hence the overriding goal of his Asian policy, that Japan remain noncommunist, economically vibrant, and firmly oriented toward the West. "Were Japan added to the Communist bloc," he told the British ambassador in December 1949, "the Soviets would acquire skilled manpower and industrial potential capable of significantly altering the balance of world power."[58]

Acheson reasoned that the only way to avert such a catastrophic outcome was through the development of alternative trading zones, in Southeast Asia and elsewhere in noncommunist Asia, to replace Japan's historic reliance on commerce with China. In January 1950 the secretary told a closed session of the Senate Foreign Relations Committee that if some way could be found to solve the "great question" of Japan's need for markets and primary products then, and only then, could American efforts to stabilize and reinvigorate the "great crescent" of nations from Japan through Southeast Asia to India succeed. Otherwise, the secretary warned, Japan could drift into the communist orbit or adopt a neutralist stance, playing West off against East. Southeast Asia, in Acheson's view, held the key to Japan's future economic health–and hence to its political and diplomatic orientation.[59] "Continuing, or even maintaining, Japan's economic recovery," noted a joint State-Defense Department report completed that same month, "depends upon keeping Communism out of Southeast Asia, promoting economic recovery there and in further developing those countries, together with Indonesia, the Philippines, Southern Korea and India, as the principal trading areas for Japan."[60]

The promotion of regional economic integration represented for Acheson the wisest policy direction for the United States in Cold War Asia, one fully congruent with the nation's fundamental strategic and economic interests. Yet its realization required nothing less than the political stabilization of a Southeast Asia that was currently wracked by revolutionary turmoil and economic uncertainty. That posed no small problem. It meant that the communist-led Viet Minh insurgency in Indochina, which presented the most serious impediment to regional peace and stability, had to be vanquished with the greatest possible dispatch, as did the communist rebellion in Malaya.

American strategic and economic interests in Europe also demanded that Southeast Asia be pacified and reconstructed. By the end of 1949 the optimism that the Marshall Plan's inception generated on both sides of the Atlantic had started to fade. France's increasingly costly colonial war in Indochina was stretching its resources to the breaking point, consuming about one-third of the French military budget and severely hampering its contribution both to the European recovery program and to European defense. The enormous dollar gap between the United States and its European trading partners posed an even more immediate threat to American interests. That trade imbalance continued to widen, reaching over $3.5 billion by mid-1949. "Unless firm action is taken," British foreign secretary Bevin implored Acheson in July 1949, "I fear much of our work on Western Union and the Atlantic pact will be undermined and our progress in the Cold War will be halted."[61] Unsettled conditions in Southeast Asia, whose tin, rubber, and other commodities had in the prewar years made the area a major dollar-earner for the European colonial powers, retarded economic recovery there and thus exacerbated the dollar-gap problem.

Acheson first became conscious of those linkages between Western Europe and the colonial areas of Southeast Asia during his tenure as undersecretary of state. During those years, guerrilla insurgencies erupted in Indochina and the East Indies when the French and Dutch governments attempted to restore full colonial sovereignty in the face of broad-based indigenous bids for independence. Acheson sympathized with the imperial powers, whose cooperation in Europe was—not incidentally—critical to U.S. strategic and economic needs. But, at the same time, he urged French and Dutch officials on several occasions to offer meaningful concessions to native aspirations for eventual self-rule. Above all, he and other top State Department officials wanted to prevent any clash of arms; they considered colonial wars of reconquest to be as anachronistic as they were likely to be self-defeating.

As secretary of state, Acheson initially stuck to the well-established script of formal neutrality, supporting neither the European imperial powers nor the nationalist movements they were seeking to suppress. Instead, he continued to call for negotiated settlements, as he believed compromise and conciliation represented the wisest course for America's allies to follow toward the colonial disputes that had long since turned violently destructive in both Indochina and the East Indies. The Dutch, however, soon forced him to choose sides, and Acheson, surprisingly to them, sided not with his dependable northern European ally but with the Indonesian independence movement. A major Dutch military offensive against the self-proclaimed Republic of Indonesia, which coincided with Acheson's return to the State Department, forced the issue. By early 1949 the offensive had failed miserably. Not only had Dutch troops proved unable to pacify the sprawling archipelago, but their heavy-handed approach to an essentially moderate nationalist movement threatened to push that movement to the left. Even worse, from Acheson's perspective, the Dutch were diverting resources from the Marshall Plan while widespread protests against their resort to old-fashioned imperial methods cast a pall over the proposed Atlantic pact at a crucial juncture.[62]

Consequently, on March 31, 1949, Acheson met with Dutch foreign minister Dirk U. Stikker, who was in Washington for the NATO signing ceremony, and read him the riot act. Speaking bluntly, the secretary said that the "deep-rooted conviction on the part of our people" was that the "Dutch were wrong" and "guilty of aggression." That conviction had produced a negative reaction within Congress that now "gravely jeopardizes the continuation of ECA assistance to the Netherlands." Only an immediate reversal of Dutch policy—meaning real movement toward Indonesian independence—could remove the specter of a U.S. aid cutoff, Acheson insisted. The Dutch government got the message and soon began the drawn-out negotiations that led, finally, to the transfer of power to an independent Indonesia on December 27, 1949.[63]

The French–Viet Minh struggle, raging since late 1946, offered no such straightforward solution. That France was by far the more indispensable ally, and the one much less susceptible to American pressure, posed one problem.

There are "limits on the extent to which one may successfully coerce an ally," Acheson observed in his memoir. "Withholding help and exhorting the ally or its opponent can be effective only when the ally can do nothing without help, as was the case in Indonesia."[64] Communist leadership of the Vietnamese independence struggle posed an even more acute dilemma. Although Acheson and the State Department's Asian experts had long recognized the need for France to offer substantive concessions to Vietnamese nationalists, they viewed the prospects of an independent regime led by Ho Chi Minh with horror. They were certain that such a regime would make common cause with Moscow and Beijing and thus facilitate the communist bloc's extension into mainland Southeast Asia. The recognition of Ho's fledgling government by the two communist powers, in January 1950, seemed to substantiate that fear. On February 1, Acheson publicly declared that the Kremlin's recognition of the "Communist movement" in Indochina "should remove any illusions as to the 'nationalist' nature of Ho Chi Minh's aims and reveals Ho in his true colors as the mortal enemy of native independence in Indochina." A State Department reappraisal of U.S. policy, completed that same day, both reflected and influenced Acheson's thinking on the subject. "The choice confronting the United States," it stated starkly, "is to support the French in Indochina or face the extension of Communism over the remainder of the continental area of Southeast Asia and, possibly, farther westward." A "failure to support French policy in Indochina," moreover, "would have the effect of contributing toward the defeat of our aims in Europe."[65]

On February 7, with Truman's firm support, Acheson's State Department announced that the United States was according diplomatic recognition to the State of Vietnam, a quasi-independent government within the French Union led by former Vietnamese emperor Bao Dai, as well as to the Kingdoms of Laos and Cambodia. Despite ample reservations and misgivings owing to the limited sovereignty bestowed on the State of Vietnam and the widespread international perception of it as nothing more than a French puppet regime, Acheson saw no choice at this juncture but to support France. He now viewed Indochina as the newest theater of the Cold War. But diplomatic support for the Bao Dai experiment was still a far cry from military support. A week and a half later the French formally requested that as well, insisting that by fighting the Viet Minh they were blocking the spread of communism into Southeast

Asia and thus acting on behalf of the West as a whole. Acheson, though wary that the United States would lose its leverage once it began providing Paris with aid, accepted the imperfect logic behind the case for military assistance. If the French chose to withdraw from Indochina, the ascendancy of Ho's Soviet- and Chinese-supported movement would be well nigh inevitable, the worldwide perception of another defeat for the West unavoidable. "We have to be careful here that the French did not get discouraged by internal difficulties at home and withdraw from Indo China," Acheson told Filipino diplomat Carlos P. Romulo. "If their troops were withdrawn there would be a real danger of the first magnitude."[66]

On April 24 Truman approved a State Department–initiated recommendation that the United States commence the provision of military and economic assistance to the French in Indochina. Acheson conveyed the welcome news to Schuman on May 8. An indication of Indochina's growing importance to overall U.S. foreign policy priorities can be gleaned from the fact that the Acheson-Schuman meeting, held in Paris, focused more attention on Indochina than on any other agenda item. A position paper prepared prior to that meeting by the French Foreign Ministry emphasized that France had reached its "dying breath" in Indochina. "The situation is such today that if massive American aid does not arrive in the shortest possible time," it warned, "the war-making potential of the expeditionary corps will suffer total collapse at the end of this year or the beginning of 1951. The evacuation of Indochina will be the only option open to us." With such high stakes at play, Schuman pressed Acheson for the immediate provision of urgently needed U.S. warplanes and naval vessels so that the French could reinvigorate their counterinsurgency campaign.[67]

Acheson's promise of up to $20 million in assistance during the final six weeks of fiscal year 1950–with more, presumably, to be programmed for fiscal year 1951–fell short of French hopes. Schuman, nonetheless, was delighted to receive a concrete commitment for U.S. matériel and relieved to hear much greater sympathy and understanding from his American counterpart on the subject of Indochina than ever before. When the foreign minister bemoaned France's "twin burden" of providing for Indochinese and European defense, and obliquely implied that its European contribution might need to be cut back, Acheson expressed not just understanding but a determination to help. "We are all agreed on [the] strategic importance of Indo-China," the secretary remarked; "if it goes, SEA [Southeast Asia] goes." Further, Acheson emphasized that the United States recognized the "close and immediate connection" that linked the turmoil in Southeast Asia to Western defense efforts.[68]

"So few problems are isolated," Acheson ruminated in an October 1949 speech. "Most are part of a very complicated mosaic."[69] Certainly that wise observation applied with especial force to the problems he found himself grappling with in Southeast Asia. Acheson's undeniable Eurocentrism did not blind him to the mounting challenges emanating from the non-Western world, as some scholars have alleged. "We will get nowhere, I think, by supporting the French as a colonial power against the Indochinese," he testified on Capitol Hill in October 1949.[70] More than most of his contemporaries, the secretary of state appreciated that burgeoning third world nationalism made any attempt to restore the old colonial order a losing proposition. Acheson's preoccupation with Europe, moreover, actually helped sensitize him to the challenges of an emergent Asia. As the costly war in Indochina drained France's treasury and limited its potential contribution to European defense, Acheson would have been extremely shortsighted to miss the interdependence between Southeast Asia and Western Europe.

He was not. To the contrary, he was quite keenly attuned to the seamless web of interests that inextricably tied the war in Indochina to the prospects for French economic recovery and political stability. One's identification of a problem, however, should never be conflated with the far more daunting task of devising an intelligent solution to it. Acheson seized on the Bao Dai initiative as the least objectionable alternative, all the while appreciating its highly imperfect nature. More than most U.S. decision makers, he appreciated that U.S. military aid to the French—no matter how generous—could not by itself resolve the core issue of meeting the legitimate demands of Vietnamese nationalists. Given the communist leadership of the dominant strand of Vietnamese nationalism and the recalcitrant attitudes of the French toward transferring genuine sovereignty, Acheson calculated that he could do little more at the moment than support Bao Dai, hold his nose, and hope for the best.

WAR COMES IN KOREA

On Saturday, June 24, 1950, Acheson was enjoying a quiet weekend at his rustic Maryland farmhouse. This early summer weekend Harewood must have seemed a particularly welcome respite after a busy week that included a commencement address at Harvard University. He devoted a couple of hours to gardening that afternoon. Then, after a good dinner with Alice, he retired early, intending to read himself to sleep. The only sounds, he recalled later, were the changing of the security detail. McCarthy's relentless attacks on Acheson had brought a flood of death threats, necessitating round-the-clock security guards at Harewood and at his home in Georgetown—a constant reminder of his status as "a controversial person," as he sometimes jokingly referred to himself.

At about 10:00 p.m. the phone that kept him connected to the White House switchboard rang. State Department duty officers conveyed to Acheson the gist of a cable just received from John Muccio, the U.S. ambassador to South Korea. It was as urgent as it was grim. Muccio reported that North Korean forces had moved across the 38th parallel and were mounting a heavy attack against South Korea. It appeared, in the ambassador's judgment, to be "an all-out offensive." Assistant Secretary of State John D. Hickerson suggested to his boss that an emergency meeting of the UN Security Council be requested for the next morning, in order to call for a cease-fire in Korea. Acheson instantly approved that recommendation, setting the wheels in motion for what would be an unprecedented Sunday session of that body.

He then phoned Truman, who was enjoying a relaxing weekend of his own at his family home in Independence, Missouri. Acheson informed the president of the alarming news from Korea. He dissuaded him from leaving immediately for Washington—the combative Truman's initial instinct. Truman endorsed Acheson's decision to seek an emergency Security Council meeting. The two also decided that the administration's top national security officials, many of whom had been out of town enjoying the early summer weekend, should be summoned to assemble in Washington the next day for a full discussion of the Korea crisis. Truman could then decide on the most appropriate response to what both men considered an unprecedented Soviet challenge.[71]

Acheson spent much of Sunday, June 25, at the State Department: reading the latest cables, receiving briefings from the department's top Asia hands, weighing policy options with his most trusted advisers, and sending instructions to U.S. diplomats at the United Nations. Reports from the field were uniformly distressing. He learned that "South Korean arms were badly outclassed." Acheson never doubted that the Kremlin's hand was behind the North Korean strike. "It seemed close to certain that the attack had been mounted, supplied, and instigated by the Soviet Union and that it would not be stopped by anything short of force," he recalled in his memoir. "If Korean forces proved unequal to the job, as seemed probable, only U.S. intervention could do it."[72] A slim glimmer of hope came with the news that the UN Security Council—which the Soviet Union, fortuitously, had been boycotting to protest the council's refusal to award China's seat to Mao's government—had voted unanimously to condemn North Korean aggression.

From the outset of the crisis, Acheson was convinced that only a forceful U.S. response to this provocation could preserve America's international credibility—in the eyes of its adversaries and, just as important, in the eyes of its allies. Allowing a communist bloc nation to vanquish an American client state without a concerted U.S. counteraction, he was certain, would encourage aggression elsewhere. Further, it would gravely undermine Washington's reputation as a resolute, dependable ally. "To back away from this challenge, in view of our capacity for meeting it, would be highly destructive of the power and prestige of the United States," Acheson reasoned.[73] Yet precisely how to respond and exactly what this attack portended about Moscow's wider intentions remained far murkier issues.

In his celebrated speech of January 1950, explaining the administration's Asian policy, Acheson had not included South Korea within the American defense perimeter he had sketched. The secretary of state had not done so for an amalgam of reasons: the United States had already moved to limit its commitments in South Korea on budgetary grounds; with the termination of America's official occupation duties, a staunchly anticommunist and pro-American government under the leadership of Syngman Rhee had become firmly ensconced there; the country never had impressed Acheson or other senior State Department officers as vital to the Cold War power balance; the United States possessed no critical security or material interests on the Korean peninsula; and, in any event, the prospect of a Soviet-sponsored incursion across the 38th parallel appeared highly unlikely. He had even testified before Congress that January, in an executive session, that should a North Korean attack occur, "We think that the [South] Korean Government can take care of any disturbances of that nature."[74] The wholly unexpected North Korean invasion, which Acheson correctly assumed to be backed by Stalin—as Soviet and Chinese documentation now confirms–challenged all elements of his previous convictions. "Here was a major attack by a Soviet satellite, highly armed, which obviously had an important relation to the entire situation which was created in the world by the Soviet Union," Acheson observed months later. It unavoidably carried profound global implications. "This was aimed at the entire position of the independent nations in the Pacific," he speculated, "the position of the Western nations, both in the Pacific and in the South Pacific; and in the Near East, and in Europe."[75]

Late on the afternoon of June 25, Acheson, along with Secretary of Defense Louis Johnson and Undersecretary of State James Webb, met Truman at the airport on the president's return from Independence. The four men discussed their preliminary thoughts about the Korean conflict while driving together to Pennsylvania's Avenue's Blair House. While en route, Truman vowed, "By God, I am going to let them have it!"[76] Following a 7:45 p.m. dinner with his senior national security advisers, Truman opened the discussion of the Korea crisis by turning to his most trusted adviser. Acheson immediately assumed a lead role, one he would maintain throughout the intense policy deliberations of the next several days. He summarized the gloomy and still confusing events unfolding in Korea and then presented the president's top defense officials with a set of specific recommendations for immediate action. Acheson first recommended that General Douglas MacArthur, the supreme commander of U.S. occupation forces in Japan, be authorized to supply the South Koreans with additional arms and other needed military equipment. He then suggested that the U.S. Air Force provide cover for the evacuation of women and children from Seoul and that it be authorized to knock out any North Korean tanks or aircraft interfering with that evacuation. Additionally, he advised that the president contemplate what extra assistance might be provided to South Korea in line with the Security Council resolution passed earlier that day. Recording his agreement with a memorandum just received from MacArthur about the importance now of defending Taiwan, Acheson next suggested that the president order the Seventh Fleet to proceed to the Taiwan Strait to deter any possible attack from the Chinese mainland. Finally, he urged an increase in U.S. aid to French forces in Indochina.

Acheson's ideas established the terms of debate for the meeting. Gen. Omar Bradley, chairman of the Joint Chiefs of Staff, speaking next, quickly voiced his agreement with each of the actions Acheson recommended. The decorated World War II commander emphasized that "we must draw the line somewhere" and ventured that the Korean fighting offered "a valuable opportunity for us to act." Following a lengthy discussion, Truman endorsed nearly all of Acheson's recommendations. He held off on issuing specific orders to the Seventh Feet, reasoning that those orders could await its arrival at the Taiwan Strait within the next thirty-six hours. The president also instructed Acheson to monitor carefully other likely spots for Soviet strikes and to prepare a statement for him to issue publicly, outlining U.S. actions.[77]

The following day, June 26, brought "steadily worsening reports from Korea." A cable from Ambassador Muccio in Seoul characterized the situation as one of "rapid deterioration and disintegration." From Paris, Ambassador Bruce reported a worrisome conversation with a senior French Foreign Ministry official. "If we do not send American troops, he thinks Korea will quickly be overrun and Western prestige irretrievably impaired," Bruce informed Acheson. After a series of conferences with State and Defense Department officers throughout the day, Acheson alerted Truman by telephone that "the situation in Korea was becoming so desperate that he would wish to hear about it firsthand and instruct us further."[78] The president, accordingly, called together the same group that had met the evening before for another Blair House conference.

Acheson, once again, spoke first. The U.S. Navy and Air Force, he began, should be authorized to "offer the fullest possible support to the South Korean forces, attacking tanks, guns, columns, etc., of the North Korean forces." In response to a question, he clarified that this military action should be confined to the area south of the 38th parallel. Second, Acheson suggested that President Truman should instruct the Seventh Fleet to block any attack mounted against Taiwan. Third, he recommended that the United States enlarge its military force stationed in the Philippines while increasing its aid to the Philippine government. Those measures, Acheson stressed, could help ensure a strong base of operations for the United States in its former Pacific colony. Fourth, he urged, as he had the previous evening, that the administration step up its aid to the French in Indochina.

Truman approved each of those recommendations at once—and without reservation. The secretary of state next handed Truman a rough draft of the statement he might issue the following day in explanation and defense of the administration's countermeasures. The president indicated that he would work on the draft later that night. Finally, Acheson informed the group that the State Department had prepared a second resolution for consideration by the Security Council; it would call on UN members to render such assistance to South Korea as was needed to repel the North Korean attack. Early soundings, he added, indicated its likely adoption. The president voiced his assent to that initiative as well.[79]

All in all, Acheson's performance at the two Blair House meetings was masterly. He had come to those crucial sessions extraordinarily well prepared. From the start of each, he set the general tone for the debate and he largely controlled the course of the deliberations that ensued. The president reflexively deferred to his judgment, endorsing each of the actions that Acheson counseled. None of the other policymakers in attendance at either of the Blair House meetings challenged or sought to alter substantively any of them. Truman alone, of course, held ultimate decision making responsibility, a fact Acheson well recognized and respected. Yet, to a remarkable extent, the program of coordinated military moves that Truman decided on in the immediate aftermath of the North Korea incursion was Acheson's program.

On June 27 Truman issued his planned public statement, prepared by Acheson, that outlined the actions he was authorizing. The fall of Seoul the next day made it clear, however, that those measures alone would be insufficient to guarantee South Korea's survival. Consequently, on June 30 Truman ordered the dispatch of U.S. ground forces to the Korean peninsula, a decision Acheson supported without reservation or hesitation. Less than five years after the termination of mankind's most devastating conflict, the United States was once again going to war.

5

THE CRUCIBLE OF WAR

The Korean conflict marked a critical turning point in the history of the postwar era. The accelerated militarization and globalization of U.S. foreign policy that accompanied it would become fixtures of the Cold War years, and after. More than anyone, Acheson deserves credit—or blame—for the far-reaching transformations that ensued. He imparted purpose, direction, and meaning to the Truman administration's post-Korea actions. If one of the hallmarks of effective statesmanship is the ability to turn problem into opportunity, to transform a crisis into a springboard for creative activity, then Acheson's stewardship of U.S. foreign policy in the immediate aftermath of the North Korean invasion surely meets that standard. He recognized that the climate of uncertainty and heightened fear ushered in by the Soviet-sponsored attack presented an unparalleled chance to push vigorously for the rapid defense buildup at home and within the Western alliance that he had long considered imperative to U.S. security.

On July 21, 1950, in extemporaneous remarks to the press, Acheson boasted with more than a hint of self-congratulation that the vigorous steps taken within the past month had greatly enhanced U.S. security and "brought about [an] extraordinary degree of unity within the free world and within this country." He observed with obvious satisfaction, and a dollop of grandiosity, "I do not recall any period of 4 weeks in the history of the United States when so much has been accomplished."[1]

TOWARD A MASSIVE U.S. MILITARY BUILDUP

Prior to the outbreak of the Korean War, Truman maintained a resolute commitment to a defense budget far more circumscribed than what Acheson and the Joint Chiefs of Staff thought necessary. Despite the stark warnings contained in NSC 68, which had reached the president's desk just two months before the North Korean invasion, Truman adhered to the belief that the nation simply needed to live within its means. It had to accept "calculated risks" in the face of the communist threat, he insisted, lest it jeopardize its fiscal solvency in a fruitless effort to achieve "absolute security." For him, America's security, and the survival of American democracy, depended on its willingness and ability to "establish world conditions under which we can preserve and continue to develop our way of life" against the challenge of "Soviet imperialism." But it was, at the same time, imperative that expenditures on defense did not permanently impair the economy or compromise "the fundamental values and institutions in our way of life." Before the Korean conflict, in sum, Truman saw himself holding the line against the advocates of a far-reaching transformation in the nation's defense priorities and expenditures. He clung to the hope that the system of collective security, embodied by the UN and the still infant NATO, would allow for the containment of the communist threat without turning his beloved country into a dreaded garrison state that would inevitably compromise traditional freedoms.[2]

Truman had appointed political loyalist and fund-raiser extraordinaire Louis Johnson to head the Defense Department largely because he felt confident that the short-tempered, bullying West Virginia lawyer, a former assistant secretary of war under FDR and a man with grand political ambitions of his own, would achieve the economizing he thought essential. The acerbic Johnson made no secret of his contempt for what he saw as Acheson's arrogance and air of superiority. For his part, the suave secretary viewed his opposite number at Defense with thinly veiled contempt. He considered Johnson not just a hopeless lightweight and political hack from the hinterlands but also someone who, as he liked to tell friends, was "nuttier than a fruitcake." The president also staffed the Bureau of the Budget with individuals who shared his conservative fiscal proclivities. They immediately raised objections to the assumptions undergirding NSC 68 and to the frightening dollar costs the program was certain to entail—and held firm in the weeks that preceded the outbreak of the Korean conflict. Johnson had signed on to NSC 68, but his commitment to the program remained less than halfhearted and he appears not to have fully grasped the document's fiscal implications.[3]

In a strong critique of that policy paper, which was forwarded to the NSC, the Budget Bureau's William F. Schaub asked if the country was now prepared to abandon the postwar trend toward prudence in government spending in favor of a strong military posture and full-scale mobilization. Pursuing those priorities would likely mean both increased taxes and increased governmental controls over the economy, Schaub cautioned. In seeking to rectify what NSC 68 identified as serious military deficiencies, he asked pointedly, was the administration prepared now to accept the real economic risks associated with a sharp spike in defense spending? Highlighting the potentially negative economic impact of such a program on the nation's productivity as well as the distortions and disruptions it might cause within the economy's civilian sectors, Schaub warned that a large military buildup would also extract a cost "in terms of the psychology and orientation of our society." A program designed to enhance America's military strength would "require measures which may seriously impair the functioning of our system."[4]

Viewed against this backdrop, the signal importance of the Korean War becomes clear. The conflict's onset immediately and decisively broke the budgetary stalemate within the executive branch that had pitted Acheson, Nitze, and the Joints Chiefs against the president and the economizers in the Budget Bureau. Could another event have played a comparable role? Obviously, we cannot know for certain, but it seems highly unlikely. What we do know is that the whole tenor of the internal policy debate changed virtually overnight with the North Korean invasion. A consensus quickly developed around the need not just to respond forcefully to Soviet-sponsored aggression in Korea but also to prepare for the possibility of additional aggressive moves by Moscow and its allies worldwide. "If we let Korea down," Truman said at one of the first post-hostilities meetings with his top advisers, "the Soviet [Union] will keep right on going and swallow up one piece of Asia after another. . . . If we were to let Asia go, the Near East would collapse and no telling what would happen in Europe."[5] The war's outbreak thus had adventitious consequences for proponents of a major U.S. defense mobilization. "It is doubtful," Acheson later reflected, "whether anything like what happened in the next few years could have been done had not the Russians been stupid enough to have instigated the attack against South Korea and opened the 'hate America' campaign."[6]

On July 6, 1950, W. Stuart Symington, chairman of the National Security Resources Board, read before an NSC meeting, with Truman presiding, a forceful statement in which he contrasted the gravity of the present international situation with "the serious current inadequacy of our own military forces." The Korean attack had come "as a surprise and a shock," Symington observed, "not only to the people of the United States and the world, but also to the people around this table, whose job it is to keep the President correctly advised." He recommended that the council quickly provide the president with a set of concrete actions and programs that he could authorize to meet "this critical danger." Viewing the nation's very survival as hanging in the balance, Symington said that the administration needed to "start now to spend more money instead of less money for our national security." He argued that the increased funds were needed to provide "vital necessities for U.S. defense." A rapid increase in U.S. military strength and in defense-related production would hearten America's allies while, he hoped, serving as a deterrent to its enemies.[7]

Acheson wholeheartedly agreed with that assessment and offered similar advice at a cabinet meeting one week later. The dramatically changed international picture offered the secretary an opportunity to push hard for adoption of the NSC 68 agenda, and push he did. In the wake of the North Korean attack, Acheson judged a rapid U.S. military buildup to be absolutely imperative. He told the cabinet that the administration now had no choice but to seek a sizable increase in the projected defense budget for fiscal year 1951 then being debated on the Senate floor. The situation the United States faced was, in his words, "one of gravest danger." Recent U.S. military reverses in South Korea were sowing doubts among America's allies—not about its intentions but about its *capabilities*. Those doubts had created a mood of "petrified fright" among Europeans. The president, he urged, should announce publicly the immediate increase in U.S. forces as well as stepped up U.S. production, and he must ask Congress for substantial additional funds to meet those essential goals. If it were "a question of asking for too little or too much," Acheson insisted, the president "should ask for too much." Truman agreed.[8]

On July 19 the president delivered a special message to Congress regarding the Korean conflict that outlined the military measures he was taking in response to this unprecedented global threat. He announced that he had authorized the secretary of defense to increase U.S. military forces beyond the levels currently budgeted; that National Guard and Reserve troops would be called up as needed; and that the Selective Service system would be used as necessary to secure additional military personnel. "The attack upon the Republic of Korea makes it plain beyond all doubt that the international communist movement is prepared to use armed invasion to conquer independent nations," he declared. "We must therefore recognize the possibility that armed aggression may take place in other areas."[9]

From that point forward, the administration embarked on a no-holds-barred military buildup, with Acheson serving as chief promoter, justifier, and cheerleader. "Military unpreparedness would be an open invitation to further aggression," he implored the House Armed Services Subcommittee; "the best hope of peace in the present situation is to make it clear that acts of aggression will be resisted, and resisted successfully." That meant, he explained, that the United States and its "Free World" allies must tap their "tremendous defense potential" by moving with "the greatest speed [to] translate that potential into defense in being."[10] During a private meeting with congressional leaders, Acheson labored to put the current crisis in historical perspective. According to his own contemporaneous record of that meeting, "I informed them that the United States Government was in the greatest danger in history, more so even than the crucial days marked by the battle of Gettysburg and the debacle at Pearl Harbor." Since "time is short" and "it is running out on us," Acheson pleaded with them to support an immediate increase in U.S. defense spending.[11] In early August 1950 Truman asked Congress for an additional $4 billion for military assistance programs, an extra $260 million for the Atomic Energy Commission, and an astounding $11.6 billion in supplementary defense spending–all emergency attachments to the military budget bill for fiscal year 1951. By the end of September Congress had approved the supplemental defense requests. Those made possible an Army of 11 divisions, an Air Force of 58 groups, and a Navy of 282 major combat vessels.[12]

Throughout August and September, Acheson made a compelling case to several congressional committees regarding the urgent need for these supplemental appropriations to the Mutual Defense Assistance Program. In personal notes that he penned in preparation for one of his appearances on Capitol Hill, Acheson outlined his thoughts about the new Soviet challenge. "We are in the position of the individual who, for the first time, on the death of a parent, hears the roaring of the cataract," he ruminated. "Today we either stand alone or we stand with friends. But in either case we stand together from the very first shot. If that is not made clear *now* and clinched with unmistakable action, the somber truth is that we stand alone—outnumbered—outresourced—with an unmanageable problem." Reflecting on America's Cold War policies to date, the secretary noted that the United States had rightly concentrated its efforts in Europe, politically, economically, and diplomatically. "As strength grows there, it grows everywhere," he wrote. "Without it, any other growth will wither." Yet Western military rearmament was still at a preliminary stage. The West remained weak relative to the huge numbers of Soviet divisions it faced in Europe, and recent events in Korea revealed a more belligerent and risk-tolerant adversary than Acheson had previously imagined. Time no longer appeared on the West's side. "The profound lesson of Korea," he reasoned, "is that, contrary to every action preceding, the USSR took a step which risked—however remotely—general war. No other action has done this—not even the Berlin Blockade." This, Acheson stressed, was the "all important *new* fact" about the international situation—and it was highly disquieting.[13]

Acheson repeatedly harped on the seminal significance of that "new fact" in lobbying the legislative branch for supplemental defense appropriations. The conflict in Korea, he acknowledged openly, had changed the "whole pattern of thought" within the administration about the immediacy and gravity of the Soviet threat. "Korea was not just another ordinary crisis," Acheson implored one group of lawmakers, "it was the first clear-cut act of military aggression since the fall of the Axis." Consequently, "American policy toward Europe, and indeed the policy of the Atlantic Community as a whole, was sweepingly modified by a new sense of danger and urgency."[14]

In confidential testimony before the Senate Foreign Relations and House Foreign Affairs committees, he admitted that Western defense efforts had thus far been wholly inadequate. "What you need are divisions, people with guns, halftracks, tactical air, and organization for command," he stated emphatically, "and in the earliest possible moment [to] build up in Europe, in being, a force which will be capable of deterring anybody from aggression . . . or, if the aggression takes place, stop it."[15] In a similar vein, he said to the Senate Appropriations Committee during a public hearing, "The defense effort required is tremendous, but we cannot afford to do less."[16]

MOBILIZING FOR EUROPEAN DEFENSE

In addition to its decisive impact on the U.S. military buildup, the Korean War also spurred an intense debate about, and accelerated planning for, the defense of Europe. The core problem faced by strategists in Washington and other NATO capitals was how to redress the substantial imbalance between Western and Soviet forces on what was still the Cold War's central front. The immediate aftermath of the North Korean offensive brought a heightened perception of threat and renewed uncertainty. Acheson, as a result, quickly came to appreciate the necessity for dispatching additional U.S. troops to Europe and for simultaneously invigorating each NATO nation's defense efforts and troop deployments. He and other top U.S. planners, civilian and military, recognized that NATO's current disposition of "twelve ill-equipped and uncoordinated divisions with little air support" constituted a woefully inadequate vehicle either for deterring or for repelling Soviet aggression. The U.S. ambassador in London, his old friend Lewis Douglas, sent a personal letter to Acheson on July 12 in which he made a powerful case for deepening the U.S. commitment to NATO forthwith. In an assessment that dovetailed with the secretary of state's own evolving view, Douglas said there was an urgent need now for more U.S. troops to be stationed in Europe and for active participation by the United States in NATO's military command.[17]

On July 22 Acheson cabled the senior U.S. diplomatic representatives accredited to all the NATO countries to instruct them to encourage their host governments to bolster substantially their commitments to the alliance in terms of troops and defense matériel. The Soviet-sponsored aggression in Korea made mandatory "the immediate objective of increased military strength." That immediate need did not conflict with the long-term goal of economic recovery, he assured them, even if a major rearmament push might require some short-run economic sacrifices. Acheson found the subsequent reports regarding the rearmament steps America's allies were willing and able to undertake rather disheartening. Clearly, the total number of forces available for deployment in Western Europe, from all of NATO's current members, would fall well short of any reasonable military plan for an adequate defense.[18]

The three most experienced U.S. diplomatic representatives in Europe, Ambassador Lewis Douglas in Great Britain, Ambassador David Bruce in France, and High Commissioner John McCloy in West Germany—all personal friends of Acheson's—each separately advised that the rearming of Germany and the integration of German units into a Western European, or NATO, army offered the only feasible means for solving the present manpower deficiency. "To defend Western Europe effectively will obviously require real contributions of German resources and men," insisted McCloy. The creation of "a genuine European army," the High Commissioner argued, "would fully integrate Germany into Western Europe and be the best possible insurance against further German aggression."[19] Acheson accepted the irrefutable logic of German participation in European defense, an abrupt volte-face on the issue for him—and a powerful indication of how fundamentally his views about European defense had changed in the Korean War's wake. "I think everyone is agreed that certainly talking about the rearmament of Germany at this time is very undesirable," he had assured the Senate Foreign Relations Committee on May 1. "That frightens the French; it also makes the Germans cocky." Less than three weeks before the North Korean attack, the secretary had similarly testified, during appropriation hearings, that the United States would continue to promote German demilitarization. What he saw as Soviet recklessness in Korea had plainly compelled a rethinking of that position. The unanimous support for German rearmament from three savvy diplomats whose judgment he valued hastened his conversion.[20]

On July 31 Acheson shared his new thinking with Truman during a one-on-one meeting at the White House. He stressed the importance of Germany's potential participation in European defense and recommended that the president authorize formal consideration of the issue through the NSC process. "The question was not whether Germany should be brought into the general defensive plan," Acheson asserted, "but rather how this could be done without disrupting anything else that we were doing and without putting Germany into a position to act as the balance of power in Europe." In other words, the issue for him was not *whether* German rearmament should be encouraged but *how.* The secretary made it clear that he was adamantly opposed to the re-creation of a national German army–as were McCloy, Douglas, and Bruce. Such an initiative, all four men believed, would only weaken European defense by stirring up frightening memories of the recent past. Truman fully agreed, offering his own historically rooted perceptions about the dangers of German domination of the European continent. Acheson emphasized that the State Department was contemplating, instead, the "possible creation of a European army or a North Atlantic army." The president gave his blessing to a careful vetting of that idea.[21]

Over the next month Acheson took a lead role in the administration's development of what came to be called the "one package" plan for bolstering European defense. The plan was to be presented at the next North Atlantic Council meeting, scheduled for New York that September. It consisted of four indivisible elements: a significant increase in the number of U.S. troops stationed in Europe; the creation of an integrated NATO military command structure; the establishment of a supreme commander for NATO forces–expected to be a high-profile American military man; and the integration of German military units into a European army within the NATO umbrella. The latter, as anticipated, proved most controversial from the first–especially for the French.

Prior to the formal opening of the North Atlantic Council meeting, Acheson held a series of meetings with the French and British foreign ministers in an effort to persuade them of the necessity of the steps the United States now considered integral to a sound European defense structure. The secretary presented his case with a combination of cool rationality and controlled passion. Time was of the essence, he emphasized. The United States anticipated "a period of great danger" occurring within the next two years, and hence it did not want to postpone decisions that it considered crucial to the defense of Europe against possible Soviet aggression. The participation of German units in NATO's defense forces constituted one of the most fundamental of those decisions; the

United States believed that any "attempt to defend Europe without German participation was impossible." Bevin, after receiving a report from the British Chiefs of Staff that mirrored Acheson's conclusion about the need for German participation, indicated general support for the American one-package plan. Schuman, on the other hand, expressed his government's "very strong and firm opposition" to any scheme that would involve German rearmament. It would cause grave psychological difficulties with the French public, owing to the bitter memories of France's recent defeat at Germany's hands, he explained, intimating that any government that sought to move in that direction could not long survive.[22]

Frustrated, if not entirely surprised, by the initial French response, Acheson nonetheless presented the American proposals to the full North Atlantic Council on September 15. The U.S. decision to deploy large numbers of additional, combat-ready troops to the European continent represented, in his words, "a complete revolution in American foreign policy and in the attitude of the American people." He vividly captured the historical significance of that commitment: "This, of course, means that if there were troubles in Europe, the US would be involved in it from the very first moment and would be as deeply committed to the repulse of any attack as any member of the North Atlantic community." But, Acheson also made clear, that commitment formed just one part of an integrated program that could not be adopted in piecemeal fashion. The secretary laid out the U.S. case for Germany's inclusion in European defense efforts in the logical, lawyerlike manner that he preferred, establishing a central premise from which all succeeding propositions flowed naturally. The defense of Europe must begin as far to the east as possible, he asserted, which meant in Germany. The loss of West Germany to the Soviets would be disastrous to the NATO nations; hence its borders must be defended. Yet they could not be secured if Germany's own participation in that defense—which Adenauer himself had recently offered—were to be blocked. Such a rejection would demoralize the German people, further complicating any defense plan. Either NATO member-states accepted that the program under discussion necessitated German involvement, Acheson asserted starkly, or else they must believe that "we should repulse Germany and insist that all of us go to even greater sacrifices to defend German territory and the German people without requiring them to make some of the sacrifices which we are going to make." It was a powerful case, presented with clarity, conviction, and fire.[23]

Yet it did not move Schuman's government an inch. By the close of the council sessions, every NATO nation–except France–had accepted or was gravitating toward acceptance of the proposed U.S. program. Unfortunately for Washington, French backing was so fundamental to the program's prospects for success that Paris could exercise a de facto veto over it. If the French did not come on board, Acheson admitted privately, "the whole situation will probably disintegrate."[24] The secretary of state was fully supportive, it bears emphasizing, of a key French initiative on the economic front that was moving forward at exactly this time. In May 1950 French Foreign Minister Schuman had proposed that the coal and steel industries of France and Germany be unified under a single authority, along with those of any other European nation that chose to join. The next month Acheson reported the administration's unqualified backing for the so-called Schuman Plan to a congressional committee, calling it "a most important and far reaching proposition" that represented "a tremendous step forward." The absence of a comparable breakthrough on the all-important security front, however, left him deeply frustrated.[25]

Following the New York meetings, consequently, Acheson and his re-vered former boss, newly installed Secretary of Defense George Marshall, privately pressed French officials hard in an effort to make them see the light. U.S. officials needed to "keep the heat on the French," Acheson insisted. The impasse, however, dragged on.[26] The problem for the French, of course, was in good measure emotional, a fact Acheson appreciated. Indeed, to humanize the difficulties France was wrestling with, he once called the attention of congressional representatives to the personal history of French defense minister Jules Moch, a man whose brother had been tortured and executed by the Germans during World War II.[27] Belgian foreign minister Paul-Henri Spaak, whose country had also been defeated, humiliated, and occupied by the Germans, observed that Acheson's plea for a rearmed Germany "troubled a great many consciences." An unanswerable question, Spaak suggests, overhung all of the resulting negotiations: "Was it wise to rearm Germany barely five years after the end of the war?"[28]

In mid-October France unveiled a half-baked counterproposal, dubbed the Pleven Plan after Prime Minister René Pleven, that quickly gained solid backing from the French Assembly. The plan consented to the inclusion of a relatively modest number of German troops, at the battalion level, in a broader European army. Acheson and other top U.S. officials found the French initiative a disappointing nonstarter because it relegated German forces to second- or third-class status while hardly boosting overall NATO force levels. "It is a very bad business," a discouraged Acheson told the Senate Foreign Relations Committee. "From a political, psychological, and military point of view, [Germany] is absolutely essential to building up this force that is so necessary in Europe"; yet the French "continually put forward proposals which humiliate the Germans." Plainly, Acheson recognized, a different U.S. approach would be required for meaningful progress on European defense issues.[29] Before the next stage of intra-allied consultations could take place at the December meetings in Brussels, however, developments in Korea had elevated the Cold War to a still more dangerous level, creating even greater urgency on the European defense front.

CHINESE INTERVENTION AND THE MACARTHUR CHALLENGE

In September and October 1950, as intra-allied negotiations over European defense plans sputtered to a stalemate, the fortunes of UN ground troops in Korea abruptly and dramatically changed. On September 15 MacArthur, whose forces had been hemmed in perilously at the narrow Pusan perimeter, engineered the successful landing of the First Marine Division at Inchon Harbor in a bold flanking maneuver. The battlefield momentum almost immediately shifted to the UN side. By September 27 Seoul had been recaptured and North Korean troops forced into full-scale retreat. That same day, following weeks of intensive debate within the State and Defense departments, the Joints Chiefs of Staff cabled a new set of instructions to MacArthur, endorsed by Marshall and Acheson. "Your military objective is the destruction of the North Korean Armed Forces," the directive read in part. "In attaining this objective you are authorized to conduct military operations, including amphibious and airborne landings or ground operations north of the 38th parallel in Korea, provided that at the time of such operations there has been no entry into North Korea by major Soviet or Chinese Communist Forces, no announcement of intended entry, nor a threat to counter our operations militarily in North Korea."[30]

Acheson fully supported the new orders; he was convinced that "no arbitrary prohibition against crossing the parallel should be imposed." He composed a key part of the growing consensus within the administration that believed the United States should not just turn back North Korea's aggression but should crush the regime and its armed forces.[31] He, more than most, relished the tantalizing prospect of not just repelling communist aggression but also scoring a major political, psychological, and geostrategic victory for the West. The sudden reversal of the tide of battle thus gave rise to a set of questions that went beyond those associated simply with the conduct of military operations above the 38th parallel. Should the United States, in seeking to destroy North Korea's military forces, also seek to destroy the Pyongyang regime? Should it strive to turn into reality the pious UN resolution of 1947 that had called for "an independent, united Korean government"? And, if so, then what risks should the American government be willing to accept in the attainment of that goal?

President Harry S. Truman consults with Acheson and Secretary of Defense
George C. Marshall on Korean War strategy, December 1950.
Courtesy of the Harry S. Truman Library

As Truman's chief diplomat, Acheson did not of course bear responsibility for issues of a purely military character. Matters of strategy and tactics were the province of the Pentagon and the commander in the field. Since the former was headed by General Marshall, the celebrated organizer of victory in World War II, and the latter was the indomitable General MacArthur, one of the most renowned and revered heroes of that war, Acheson's intrusion onto their turf would have been wildly inappropriate. Yet he remained the president's most trusted adviser and to the extent that war-fighting strategy and tactics impinged on larger issues of Cold War geopolitics—as they inevitably did in the Korea case—his views carried weight with the commander in chief in the White House. In that regard, Acheson's influence on the decision to widen U.S. war goals proved especially important. Following the military success at Inchon, he proposed lobbying the UN General Assembly (to avoid a certain Soviet veto in the Security Council) for a resolution that would allow UN forces to enter into and remain within North Korea until both halves of that divided country were reunified under a democratic government. After receiving a green light from Truman, the secretary helped engineer the passage of precisely such a resolution on October 7, by a vote of forty-seven to five, with seven abstentions. The original Security Council enabling resolution had called simply for the repulsion of North Korean aggression. With Acheson's strong backing, the General Assembly was now sanctioning a far more expansive war aim: Korean unification under UN auspices.

MacArthur assured Truman, during an impromptu meeting at Wake Island in mid-October, that the war was already won and that Chinese or Soviet intervention at this stage was exceedingly unlikely. CIA and State Department intelligence reports rendered similar judgments, despite private warnings from Beijing that it would not permit UN troops to move too close to the Yalu River, the natural boundary between North Korea and China. "While full-scale Chinese Communist intervention in Korea must be considered a continuing possibility," the CIA observed, "a consideration of all known factors leads to the conclusion that, barring a Soviet decision for global war, such action is not probable in 1950."[32] Acheson, along with other top administration strategists, chose not to question those complacent assessments. Although he admitted privately that moving north entailed some risks, he emphasized that "there had been risk from the beginning and at present," and "a greater risk would be incurred by showing hesitation and timidity."[33] On October 26, however, China's People's Liberation Army (PLA) troops unexpectedly attacked and routed a contingent of South Korean forces as they approached the Yalu River. The next day another large force of PLA troops engaged South Korean and U.S. units just south of the Yalu. After four days of heavy fighting, the Chinese forces withdrew. Despite these worrisome probes, Acheson's support for MacArthur's advance did not fundamentally change.

In retrospect, it is clear that Beijing was sending a strong message: that it was fully prepared to intervene militarily if its borders appeared threatened by UN troop movements. Truman, Acheson, and other top U.S. officials chose, nonetheless, to ignore those signals, essentially deferring to MacArthur's assurances that UN forces could achieve a stable defensive position at the Yalu and that the recent Chinese moves amounted to mere bluffing. British and Canadian diplomats certainly read the situation that way. Foreign Ministers Ernest Bevin and Lester B. Pearson made several fruitless démarches to Acheson, urging that he support the establishment of a demilitarized buffer zone well south of the Chinese border so as to assuage Beijing's suspicions about MacArthur's intentions and thus prevent a full-scale Chinese intervention. Acheson responded that the offensive should first be allowed to run its course.[34] The administration, in Acheson's retrospective appraisal, missed its last chance to rein in the "Sorcerer of Inchon" during the critical weeks that followed the initial Chinese military probe of late October. By the end of November, it was too late. On November 27 a massive force of 300,000 Chinese soldiers poured forth from hidden positions in mountainous terrain within North Korean territory to shock the advancing UN armies and force their retreat. What ensued, as Acheson reflected bitterly—but honestly—in his memoir, was "the greatest defeat suffered by American arms since the battle of Manassas and an international disaster of the first water [*sic*]."[35]

Acheson's contribution to this debacle, in which the prospect of a spectacular politico-military success overnight turned into the sober reality of a crushing politico-military defeat, has long fascinated observers of his career, and students of American foreign policy decision making more broadly. Why would a man renowned for his probity, prudence, and maturity of judgment act so rashly in this instance? Why did he not recognize the manifest dangers of the administration's military policy and at least inject some cautionary words into the internal debate? And why would Acheson so cavalierly discount Chinese and third-party warnings while lending his support to a headlong march to the Yalu that risked much for relatively little additional gain? After all, the establishment of a demilitarized, buffer zone well south of the Yalu– and Britain's Bevin proposed just that course–could have assuaged China's suspicions while allowing for a consolidation of the smashing victory already achieved against Soviet-sponsored aggression. That would have safeguarded what already ranked as one of the most impressive Cold War victories to date for the United States and the West. Instead, the enormous gains achieved since the early fall were squandered by the foolhardy and needlessly provocative overreaching of the late fall. Acheson, in his memoir and other reflections, claims that he fell victim to a combination of faulty intelligence and groupthink, that he was guilty of undue deference to the military and a disinclination to challenge the assurances of a commanding general who had successfully defied far greater odds earlier with his brilliant Inchon maneuver. Those doubtless exerted an important influence on his behavior. But surely deeper factors were also at work.

For one, Acheson had long relished risk-taking. Throughout his professional life he had courted sizable risks, from his earliest legal case at The Hague tribunal and later defiance of FDR through his frontal challenges to Soviet interests in the Turkish crisis of 1946, the German reintegration and rearmament initiatives, and, not least, the Korean intervention itself. Nearly all had paid off handsomely. Considered against that pattern of decision making, Acheson's endorsement of MacArthur's reckless advance toward the Chinese border might be seen as but one more calculated risk undertaken by an individual whose lifelong winning streak–his defiance of FDR excepted–had inured him to the possibility of failure. An individual whose past history of risk-taking has almost always yielded success typically becomes less cautious over time in weighing gain against risk, thereby feeling less constrained by the possibility of miscalculation or chance of a major setback. The only serious obstacle to reunification under a pro-American government was China, moreover, a country whose military prowess Acheson had long disparaged.

Finally, the temptation of a potentially huge payoff for the United States, for the Truman administration, and for himself personally—and not just internationally but at home—must have appeared irresistible to the embattled secretary of state. Acheson had become "the symbol of appeasement everywhere in Asia," in the cruel words of *Life*, the nation's largest mass-circulation magazine. Attacks on his competence and integrity had snowballed after the Korean War's outbreak, with Senator Kenneth Wherry charging that he had "the blood of our boys in Korea" on his hands.[36] Acheson would not have been human if that brutal political environment had not exerted some influence on his approach to MacArthur's "final" offensive. Had he recommended reining in a general who was the darling of the political right and who remained enormously popular with the public at large, then surely that position would have been leaked to the press at some point, further soiling his image and reputation. By going along with the general's strategic gamble, however, whatever private reservations he might have harbored in the aftermath of China's warnings and military probes, Acheson could share in the acclaim sure to follow a successful outcome. That could have undercut his critics, putting them for once on the defensive. It likely seemed a highly appealing prospect.

Whatever the precise mix of reasons that led him to back MacArthur's roll of the dice, Acheson clearly bears major responsibility for the military and political calamity that resulted. If the secretary of state deserves great credit for the administration's prompt and effective response to the Korean challenge in June 1950, as he does, then he deserves substantial blame for the debacle of November 1950. The former achievement will forever be tainted by the foolish recklessness that followed—probably the most grievous blunder of Acheson's tenure as secretary of state. It was one, moreover, whose consequences overshadowed his remaining two years in office.

Acheson was stunned by the entry of Chinese forces into the conflict, a development he later described as "an incalculable defeat to U.S. foreign policy."[37] Chinese intervention constituted not only the gravest international crisis he had yet faced as secretary of state but a deep personal one as well. Alice Acheson recalled later that she had never seen her husband so depressed—or so anxious about the possibility of general war.[38] Nonetheless, he chose to face head-on the consequences of the jarring setback that he helped bring about, urging

Truman that the United States must salvage what it could from the wreckage of the administration's Korean policy. He quickly reached the view that the United States could not withdraw from Korea without diminishing its credibility in the eyes of allies and enemies alike, but neither could it achieve a military victory over numerically superior Chinese armies—at least not without sacrificing allied solidarity and broader global interests. "One imperative," he advised Truman, "is to find a line that we can hold, and hold it." To the president and the Joint Chiefs of Staff, he insisted that Korea could not now be abandoned. "There is a danger of our becoming the greatest appeasers of all time if we abandon the Koreans and they are slaughtered," he argued; however, "if there is a Dunkirk and we are forced out, it is a disaster, but not a disgraceful one." With his critics now baying loudly for his head—in mid-December Republicans in the House and Senate declared that the secretary had lost the country's confidence and called for his removal from office—Acheson held fast to that position. By early January 1951 he and Marshall had guided the president to a new, much more modest and realistic war goal: a cease-fire leading to negotiations aimed at the restoration of the antebellum status quo. The United States needed to restore confidence among its allies, he emphasized, "so that we can get results in our European defense plans."[39]

Not without irony, Chinese intervention gave a significant boost to the two broader foreign policy initiatives Acheson considered most urgent at this juncture of the Cold War: the strengthening of NATO and the acceleration of the nation's defense mobilization. On December 18–19, the NATO Council met at Brussels to consider the proposals introduced by Acheson three months earlier. The secretary described the atmosphere at the Belgian capital as "tinged with fear," and many hushed corridor discussions were devoted to the danger of general war. That crisis atmosphere smoothed the path toward the council's unanimous acceptance of the U.S. proposal to appoint Gen. Dwight D. Eisenhower as the first supreme commander of an integrated NATO command structure. It also facilitated incremental progress on the all-important question of German rearmament. France agreed to modify its Pleven Plan so that German forces, organized in regimental combat units of five to six thousand men, could be integrated into a European army—or European Defense Community (EDC), as it was officially dubbed. NATO member-states consented to commence negotiations toward that end shortly in Paris. The conferees also agreed to open another negotiating track on the German rearmament front; this one to be conducted by the U.S., UK, and French high commissioners in Bonn and to focus on the inclusion of German military forces within NATO. From Acheson's perspective, the movement forward was frustratingly slow. Nevertheless, the Brussels meeting constituted a watershed in Western defense planning since all NATO nations were now committed in principle to German rearmament.[40] During a Washington press conference, on December 22, Acheson said that Brussels marked "the conclusion of a chapter in a long book." With NATO's organizational structure now intact, it was time to "go to work to put real muscle and real bone into it."[41]

Chinese entry into the Korean conflict also served to strengthen the hand of those administration officials, like Acheson, who desired an even more extensive U.S. defense buildup. At an NSC meeting of November 28, just days after massive waves of Chinese troops attacked allied armies south of the Yalu, Truman endorsed a council recommendation that Congress be requested to support another $16.8 billion in supplemental defense spending. Given what seemed a dire wartime emergency, Congress wasted little time in rubber-stamping the president's expansive request. The resulting supplemental appropriation bill, it bears emphasizing, authorized a sum greater than the *total* defense budget Truman had originally submitted for all of fiscal year 1951. Still, not even that dollar figure proved sufficient for Acheson and other advocates of a truly robust military buildup, and those advocates were now in the ascendancy. The uniformed military decided that the four-year time frame for the planned expansion conceived in the immediate aftermath of the North Korean attack was simply no longer adequate. Instead, the program's timetable needed to be accelerated dramatically so that the force goals established for 1954–and those had been set just months earlier–could, and should, now be achieved by 1952.[42]

At an NSC meeting on December 14, Acheson made clear his conviction that the nation needed the greatest possible defense enhancement in the shortest possible time. "It would not be too much if we had all the troops that the military want," he exclaimed. "If we had all the things that our European allies want it would not be too much. If we had the equipment to call out the reserves it would not be too much. If we had a system for full mobilization it would not be too much. . . . The danger couldn't be greater."[43] As he remarked at an off-the-record meeting with the Advisory Council of the National Association of Broadcasters that same day, "War may come at any moment." The North Korean attack proved, Acheson told the broadcasters, that "the Soviet Union was willing to go to war, if necessary, to achieve their objectives."[44]

By January 1951 Congress had approved total defense appropriations for fiscal year 1951 amounting to $42.9 billion, more than tripling Truman's pre–Korean War request. Still, military planners wanted more and Truman's secretary of state lent them his unqualified support. An assessment by the Joint Chiefs of Staff, circulated that same month, proclaimed solemnly that "the United States faces today one of the greatest dangers in its history." In view of the relative weakness of America and its allies in the face of the Kremlin's "aggressive expansionist activities," no policy other than one devoted to a sizable growth in the American military establishment could be countenanced. Such a policy, the Joint Chiefs concluded, must include "a coordinated and integrated crusade against Kremlin-dominated communism everywhere" and "a rapid, resolute build-up of the tangible military power of the United States and its allies."[45]

As its defense buildup surged forward, the Truman administration faced another agonizing dilemma in Korea. The ongoing fighting there had taken a favorable turn early in the new year. By February MacArthur's forces had regained the offensive and were once again beginning to move north toward the 38th parallel. The new, sharply circumscribed war aims adopted by his superiors in the White House and Pentagon never sat well with the imperious and vainglorious MacArthur. He remained wedded to the notion that total victory could, and should, be achieved—even if that objective necessitated an all-out clash of arms between the United States and China. The outspoken commander also did not shy away from venting his belligerent views in public declarations, statements to the press, and private communications with supporters. Plainly, to the dismay of Truman, Acheson, Marshall, and the Joint Chiefs, MacArthur believed himself entitled to the unhampered freedom essential to destroy the military capabilities of what he considered the principal enemy: China. Acheson, for his part, saw China as "the second team" and worried that full-scale war with Beijing would serve only the Kremlin's purposes by diminishing America's ability to fight the Soviet "first team." Moreover, as he remarked in a meeting with Marshall and the Joint Chiefs, "If our resources are devoted there [China], we cannot build up strength in Europe."[46] Marshall's Pentagon sought to hem MacArthur in with explicit directives but never fully succeeded.

Increasingly defiant of presidential authority, MacArthur finally crossed the line with an unauthorized ultimatum to Beijing, on March 24, and a subsequent letter to Republican Representative Joseph Martin in which he bridled against the restraints Truman was imposing on him. When Martin shared the letter with the press, Truman recognized that his choices were either to fire MacArthur for insubordination or to violate the constitutional principle of civilian control over the military. On April 9, 1951, the president announced publicly that he was relieving MacArthur of all his commands.

In so acting, Truman enjoyed the unqualified backing of Acheson, Marshall, and the Joint Chiefs. Acheson believed that MacArthur's insubordination "had raised a question of the most serious possible nature," one that "went to the very center of power and the exercise of power." The core constitutional issue could not have been plainer, in his judgment: the president "speaks as Commander-in-Chief. He gives the orders and they must be carried out. There is no question about that." Truman and his chief military and civilian advisers were well aware that firing a popular general in the middle of a war could unleash political bedlam, but they saw no alternative and were prepared to ride out the storm.[47]

MacArthur returned home to a hero's welcome. Polls revealed the dismissed general's continuing popularity; the president, in embarrassing contrast, suffered from steadily sinking public support. The episode gave its critics another excuse to berate the administration. Senator McCarthy, as was his style, went for the jugular. At first, he placed blame for the MacArthur flap squarely on Truman's shoulders. "That son of a bitch should be impeached," he huffed in late April. McCarthy went so far as to hint that the chief executive might have been drunk on bourbon, his favorite spirit, when he fired MacArthur. Shortly thereafter, the bumptious senator backed away somewhat from that profane assault, which was outrageous even by his standards. McCarthy told a friendly home crowd in Cudahy, Wisconsin, that the real problem was Truman's secretary of state. Truman was president "in name only," he remarked; "the Acheson group has almost hypnotic power over him." It was Acheson—"the heart of the octopus," as McCarthy termed him—who truly needed to be impeached. A month later, on the Senate floor, McCarthy once more lashed out at Acheson and his "lace handkerchief crowd," calling again for the secretary of state's impeachment. He melodramatically introduced the figure of Bob Smith, an ordinary soldier just returned from Korea without his legs, and said that just as soon as Smith had been fitted for artificial legs he should walk over to the State Department and confront the traitorous Acheson. "He should say," McCarthy cried, "'Mr. Acheson, if you want at long last to perform one service for the American people you should not only resign from the State Department but you should remove yourself from this country and go to the nation for which you have been struggling and fighting so long.'"[48]

Yet, for all of the scurrilous charges hurled at Truman and Acheson, the administration managed to ride out the storm. Extended hearings, demanded by Congress, allowed top military leaders to explain effectively and dispassionately the factors that lay behind Truman's decision to relieve MacArthur. Acheson himself endured nine solid days of questioning from often-hostile legislators. The secretary acquitted himself well, using the sessions as an opportunity to outline and defend the administration's overall Asian policy. He emphasized that "all of the President's advisers believe the course we are now following gives us the best chance of stopping hostilities and ending the aggression in Korea." The alternative course of action called for by MacArthur and his supporters carried enormous risks. "Against the dubious advantages of spreading the war in an initially limited manner to the mainland of China," Acheson explained patiently, "there must be measured the risk of a general war with China, the risk of Soviet intervention, and of world war III, as well as the probable effects upon the solidarity of the free world coalition." There were no compelling reasons to court such risks, moreover, since "time is on our side if we make good use of it." The secretary of state's confidence grew from his conviction that the United States and its allies boasted far greater productive potential than their enemies—the fundamental premise, of course, of NSC 68. "We and our allies have the capacity to out-produce the Soviet bloc by a staggering margin," he asserted. "There is no doubt about that. Our capacity to produce has been set in motion and is rapidly getting to the point where its output will be vast and its effect significant."[49]

DEEPENING COMMITMENTS IN ASIA

With the onset of the Korean War, America's commitments across the Asian continent deepened appreciably–from the Korean peninsula to Taiwan and Japan and from the Philippines to Indochina. Within days of the North Korean strike, Truman announced that the United States was not just intervening with military force on behalf of South Korea but also was dispatching the Seventh Fleet to the Taiwan Strait, increasing its aid to the Philippines, and stepping up its military support to the French in Indochina. The United States thus simultaneously insinuated itself into four separate Asian conflicts. Acheson, who had strongly advocated each of those actions at the crucial Blair House meetings, believed it essential for Washington to signal its resolution by providing a more effective containment shield to areas that suddenly appeared much more important to the overall Cold War power balance. He was not blind to the civil war elements that obtained in all four of those struggles. Both South Korea and North Korea, after all, had been regularly threatening military action against the other well before Pyongyang launched its offensive on June 25; neither Korean government was willing to accept division of the homeland as permanent. Across the Taiwan Strait, the rival governments of Mao and Chiang had also rattled sabers at each other with some regularity. They could agree on little except for the fact that there was only one China. The struggle between the American-supported regime in Manila and the Hukbalahap insurgents, similarly, was an internal struggle, one among different groups of Filipinos over what type of government would rule the islands and in whose interests. In Indochina, the fight essentially pitted Vietnamese nationalists against French colonialists. Acheson appreciated those nuances but saw the need to affirm the credibility of U.S. commitments in Asia as a global priority that simply overrode local particularities.

The Korean War also provided a powerful impetus for the negotiation of a final peace treaty with Japan. Acheson considered the treaty, which was signed in San Francisco on September 8, 1951, to be the major diplomatic achievement of that trying year. It stands, as well, as the single, unqualified triumph of his Asian policy. Yet, ironically, the nuts and bolts of the negotiating process were handled not by Acheson himself–although he set the basic parameters–but by a man he detested and who would ultimately replace him as secretary of state: the dour and ambitious John Foster Dulles.

A prominent Wall Street attorney, leading Republican foreign policy spokesman, and former New York senator, Dulles represented a brand of conservative internationalism that in key respects was little distinguishable from Acheson's liberal internationalism. In terms of style, temperament, and personality, however, the two lawyers could not have been more different. Acheson found Dulles, a pious Presbyterian who tended to wear his religion on his sleeve, to be self-righteous and humorless; for his part, Dulles thought Acheson arrogant and condescending. Initially, Acheson resisted the proposal, advanced by Vandenberg and others, that Dulles be offered an appointment as a State Department adviser to help shore up the administration's faltering bipartisan bona fides. "Has he lost his mind?" Acheson exclaimed when reading a recommendation to that effect from deputy James Webb. But the secretary's pragmatism soon overcame his visceral distaste for the sanctimonious Dulles. He came to appreciate the political utility of having so prominent a Republican inside the tent; the latter's involvement in Asian diplomacy, in particular, could help protect the administration's most vulnerable flank from the relentless hammering of GOP critics. Consequently, in April 1950, Acheson offered Dulles a position as a State Department consultant. Dulles immediately accepted.[50]

Acheson and Dulles thought in similar terms about Japan. Each viewed the former adversary as Asia's prime Cold War prize, based on its advanced industrial infrastructure, strategic location, and highly skilled workforce, and worried that it formed a major target for Soviet subversion or aggression. The two were agreed, consequently, that Tokyo's alignment with the West could be an enormous asset to the United States, its drift into the communist orbit a calamity. The secretary of state and his new Republican colleague also found themselves in strong accord on the need to fashion a liberal peace settlement with Japan that would help ensure its loyalty to the West while facilitating its economic integration into the international capitalist system. Achieving those aims, they were convinced, meant guaranteeing both Japan's security and its unfettered access to critical raw materials and foodstuffs. "Japan is, with Germany, one of the two great assets that the Soviet power seeks for exploitation in aid of its aggressive policies," Dulles emphasized in a December 1950 memorandum to Acheson. It was the one country within East Asia, he contended, whose loss could upset the current balance of power.[51] Acheson could not have articulated the stakes at risk in Japan any more succinctly himself.

Shortly after the outbreak of the Korean War, Acheson pushed hard for opening negotiations with Japan aimed at reaching agreement on an acceptable peace treaty and accompanying bilateral security pact. He and Truman agreed that Dulles should serve as the principal negotiator, in part to prevent yet another sensitive Asian issue from becoming a target of partisan sniping. On September 8, 1950, Truman approved a memorandum to that effect, drafted by Acheson and approved by Secretary of Defense Johnson. Dulles commenced preliminary work on a draft treaty that autumn. The rapidly shifting course of the war in Korea, however, led the Pentagon to withdraw its support for immediate negotiations. Since Japan served as an essential staging area for military operations on the Korean peninsula, the Joint Chiefs of Staff expressed wariness about jeopardizing that role by a premature agreement. Following the entry of Chinese forces into the conflict in December 1950, Acheson argued forcefully that it would be imprudent to hold off negotiations with Japan any longer; he feared that doing so might put in peril the broader goal of ensuring Japan's long-term commitment to the West.[52]

During a private meeting with George Marshall, on January 8, 1951, Acheson persuaded the secretary of defense that further delay would be too risky. They jointly drafted a set of presidential instructions for Dulles, which Truman approved without substantive change two days later. In his letter to Dulles, dated January 10, Truman designated the Republican foreign policy expert a special representative of the president with the personal rank of ambassador and authorized him to visit Japan and other Pacific region countries to discuss the general basis for a peace settlement. The president's instructions underscored the intention of the United States to "commit substantial armed force to the defense of the island chain of which Japan forms a part" and its concomitant desire that Japan "should increasingly acquire the ability to defend itself." Truman's directive also expressed the government's willingness to enter into mutual assistance arrangements with the other Pacific island nations, including Australia, New Zealand, Japan, and the Philippines.[53]

Armed with those broad guidelines, Dulles traveled to Japan in late January and, during a series of talks with Prime Minister Yoshida Shigeru, effectively laid the groundwork for a mutually acceptable accord. Dulles proved himself adept at the give-and-take of the diplomatic art, displaying a shrewd eye for the fundamental needs of his interlocutors and for what could be compromised— and what could not. Yoshida's adamant opposition to rearmament and the reluctance of the Filipinos, Australians, and New Zealanders to enter into a Pacific-wide security agreement that would include Japan, their recent enemy, forced essential modifications in the U.S. negotiating tack. By the spring of 1951 Dulles and Acheson concurred that the United States should pursue three separate security agreements—with Japan; with the Philippines; and with Australia and New Zealand—rather than one all-inclusive Pacific pact. They also acknowledged that any movement toward Japanese rearmament would remain politically unfeasible for some time.[54]

MacArthur's firing temporarily threatened to derail progress on the treaty. After awakening Dulles late on the evening of April 10 and having him rush to Acheson's P Street house, the secretary personally delivered the shocking news that the Republican Party's favorite general was about to be dismissed. After expressing his regret about the decision and casting blame on the administration for the rupture with MacArthur, Dulles nonetheless consented to fly to Tokyo immediately and reassure Yoshida that a peace treaty with Japan remained a top U.S. priority. The Japanese welcomed his words of reassurance. Once again, Dulles proved a reliable team player and drew Acheson's grudging gratitude.[55]

From that point on, the treaty process moved forward expeditiously. The Pentagon and the British government posed the only serious obstacles to the treaty terms desired by Dulles and Acheson's State Department. The special representative's face-to-face meetings in London with the new British foreign secretary, Herbert Morrison, helped deflect British reservations about the treaty. Acheson's timely appeals to Truman, capitalizing as usual on his special relationship with the president, led the military to withdraw its objections. To cite but one key instance, the secretary effectively undercut the Joint Chiefs' bid to maintain indefinitely the legal right to utilize Japanese military facilities in the prosecution of the war in Korea with a highly pragmatic counterargument. On June 29, during a White House meeting with Truman and senior Pentagon representatives, Acheson observed, "There is very little risk that [the Japanese] would not act sensibly and cooperatively." Moreover, "in this case as in so many others the United States could not rely on mere arbitrary authority to control other people, but had to do it by persuasion." Truman, as he usually did, came down on Acheson's side.[56]

The overriding issue, Acheson had advised Truman prior to that meeting, is "not only the military position in and about Korea but also the requirement that Japan should continue to be a bastion that is friendly." Two months later, on the eve of the San Francisco ceremonies, he restated that controlling assumption in another strongly worded memorandum to the president. "The future alignment of Japan as between the free world and communism," the secretary declared, "is an issue second in importance perhaps only to Germany."[57] Acheson was not insensitive to Japan's military value. To the contrary, he labored successfully to help forge a U.S.-Japanese bilateral security agreement–separate from the multilateral peace treaty–that would permit the United States to maintain both military basing rights within Japan and, to Yoshida's disappointment, occupation authority over Okinawa.

The gala signing ceremony at San Francisco's Opera House, the same venue at which the historic UN charter was signed five and a half years earlier, must be termed a personal triumph for Acheson. He ensured, in advance, that the rules of procedure under which the conference would proceed virtually precluded participant nations from seeking to alter any elements of the treaty. Acheson's chief fear in the days before the official conference opening, on September 4, was that the Soviets or their allies would seek to disrupt the proceedings by advancing alternative clauses and putting them up for a vote. By wielding his chairman's gavel with firmness and holding to the U.S.-written rules of procedure that he himself admitted were "severe," Acheson managed to squelch dissenting voices while achieving the broad support he sought.[58]

In the end, the United States, Japan, and forty-seven other nations signed the treaty that Dulles negotiated and that Acheson had overseen from its inception; among the attending nations, only the Soviet Union, Poland, and

Czechoslovakia refused to do so. Following the official signing, Acheson closed the conference with some characteristically gracious and eloquent remarks. He said it was fitting that all the grim memories of the recent war "should culminate today in this act of reconciliation; because what you have seen this morning is something unique in history. You have seen an act of greatness of spirit, a true act of reconciliation." It was an act, he told the delegates, "in accordance with the fundamental moral principles of the great spiritual teachers and leaders of all nations and of all religions." Acheson repeatedly stressed the word "reconciliation" throughout his address, doubtless seeking to contrast this treaty with the failed Versailles treaty that remained a sobering object lesson for him and so many statesmen of his generation. He ended, as he so frequently did in important speeches, with a biblical reference. "May the peace of God which passeth all understanding," he prayed, "be amongst us and remain with us always."[59]

The Japanese peace treaty constituted a critical element in Acheson's Cold War grand strategy. The secretary of state considered it a "great forward step" toward what he identified as perhaps the most important priority of all for the United States: "the reincorporation of our former enemies, Germany and Japan, into defensive alliance with us." As he remarked during an off-the-record speech at the National War College, a month before the San Francisco conference, the United States was striving to erect an interdependent structure of nations within the western Pacific. The reintegration of a nonaggressive Japan into the Asian-Pacific community, together with America's about-to-be-concluded treaties of alliance with the Philippines and Australia–New Zealand, promised to lay a strong foundation for that structure. The overarching goal, as Acheson envisioned it, was to forge an "arch of defense" in the western Pacific "into which each nation will be so tied into the efforts of every other nation that fear between them will not exist and no one nation can conduct an independent military course."[60] It was a strategic vision that seamlessly blended Wilsonianism with Cold War geopolitics.

MIDDLE EAST TRAVAILS

As the Korean War dragged on inconclusively throughout 1951 and 1952, the United States found itself faced concurrently with a set of perplexing new challenges in many other parts of the developing world. Mounting instability and revolutionary nationalism in Southeast Asia and the Middle East, in particular, posed major obstacles to Acheson's efforts to forge a stable postwar order–and to ensure a preponderance of American power within that order. The Middle East, a region he had dealt with only sporadically as undersecretary, proved especially vexing. Like other top administration strategists, Acheson recognized that vital U.S. security and economic interests were at stake there. The region's distinction as the world's richest source of petroleum, a resource imperative to the wartime and peacetime strength of the West, made its orientation crucial to the overall balance of global power. By 1950–1951, oil was fast supplanting coal as Western Europe's basic energy source, and 70 percent of Western Europe's oil by then was being imported from the Middle East. Plainly, any disruption in the supply of cheap Middle Eastern oil would deal a severe blow both to the European recovery plan and to NATO's military rearmament efforts. Furthermore, the region factored heavily in all U.S. war-fighting plans. If the Cold War ever turned hot, Pentagon planners counted on U.S. access to military bases in Turkey, Egypt, and North Africa in order to deliver punishing aerial assaults against Soviet military and industrial targets.[61]

Given such high stakes, Acheson and other top U.S. diplomatic and defense officials naturally judged it essential that the Middle East remain linked closely to the West and that the Soviet Union be prevented from either initiating overt aggression against the area or gaining economic or political inroads there. Yet endemic regional turmoil rendered the achievement of those goals highly elusive. The unreconciled hostility of Arab and Muslim governments to the newly created state of Israel roiled the entire region. In addition, many of those governments were responsive to the rising tide of indigenous nationalism. That generated bitter resentment, in a number of instances, toward the European powers that had long dominated the region, controlled key resources, and curtailed local self-governance. In Egypt, for example, nationalists demanded that Britain begin the immediate evacuation of all its forces from that ancient land and that it relinquish control over the Sudan as well. Since the British base at Suez remained a linchpin in U.S. military-strategic planning, the increasingly intense dispute between Cairo and London inevitably affected Washington's interests as well. Acheson, who strove without success to initiate tripartite negotiations between the Egyptians, the British, and the Americans, feared that this impasse could seriously undermine the Western position in the Middle East. "We consider Egyptian nationalism" a "deeply-rooted movement which will neither subside nor alter its course by mere time," Acheson told British foreign secretary Anthony Eden in December 1951. "What we could do in 1882 would not be acceptable to world opinion in 1952," he added–perhaps somewhat ruefully.[62]

The British-Iranian dispute, which erupted in the early months of 1951, proved even more worrisome to Acheson and other top Truman administration officials. On March 7 a religious fanatic assassinated moderate Iranian prime minister Haji Ali Razmara. His death brought an end to whatever flickering hopes remained in London, and Washington, that the British-owned Anglo-Iranian Oil Company (AIOC) would reach a profit-sharing arrangement satisfactory to the burgeoning Iranian nationalist movement. The powerful AIOC, one of the titans of the international oil industry, had long controlled the extraction, refining, and distribution of Iran's most valuable resource. To the consternation of the Iranian National Front and its popular leader, Mohammad Mosaddeq, the company showed no inclination to share its lucrative profits more equitably with the host country–and the British government fully backed the rigid stance of a company in which it was the majority shareholder. The fiery Mosaddeq succeeded Razmara as prime minister on April 28, 1951, and just days later Iran's parliament, the Majlis, issued a decree nationalizing the AIOC's oil fields and refineries. An ominous showdown suddenly loomed in an area of great strategic and economic importance to the United States.

The ensuing crisis impaled Acheson and the Truman administration on the horns of a cruel dilemma. On the one hand, Anglo-American solidarity formed the cornerstone of Acheson's Middle Eastern policy. On the other hand, the secretary of state feared that a British resort to force would push Iran's nationalists further to the left, with the Iranian communist party (the Tudeh) and Russia winding up as the prime beneficiaries. The day before Mosaddeq's ascension to power, Acheson implored British ambassador Sir Oliver Franks not to adopt too inflexible a position on the oil dispute, lest Britain risk the nationalist movement "immediately being captured by the U.S.S.R."[63] While Acheson took a firm stand against any military solution to the conflict, however, he also staunchly opposed nationalization. In a statement issued on May 18, the State Department thus tried to straddle this delicate issue by professing America's sympathy with the Iranian desire to receive a larger share of the oil profits generated by AIOC and to acquire greater control over the company's operations, but declaring its opposition to "any unilateral cancellation of clear contractual relationships."[64]

Two days earlier Acheson had alerted the NSC to the gravity of the Iranian-AIOC stalemate. The participants at the meeting, including the president, were agreed that Iran's continued alignment with the West remained imperative to U.S. security interests in the Cold War. Truman, consequently, accepted Acheson's recommendation that W. Averell Harriman, the experienced diplomatic hand and businessman, be dispatched to Iran as the president's special emissary in an effort to help mediate between Mosaddeq and AIOC managers. The Harriman mission was necessitated, in Acheson's view, by the possibility that a failure to resolve the oil dispute could strengthen the Tudeh and lead eventually to Tehran's drift into the Soviet orbit. Although well aware of the indigenous causes of the petroleum controversy, Acheson nonetheless gauged its broader significance in Cold War terms. According to a formal NSC assessment, which echoed Acheson's own appraisal, the "loss" of Iran "would seriously endanger the security of the entire Middle Eastern area and also Pakistan and India," lead to the denial of Iranian oil to the West, and jeopardize Western access to other regional oil sources. "These developments would seriously affect Western economic and military interests in peace or in war," the NSC report warned, "in view of the great dependence of Western Europe on Iranian oil, particularly the refinery at Abadan."[65]

The Harriman party arrived in Tehran on July 15, only to be greeted at the American embassy by an estimated ten thousand demonstrators protesting against both the AIOC and the diplomatic mission itself. It was not an auspicious beginning. The British, moreover, resented their ally's interference and had only acquiesced reluctantly to this mediation effort. Over the course of two weeks of intense discussions with Mosaddeq, hereditary monarch Reza Shah Pahlavi, British diplomats, and AIOC representatives, Harriman labored in vain to devise a formula that might facilitate a compromise settlement. In personal, handwritten notes, he complained that the AIOC was widely viewed within the industry as the "most rigid and unrealistic" of the large oil companies and sardonically described his talks with the two sides as "Alice in Wonderland or the 20th century hitting the 18th in head on collision." Harriman recognized that "Iran is united in wanting to get AIOC out" but found the aging, flamboyant Mosaddeq, while personally charming, to be a demagogic politician who could not grasp the intricacies of the petroleum industry's supply and distribution norms. Some degree of compromise with the company was essential, the U.S. envoy repeatedly stressed to Mosaddeq, since the loss of oil revenues would plunge his country into an economic abyss. Harriman's sympathies, it bears note, actually lay more with the Iranian nationalists whose lack of business acumen and realism he decried than with a corporation whose attitude he considered "autocratic" and whose profit-sharing arrangements with the Iranians he privately disparaged as "grossly inequitable."[66]

On August 22 the British and Iranians suspended negotiations, a development that further strengthened Mosaddeq's hand with the Iranian people. As tensions rose, Harriman and Acheson again urged the British to resist the temptation to use force—an approach the Americans were certain would be entirely counterproductive. On September 8 Britain dispatched four additional destroyers to the Persian Gulf in an old-fashioned display of saber rattling. London also suspended Iran's trading and financial privileges. In response, Iranian troops occupied the Abadan refinery at the month's end, expelling all AIOC personnel. British prime minister Clement Attlee appealed personally to Truman for U.S. understanding for and support of Britain's predicament, arousing suspicions in the State Department that London was contemplating some form of military reprisal. Acheson believed strongly that continued negotiations were imperative. On October 10, during a meeting with Truman, he broke down the key issues into the two most basic ones: whether Iran would permit AIOC personnel back into the oil fields and refineries and the question of "who gets what from whom in regard to the financial aspects." With regard to the latter, the secretary proposed that a 50-50 split in profits between Iran and the AIOC appeared the most "reasonable result" to shoot for; that would be consistent, moreover, with the recent agreement between Saudi Arabia and the Arabian-American Oil Company (ARAMCO). Acheson also recommended that the British be implored to accept the Americans as "brokers" in an effort to "try to move Mossadegh toward a 50-50 split." Truman agreed, indicating that he saw no alternative.[67]

It was a classic Acheson approach to a seemingly insoluble dispute, honed during his decades as a corporate lawyer: split the difference between the two antagonists, appeal to both in terms of the pernicious consequences of *failing* to reach a compromise settlement, and, above all, keep the two sides talking to buy time. But, in this case, the divergent interests, mutual suspicions, and bad faith separating the two contending parties simply proved insurmountable. The election of a conservative government in the United Kingdom in late October, which brought the indomitable Winston Churchill back to power, further complicated the situation. Had he been prime minister earlier, Churchill blustered to Truman, in January 1952, "there might have been a splutter of musquetry, but [Britain] would not have been kicked out of Iran."[68]

Still, Acheson helped keep the two sides talking well into 1952, utilizing the World Bank for a time as a mediator. A discussion with Foreign Minister Eden, in January 1952, epitomizes the secretary's modus operandi. Acheson emphasized that it was "very important to keep the discussions with Iran going and not to reach a dead end." When Eden and his associates complained that the Americans were exaggerating the likely impact within Iran of an oil deadlock, Acheson replied firmly that U.S. experts were convinced that "a gradual weakening of the economy" would surely follow, along with increased influence for the Tudeh Party. "If Iran did not occupy its peculiar geographic location," Acheson said, "the problem would be much easier." But in view of the proximity of Iran to the Soviet Union, he believed U.S. fears to be well warranted. In response to his British interlocutors' insistence that submitting to Mosaddeq's "blackmail" would have "catastrophic" effects on other British overseas operations, Acheson calmly reemphasized the need for additional negotiations. "We must find a settlement with which we can live," he stressed.[69]

Behind the Iranian powder keg and the Anglo-Egyptian standoff lay a stubborn historical reality: Britain's rapidly declining economic and military power and its fast diminishing regional prestige. Newly emboldened nationalist regimes in Iran and Egypt were challenging British hegemony in the Middle East in a manner that few Western diplomats would have thought conceivable

Acheson meets with Iranian prime minister Mohammad Mosaddeq, October 1951.
Courtesy of the Harry S. Truman Library

just a few years earlier. Plainly, Acheson would have much preferred to work in tandem with London to protect vital Western interests in the region, maintaining a low profile in the Middle East while concentrating finite U.S. energies and resources on Western Europe and East Asia. By early 1951, however, Acheson recognized that the United States could no longer afford a Middle Eastern policy based on deference to its British ally. Too close an identification with a faltering and unpopular colonial power could be dangerously counterproductive; the secretary of state worried about Washington being tainted with guilt by association. Efforts to form some sort of anti-Soviet, regional defense pact–first under the proposed Middle East Command (MEC) and then under the proposed Middle East Defense Organization (MEDO)–foundered in the early 1950s on the anti-imperial sentiments coursing through the Arab and Muslim world.

Acheson recognized, albeit reluctantly, that Washington more and more needed to take the lead on Middle Eastern issues. The State Department's regional specialists were agreed that Britain's eroding power and prestige necessitated a leadership role for the United States lest the forces of revolutionary nationalism and anti-imperialism become determinedly anti-Western, neutralist, or even pro-communist. "Anglo-American solidarity on a policy of sitting tight offered no solution," Acheson observed sardonically in his memoir, "but was like a couple locked in warm embrace in a rowboat about to go over Niagara Falls."[70] What, precisely, the administration could do to harness powerful nationalistic currents for the benefit of the West in the Cold War, however, was unclear to Acheson and other leading U.S. strategists.

DIPLOMATIC ENDGAME

Despite the growing absorption with third world flash points that marked Acheson's final two years in office, Western Europe still impressed him as the Cold War's most critical theater. Western Europe's alignment with the United States, in Acheson's view, constituted the indispensable building block for a world order based on the preponderance both of American power and of Western values. The secretary of state's reasons for attributing primacy to the Old World remained much as they had been when he first rose to prominence as a spokesman for the Committee to Aid the Allies in the early months of World War II. Its mix of critical resources, advanced industrial infrastructure, technological prowess, and skilled workforce made Western Europe, simply put, pivotal to the overall balance of world power. Were it to be conquered or co-opted, either by Nazi Germany in the 1940s or Soviet Russia in the 1950s, Acheson feared that the fulcrum of power would tip decisively toward America's enemies.

These were not private fears, quietly shaping policy decisions while being withheld from the American public. Quite to the contrary, Acheson was as explicit in public about the geopolitical vision animating the administration's foreign policy as he was behind closed doors. In an address delivered in Washington in late December 1950, for example, Acheson outlined with remarkable clarity and precision why he considered the policy choice, favored by some leading Republicans, of retreating to the Western Hemisphere and adopting a largely defensive stance toward the Soviet Union to be a calamitously self-defeating option. Such a retreat would "enable the Soviet Union to make a quick conquest of the entire Eurasian land mass," he said emphatically. That would, in turn, "place at the disposal of the Soviet Union a possession of military resources and economic power vastly superior to any that would then be available to our home security. It would give the Soviet Union possession of a strategic position which would be catastrophic to the United States."[71]

In the opening months of 1951, a highly partisan debate erupted on Capitol Hill as prominent Republicans, including former President Herbert Hoover and Senators Taft, Wherry, and Bridges, voiced opposition to the Truman administration's plan to dispatch additional U.S. combat forces to Europe. They insisted that America's air and atomic supremacy would be sufficient to safeguard U.S. national security and that the stationing of more troops on European soil was neither necessary nor consistent with American traditions.

In eloquent testimony before the Senate, Acheson frontally attacked such views as dangerously wrongheaded, offering a succinct restatement of his longstanding position on Western Europe's vital importance to U.S. security:

> Outside of our own country, free Europe has the greatest number of scientists, the greatest industrial production, and the largest pool of skilled manpower in the world. Its resources in coal, steel, and electric power are enormous. It has a tremendous shipbuilding capacity, essential to control of the seas. Through its overseas connections, it has access to a vast supply of raw materials which are absolutely vital to American industry. As an ally, Western Europe represents more than 200,000,000 free people who can contribute their skills, their resources, and their countries to our common defense. Under the heel of an aggressor, Western Europe would represent 200,000,000 slaves, compelled to bend their energies and employ their resources for the destruction of the United States and the remainder of Western Civilization.[72]

Adequate numbers of ground troops, Acheson insisted, were essential to the defense of Europe. Accordingly, it was imperative that the United States play its part in ensuring that NATO produce sufficient armed forces to deter any Soviet attack—or to repel one once begun. "Our allies are building their forces *now*," he exclaimed; "the time for our own contribution is *now*." He and other administration witnesses argued that the presence of four extra

U.S. divisions could contribute significantly to that fundamental goal and that such a commitment would also reassure its alliance partners about U.S. resolve, thereby encouraging stouter defense commitments from the European nations themselves. He thus drew attention to the great psychological value of a muscular U.S. commitment. Repeating a point made earlier by Marshall, Acheson emphasized that "the spirit" of American participation in Western European defense "is, in the final analysis, directly related to the morale of this entire operation, and morale . . . is the vital ingredient of our security system."[73] On April 4, 1951, the Senate bowed to that logic, approving by a narrow 49-43 vote the administration's plan to commit immediately four additional U.S. divisions to European territory. The so-called Great Debate was over.

During the winter and spring of 1951, the much trickier question of German rearmament absorbed even more of Acheson's energies. It will be recalled that at the NATO Council sessions of December 1950, member-states agreed in principle on the priority of German rearmament. Yet, to the secretary's frustration, NATO made scant progress toward the attainment of that goal in the months following the Brussels meeting. Instead, French leaders again raised objection after objection to the actual reconstitution of a semisovereign, rearmed West Germany. The historical enmity and distrust between France and Germany proved a stubborn obstacle to what Acheson saw as a military and political necessity; the passions of French politics compounded the problem. Where Acheson saw opportunity, the French saw little but risk: the risk that a revived West Germany might seek reunification and the return of lost territories, the risk that a remilitarized Germany might over time come to dominate continental Europe once again, and the risk that any movement to reconstitute German military strength might spark, rather than contain, the Kremlin's aggressive impulses. Acheson reluctantly accepted that any movement forward must await the results of the French national elections of June 1951. He took some solace in the ratification of the European Coal and Steel Community that April, a significant step toward both European economic integration and Franco-German rapprochement. Developments on the military front, however, appeared much less promising. "Everything in Europe seems to move with maddening slowness," Acheson complained in a personal letter to his close friend, Yale president A. Whitney Griswold.[74]

Following the French elections, which brought a resurgence of the Right and thus reduced parliamentary support for running any risks vis-à-vis Germany, Acheson determined that a fresh initiative was needed to break the negotiating impasse. He reached the decision that it was now time for the United States "to really make a bet on the EDC."[75] In an insightful and comprehensive memorandum that he drafted on July 6 and circulated among his State Department brain trust, Acheson put his finger on the core dilemmas posed by the German rearmament issue. The Truman administration believed that an adequate defense of Western Europe was "pretty hopeless" without "enthusiastic German participation," he wrote. Therefore, the rearming of Germany "cannot be long delayed." Yet two huge roadblocks loomed. Acheson recognized that, on the one hand, Paris would seek to block Bonn's rearmament unless it received "adequate safeguards" that the formation of German military units would not, at some future point, jeopardize French security. On the other hand, he recognized that Adenauer's government would not cooperate effectively in collective Western defense efforts unless the Federal Republic were treated as an equal and unless it soon regained as much sovereignty as possible.

How to square that circle posed the great challenge. Acheson reasoned that only an integrated approach that simultaneously assuaged French fears while meeting West Germany's needs had any chance of success. He recommended, consequently, that the United States push for a European Defense Community that would permit the immediate mobilization of German military units while insisting that the envisaged continental army be placed under the control of NATO's supreme commander, General Eisenhower. The European army concept, in short, would be harmonized with the wider Atlantic defense effort; crucially, the EDC would be subordinate to, rather than independent of, NATO's command structure. According to Acheson's proposed scenario, which owed much to the advice of McCloy, Bruce, and Eisenhower, France and Britain should be urged to join with the United States in replacing the occupation regime in West Germany with a new set of contractual agreements. Those would return to the Federal Republic full sovereignty over nearly all internal and external affairs. The occupying powers would retain just a handful of residual powers—over Berlin, most importantly, as well as over any future unification negotiations.[76]

Acheson's proposals formed the basis for an important meeting held at the Pentagon, on July 16, 1951, with Marshall and his senior aides. As Acheson recorded after the meeting, "I stressed the importance of going forward simultaneously with the European defense force idea, the restoration of German sovereignty, and the raising of German troops."[77] After receiving the necessary support for that approach from the Defense Department, he then drafted a memorandum for Truman's consideration that formally recommended the adoption of this new policy tack. Dated July 30, the memorandum was jointly signed by Acting Secretary of Defense Robert Lovett, Marshall's deputy. In it, the two men explained the rationale for throwing Washington's weight behind these three distinct initiatives as part of an integrated strategy aimed at breaking the current stalemate. Because of the wary attitudes of the British, Dutch, and certain other NATO partners toward continental integration—attitudes born of concerns about preserving the traditional prerogatives of national sovereignty—the Acheson-Lovett memorandum emphasized that progress toward Western European integration could be achieved only through "the broader framework of the North Atlantic community." Acknowledging the complexities involved in establishing such supranational institutions and patterns of authority, and the time needed to do so, they proceeded to outline a remarkably cogent vision of what the United States was ultimately seeking to achieve. "Under this pattern Continental European arrangements can be utilized to offset the individual fears of the French and the Germans," Acheson and Lovett reasoned, "while the broader North Atlantic Treaty Organization relationships, in which the United States participates, can be utilized to mitigate British and other fears of Continental European integration."[78] Truman immediately signed off on the new approach, giving Acheson the full presidential backing he had come to expect from the man with whom he had worked so long and so closely. In his memoir, Acheson termed the adoption of this strategy "an epoch-making series of decisions."[79]

The secretary of state hoped that sufficient progress could be made soon on all three fronts that the NATO Council meeting, scheduled for November 1951, in Rome, could reach firm commitments about the EDC and German rearmament programs. Once again, however, Acheson overestimated Washington's ability to ease the deeply rooted animosities between France and

Germany—and to navigate the treacherous political waters that sprang from them. During meetings in Washington that September, Acheson persuaded the British and French foreign ministers of the need to bring an expeditious end to the occupation regime in West Germany. He pressed, with some success, for a quick restoration of the essential attributes of sovereignty to the Bonn government. Cutting to the heart of the matter, Acheson insisted that the three Western occupying powers needed to decide whether they were going to treat Germany as an ally or an enemy. That signal achievement was not matched, however, by a commensurate breakthrough either on the proposed continental army or on the recruitment of German military units for it.[80]

On November 30, following the conclusion of the Rome Council meeting, Acheson shared his frustrations with Truman in a lengthy, top-secret letter. "Big problems remain unsolved and will need the most energetic work over the next 60 days, if we are to solve them," he confessed. Acheson lamented, in particular, the present "confusion and strain" surrounding the establishment of a European army and the splits within the French government that made any forward movement difficult. He complained as well about "slippages" from member-states in meeting their individual contribution targets to NATO force goals. The secretary ended on a less somber note, though, expressing the conviction that all of the member-states now at least understood the urgency of the issues facing the alliance. He told Truman that "final action" on the conjoined issues of NATO's force goals, German rearmament, and the EDC must occur at the next council meeting.[81]

The disappointing results of the Rome sessions thus significantly raised the stakes for the next meeting of the NATO Council, scheduled to open on February 20, 1952. In the contemporary assessment of Canadian foreign minister Lester B. Pearson, the upcoming meeting at Lisbon "may be the decisive meeting in NATO history."[82] Acheson recalled, "Lisbon was to be the supreme gamble upon which we would stake our whole prestige, skill and power."[83] The gathering at the Portuguese capital could be considered "Acheson's Yalta," in the words of historian John Lamberton Harper, "the culmination of his career as a statesman."[84] The breakthroughs reached, there, in key respects, indeed represent the capstone of Acheson's European policy.

Using all the powers of persuasion that he had refined during a lifetime immersed in law, politics, and diplomacy, Acheson was able to broker a series of compromises that satisfied Paris without hopelessly alienating Bonn. West Germany responded to Acheson's persistent hectoring by agreeing reluctantly to make a substantial financial contribution to collective Western defenses while accepting certain frustrating security controls. France, for its part, promised to increase its military spending—in return for a pledged U.S. aid package of $600 million. According to Acheson's hard-won compromise formula, France would field an EDC force of twelve divisions, roughly equivalent to the contingent Germany had pledged to provide. Key to the bargain was Acheson's success in convincing France, and the other NATO nations, that the European army concept would not just harness Germany's manpower for the defense of Western Europe. It would also serve to constrain Bonn from developing military strength independent of the integrated, multinational command structures of NATO and the EDC. With that supremely vexing issue finally resolved, the Lisbon conferees were able to reach accord on each of the other major issues on the agenda. They agreed to raise, by the end of 1952, the number of combat-ready divisions to be made available, within one month after the outbreak of war, from the present thirty-four to fifty-five. The North Atlantic Council also endorsed the pending entry of Greece and Turkey into the alliance, another cardinal U.S. priority.[85] At the end of the meeting, Acheson cabled Truman exultantly, "We have something pretty close to a grand slam."[86]

But the euphoria proved short-lived. On March 10, 1952, the Soviet Union transmitted a bombshell in the form of a diplomatic note that proposed a series of steps leading to Germany's unification. Largely a ploy to divide the NATO allies, the Kremlin's initiative roiled the post-Lisbon waters of allied harmony for the next several months. "The Soviets are playing their heaviest cards as one expected they would," McCloy wrote Acheson, "to deflect our policy of Western European integration."[87] Acheson agreed completely. He decided to treat the Soviet note as the propaganda he was certain it was. Under his direction, a semicomical duet ensued, quickly dubbed "the battle of the notes," in which each superpower vied to be the true champion of German unification—when, in fact, each feared the potentially destabilizing effect of a united, resurgent Germany and had no serious interest in risking its emergence. "We believe strongly," Acheson cabled key U.S. diplomatic representatives in Paris, London, and Bonn, "that our main purpose is to drive ahead with the signature and ratification of the EDC and the contractual relations with Germany, and that we should not permit the Russians to accomplish their obvious purpose of frustrating both by delay."[88]

Yet allied haggling over what struck Acheson as minor matters threatened to derail the signing of those two landmark agreements, much to the secretary's frustration. On May 22, following a meeting with Truman, Acheson made a last-minute decision to travel to Europe personally to help resolve those disputes and to participate in the separate signing ceremonies, scheduled for Bonn and Paris. Not until the morning of May 26, the very day that the contractual agreements with West Germany were to be initialed, did Acheson's personal intervention finally help break the negotiating logjam. Almost immediately, he cabled Truman with the good news, joking, "We have gone through greater emotions than any mystery story could provide." Focusing, as was his wont, on the big picture, he commented, "I think we have reason to be pleased. For now we have successfully completed another phase in our postwar policy: containment of the new threat with the cooperation of our former enemy."[89]

On May 26 the contractual agreements with Germany were signed in Bonn with great fanfare. The next day the EDC treaty was signed in Paris to equal acclaim. Those agreements represent signal—even crowning—achievements for the Truman administration's European policy. Yet the administration's lame-duck status combined with the onset of the 1952 presidential election campaign ensured that they would be the administration's last substantive achievements. Throughout the summer and autumn of 1952, Acheson watched helplessly, his frustration building, as a growing number of French politicians pledged to vote against ratification of the EDC. As an official whose tenure in office was fast coming to a close, he had no cards left to play. Years later he speculated ruefully that had the sands of time not run out on the Truman administration those problems might have been averted.[90]

But they did run out. On November 8, just four days after Eisenhower crushed Democratic nominee Adlai Stevenson to become the president-elect, Acheson voiced his disappointments with the course of European developments since Lisbon. "That France is a cornerstone in the edifice which we would be happy to see constructed in Europe should be apparent," he observed plaintively in a cable to Ambassador James Clement Dunn. Yet despite Washington's heroic patience with the French and despite the fact that it agreed with French views and positions 90 percent of the time, "our relations with France have never been more complicated or more tense since we had to deal with De Gaulle." The core problem, Acheson believed, stemmed from the unalterable fact that "European security and thereby our own rests on France and Germany and not on France or Germany."[91]

A few weeks later a still reflective Acheson shared his disquiet about European developments during an appearance before the cabinet of Canadian prime minister Louis St. Laurent. "Last May that continent was on the threshold of a most brilliant future based on closer political and economic integration," he remarked. Acheson cited the Schuman Plan and the EDC, in particular, as shining emblems of that progress. The momentum had now stopped, he lamented, and a "paralysis" had set in that filled him with "foreboding about the future."[92] He spoke in strikingly similar terms during a private conversation with Jean Monnet, president of the High Authority of the European Coal and Steel Community and an apostle of European integration. "Last June, I had hoped and believed that there was a spirit and momentum toward European unity, including ratification of the EDC," he told Monnet, "which in the year 1952 would carry all of these matters so far along the road that neither Soviet obstruction nor the natural hesitancy of nations could prevent the accomplishment of something almost unparalleled in history." Now, he ruminated sadly, it seemed that "the momentum had been lost, retrogression had set in, and that we might now be on the very verge of complete disaster." When his French interlocutor asked Acheson to help stem the negative tide, the secretary responded with resignation. "I did not see that there was very much, if anything, that I could do now," he said, "representing an administration which had only a few weeks of responsibility left."[93]

Acheson's final weeks in office were bittersweet. His melancholia about trends in Europe and frustrations with the important tasks that remained incomplete mixed with justifiable pride in what he had accomplished during four crisis-filled years as the nation's chief foreign policy officer. In accepting his formal resignation, to take effect—with the president's—on January 20, 1953, Truman wrote Acheson a warm and touching letter. "You have been my good right hand," the president said appreciatively. "Certainly no man is more responsible than you for pulling together the people of the free world, and strengthening their will and their determination to be strong and free. I would place you among the very greatest of the Secretaries of State this country has had."

Acheson reciprocated by hosting, with Alice, a final luncheon for the Trumans, the president's White House staff members, and his cabinet officers at their Georgetown home. It immediately followed Eisenhower's inauguration and represented a kind of last hurrah for the departing Democrats. Following lunch, the obligatory cocktails, and boisterous chants of "We want Harry!" Acheson traveled to Union Station to say his final farewells to the president he had come to respect so greatly. A very different life awaited both men. For Acheson, who had been at the center of power for most of the past dozen years, rekindling his legal career and adjusting to private life in a city and government now dominated by Republicans would prove exceedingly hard.[94]

6

ELDER STATESMAN

Perhaps more than any secretary of state before him, Acheson remained actively involved in the intricacies of international affairs long after his tenure in office had concluded. During the eighteen years spanning from the end of the Truman administration to Acheson's death, his was a vital, informed, and influential voice on the foreign policy issues of the day. Over time, he became increasingly opinionated and sharp edged. Naturally, he focused most of his attention on those matters still close to his heart from his days in power, especially European and NATO issues and U.S.-Soviet relations. But the ex–secretary of state made sure that he was heard on a range of other international flash points as well: from the Middle East to Latin America, and from Southeast Asia to Africa.

During the Eisenhower years, Acheson became a self-styled and self-appointed critic of what he saw as a period of misdirection, false steps, and blunders on the diplomatic and strategic fronts. When the Democrats returned to power in 1961, he quickly reverted to the more familiar and comfortable role of policy insider. A frequent visitor to the White House once again, after having been frozen out by Eisenhower, Acheson became a policy adviser and occasional diplomatic envoy for Presidents John F. Kennedy and Lyndon B. Johnson and participated in a number of key policy meetings during crises over Berlin, NATO, Cuba, and Vietnam. His late conversion to the anti–Vietnam War cause, in early 1968, played a significant role in Johnson's decision to seek peace negotiations with North Vietnam. When the Republicans returned to power in January 1969, even President Richard M. Nixon, once a vicious political foe, welcomed advice from the Democratic elder statesman. Acheson seemed an Olympian figure by then, one widely hailed, even by those who had ofttimes disagreed with him, as an uncommonly sage foreign policy analyst. The publication, in 1969, of Acheson's monumental memoir of his service during the Truman years, the grandiosely titled *Present at the Creation*, which garnered a prestigious Pulitzer Prize, strengthened his reputation and stature. At his death at age seventy-eight, Acheson had become a near-legendary figure, one who seemed to embody an earlier, and presumably much simpler, era of American global dominance. Democrats and Republicans alike, to this day, seek to appropriate his image and invoke his name.

IN EXILE—AND IN OPPOSITION

Acheson's first act as a private citizen was to escape Washington for a long winter vacation in Antigua, a charming and, at the time, quite unheralded and remote island in the British West Indies. He had first visited there several years earlier and instantly fell in love with its beauty and easy-going ambience. Acheson would return there often, finding it an exceptionally soothing and rejuvenating retreat. With Alice and old friends Archibald and Ada MacLeish at his side, he found his two-month sojourn in Antigua, in early 1953, the ideal prescription for putting the maelstrom of Washington politics—and the travails of four arduous years at the center of it—behind him.

Acheson spent much of his time reading, in typically eclectic and voracious fashion. He found the published letters of John Adams and Thomas Jefferson especially engrossing, doubtless hearing resonant echoes of his own experiences in the reflections of the two wise elder statesmen. He heartily recommended them to Truman, in the first of what was a long series of personal letters to his former chief. Acheson also delighted in the Oliver Wendell Holmes–Harold Laski correspondence, Edith Hamilton's survey of Old Testament prophets, a biography of Abraham Lincoln, and the works of Henry David Thoreau, among other books. "Life here is too pleasant, easy and lazy to be in any remote way moral," he joked in a letter to longtime friend and former State Department associate Philip Jessup. "But it is lovely."[1] To law partner Ned Burling, he wrote, "We are resting deeply and happily. This is the ideal place to make you unable to remember what you came to forget."[2] To numerous correspondents, Acheson lauded his quiet retreat as idyllic, one that allowed him to read at his leisure, swim three times a day, lie in the sun, and enjoy cocktails and dinner with Alice and assorted friends. "I am brown, saturated with sun, salt water, and rum; possessed of only three articles of clothing–shoes, shorts, and shirts . . . ; and full of reading such as I have not done for twenty years," he proudly proclaimed in a letter to former executive assistant Jeffrey C. Kitchen.[3] He even professed to enjoy being "the forgotten man," writing Burling that "everything conspires to protect my anonymity."[4]

The man who had made so much news himself over the past several years now took solace in his remove from it. The *New York Times* arrived a week late–"late enough to seem like history," he mused–and he had no access to radio or television on his Caribbean outpost.[5] What he did learn about the actions of his successor, John Foster Dulles, troubled him, however, particularly Dulles's efforts to hound some loyal State Department employees from office on spurious disloyalty charges. "I cannot understand what Foster is up to in the [John Carter] Vincent case," he complained to Jessup, referring to the new secretary's efforts to sacrifice a China expert Acheson held in high esteem for the sake of the Republican right. "Or indeed on several other matters," he sneered. In another letter to his ex-colleague, Acheson observed sardonically, "So far as the news is concerned . . . I can only say that I like what I drink better than what I read."[6]

After returning to Washington in late March, Acheson began to express deeper misgivings, in his private conversations and personal correspondence, about what he characterized as the Eisenhower administration's serious missteps and ethical lapses. "The political atmosphere in Washington is unbelievable," he wrote the MacLeishes on March 26. Close friends in the press, Acheson confided, were telling him that "it has taken sheer genius to get things as balled up in two months as our new masters have done." Eisenhower seemed to be "caught in an ice floe moving to the right," he lamented. "On one side is McCarthy who has no limit, only infinity; on the other side Taft, Ike's protector, whose limit is not yet in sight."[7]

On April 14 Acheson elaborated on those concerns in a lengthy missive to Truman. Describing himself as "a spry and very lazy lad of sixty summers,"

Acheson bemoaned the new Republican administration's "terrible retrogression," especially on governmental personnel issues. "Ike is presiding over something which is corruptive on a really great scale," he charged. Acheson had always insisted that competent civil servants must be protected from crass political litmus tests; he expressed outrage at Eisenhower's and Dulles's abject failure to ensure such protection. Instead, they were appeasing the Republican Party's right-wing by purging capable government officers simply because of their close association with the Truman administration's foreign policies. "The studied appeasement of the Hill which is now going on at the expense of the best civil servants we have—certainly in State—is not only criminal but frightening in what it may mean regarding the quality of advice which the Secretary of State, and ultimately, the President will receive," he railed. Acheson highlighted, in particular, Dulles's evident willingness to sack Acheson's friend Paul Nitze just to placate Republican congressional leaders who appeared determined "that all who worked with me be changed or fired." He declared flatly, "This seems to me plain cowardice and utter folly."[8]

Throughout the spring and summer of 1953, as he slowly reentered his old law practice with Covington and Burling, Acheson's private comments about the Eisenhower administration grew increasingly venomous. In a letter to Truman that May, Acheson sarcastically referred to Ike as "the Great General." He complained that the new president was abdicating his executive responsibility, deferring instead to a government by Congress that was being led "by the most ignorant, irresponsible, and anarchistic elements."[9] In early August, he confided to Lucius Battle, his former State Department executive assistant who had become like a son to the Achesons, that he was disgusted with the personnel purge Dulles was carrying out in the State Department. "What is happening to our friends in the Department—and to the place itself—is very bad and gives one contempt for the cowardly fools who are doing it," Acheson ranted. "Dulles's people seem to me like Cossacks quartered in a grand old city hall, burning the panelling to cook with."[10]

Acheson's major criticisms of the Eisenhower-Dulles foreign policy, on substantive grounds, derived from his distaste for the budget cutting that Ike had made the hallmark of his "New Look" defense strategy. Acheson continued to believe that a stout defense, anchored by strong relationships with

America's NATO allies, formed the surest route to a more secure America. Yet Eisenhower, in his judgment, was foolishly capping defense spending at a time when the bolstering of overall Western military power remained an imperative need. Even worse, the new chief executive's kowtowing to his party's irresponsible, McCarthyite elements permitted reckless criticisms of the allies upon whom American security in the Cold War ultimately depended to go unchallenged. "The White House must discredit the demagogic isolationist wing of the Republican Party, which wishes to insult and separate us from our allies," he wrote Truman. Acheson saw one of the major achievements of their tenure–the building up of a powerfully unified Western coalition–suddenly at risk. "Our policy was to create strength by binding ourselves and our allies both economically and militarily," he reflected in a discursive letter to Truman. "It is essential to continue that policy." The evident inclination of the Eisenhower administration, prematurely in his view, to consider direct negotiations with the Soviets over Germany and other issues also disquieted Acheson.[11]

On October 1, 1953, Acheson broke his self-imposed public silence on foreign policy matters with the delivery of a major speech in New York, at the Woodrow Wilson Foundation's annual awards dinner. Although phrased discreetly and presented diplomatically, the address nonetheless amounted to a blunt critique of the direction of U.S. foreign policy under Eisenhower and Dulles. Acheson began with a self-congratulatory overview of the successes of U.S. grand strategy in the early Cold War. Placing the Truman administration's achievements within the broad sweep of modern history, Acheson said that "a coalition to resist the imposition by a powerful state of its hegemony upon others" had emerged five separate times in the past four hundred years: first, to combat Louis XIV's efforts to bring Europe under French control in the seventeenth century, and then to resist, in turn, comparable efforts at dominance by Napoleon, Kaiser Wilhelm, Hitler, and Stalin. He called the latter the greatest threat of all and hence lavishly praised the recent construction of an effective anti-Soviet coalition–in the face of the daunting challenges posed by a war-torn Europe–as a "vast and triumphant accomplishment." The result of that effort? "Equilibrium has been created," he proclaimed proudly. "Strength has told." The essential task at present, according to Acheson, was to preserve that coalition. "To sustain it and to strengthen it must be the foundation of our foreign policy," he insisted. "The most unforgivable of mistakes would be to falter in a policy just as developments prove its rightness and success."

Although he never mentioned Eisenhower or Dulles by name, Acheson's disdain for their neglect of alliance relationships shone through unmistakably in his speech. "Whoever portrays us as the sole repository of wisdom and resistance to tyranny, and who portrays our allies as something considerably less so," he declared, "does the coalition a great disfavor." He implied that the all-important "responsibility of leadership" was being forfeited, putting the cohesion of the Atlantic alliance in peril. Acheson took a clear swipe as well at arch-nemesis McCarthy, also unnamed, for adopting the very totalitarian methods of America's principal adversary. "Each day," he lamented, "presents too many examples of callousness, cynicism, indifference to the values of truth, fairness, restraints, free thought, free expression, free inquiry." In a particularly revealing passage, Acheson attributed the shortcomings of current U.S. policy to the absence of any moral core. The United States, above all, stands for freedom, he emphasized; and that commitment to freedom constituted the indispensable key to its Atlantic partners' acceptance of American leadership as wise, benign, and unselfish. "Without this idea, we are to them just another powerful nation, bent upon interests which are not theirs," Acheson warned. "If we are narrow, dogmatic, self-centered, afraid, domineering and crabbed, we shall break apart the alliance on which our future depends."[12]

Influential Democrats lauded the speech. Adlai Stevenson, among others, admired Acheson's eloquent restatement of basic principles—and told him so. The Woodrow Wilson Foundation address marked a first, tentative step toward Acheson's return to the public arena. Yet it was followed by several more months of silence. As he wrote Battle in early December, the New York speech was "the only break in my resolution to remain quiet. I am staying, I hope, out of the field of political controversy, although that is hard."[13]

Acheson clearly longed to reenter the public arena, a fact his closest friends well recognized. Paul Nitze, with whom Acheson lunched regularly at downtown Washington's elegant Metropolitan Club, intensively debated foreign affairs with his former boss during Acheson's early years out of power and found his insights about, and passionate engagement with, international politics wholly undiminished. Felix Frankfurter, whose friendship with his former student had deepened substantially since he moved to Washington, in 1941, to take up his seat on the Supreme Court, knew—and loved—Acheson as much as anyone outside his immediate family. A fellow Georgetown resident, the justice had been meeting Acheson at his P Street home virtually every workday for the past decade, from whence the two proceeded to walk much of the way to work together. Acheson towered over the diminutive Frankfurter and the unlikely Mutt and Jeff duo, invariably absorbed in vigorous conversation, had become a familiar sight to neighbors and passersby on the streets of Georgetown and Foggy Bottom. The Jewish justice delighted in joining the Achesons every Christmas Eve for their boisterous family tradition of singing Christmas carols. Frankfurter worried, during this period, that his good friend's transition from dealing with the great affairs of state to practicing law had once again been a huge letdown for him.[14]

Indeed, many of Acheson's private letters from this period remark on the painfulness of that adjustment. "My professional life is stubbornly slow in developing," he admitted in one. "The practice of the law goes very slowly indeed," he confessed in another. Although he found himself working on various briefs which he characterized as "amusing," Acheson added with more than a hint of resignation that they hardly involved "the main conflicts of our time."[15]

It was "the main conflicts of our time," however, to which Acheson was drawn—and about which he thought he still had much to contribute. Dulles's use of the term "massive retaliation," in early 1954, as an awkwardly bombastic description of the administration's defense strategy, offered Acheson an opening. On March 28, 1954, he penned a sharp critique for the *New York Times Magazine* of what he depicted as the Eisenhower administration's dangerous overreliance on the threat of nuclear retaliation. The polemical essay, in which Acheson took off his gloves for the first time and really pummeled his successors, delivered a stinging rebuke that gained considerable attention and sparked much debate. He had "become too worked up over the fraud of the New Look to be quiet any longer," Acheson explained to Truman.[16] The man who for a time had been persona non grata, even in Democratic circles, because of the persistent McCarthyite smears trained against him, was back.

From that point onward, Acheson offered the most incisive, sustained, and withering critique of the Eisenhower-Dulles foreign policy of any major

Democratic figure. He had donned his most partisan hat–and found that it fit him surprisingly well. Over the next several years, Acheson unleashed a barrage of essays, articles, speeches, opinion pieces, position papers, and the like that blasted the misdirection of the Eisenhower administration's foreign policy. He proved himself as adept in the role of polemicist as he had been in the role of diplomat. Of course, those distinctive roles demand quite different skills and approaches. If the task of a diplomat is typically that of minimizing differences with both adversaries and with allies so as to uncover some common ground, that of the partisan is to magnify and exaggerate differences between the positions of the party in power and the opposition party eager to replace it. Acheson's steady stream of well-reasoned and gracefully written invectives against Eisenhower and Dulles displayed his smooth transition to the latter role.

Of course, there *were* significant policy differences between Acheson and his successors; he was not simply inventing them to bolster his beloved Democratic Party. Acheson believed that the new administration had foolishly repudiated the logic of NSC 68, artificially lowering defense budgets for political reasons and thereby leaving the West with a much less robust defense than current conditions required. The greater dependence on nuclear retaliatory power that flowed from that budget cutting, in his view, had increased the danger of a blowup with the Soviets and aroused deep-seated anxieties among America's European allies. Moreover, he believed the administration had needlessly hectored France, a crucial if touchy ally, rather than seeking to reassure it–as he had done. Acheson placed the blame for the French Assembly's defeat, in August 1954, of the EDC treaty he had worked so hard to hammer out, on Dulles's undiplomatic heavy-handedness. "Europe seems to be unraveling fast," he fumed in a private letter of early 1955. "I am afraid that we have had our chance and have lost it. I doubt whether it comes again."[17]

The continuities between the Truman and Eisenhower administrations, in terms of certain foreign policy basics, must nonetheless also be acknowledged. Both administrations assessed the nature of the Soviet threat in comparable terms, insisted on the maintenance of strong countervailing Western military power, and accepted the need to contain the spread of communist influence on every front. Acheson's partisan inclinations–and it bears emphasizing that he *always* saw himself as a loyal Democrat—led him to accentuate deliberately all policy disagreements. His personal distaste for the manner in which Eisenhower and Dulles had so cavalierly fired a handful of former State Department associates and for the way in which they had silently acquiesced in McCarthy's unconscionable assault on the integrity of Marshall—the man Acheson looked up to as the greatest living American—doubtless fed his venom as well. Perhaps Frankfurter captured Acheson's deepest feelings best when, in a personal letter to the latter, he described Dulles's gravest shortcoming as stemming not from "intellectual limitations" but rather from the "defects of character that put brakes on [his] intellectual capacities." For Acheson, character and integrity counted for everything; Dulles, in his harsh but deeply felt appraisal, possessed insufficient amounts of either.[18]

At the start of 1955 Acheson assumed an altogether new role: that of book author. His sprightly written and passionately argued *A Democrat Looks at His Party*, published in November of that year, was the first of what would be a steady stream of books—on politics, on foreign policy, and on his own life and career—that would punctuate Acheson's post–secretary of state years. The book involved "some philosophizing on the past, present, and future of the Democratic party in American life," he explained modestly to a friend during its preparation.[19] The genesis of *A Democrat Looks at His Party*, in Acheson's retelling, lay in a late-night conversation with a wealthy Republican businessman and client. After numerous scotches and much friendly bantering, his client remarked that he found it baffling that a man as "intelligent and experienced" as Acheson belonged to the Democratic Party. "How can this be?" he asked. The book represented Acheson's extended response to that blunt question. Making the case for the defense in his best lawyerly style of argumentation, Acheson enumerated all the factors that lay behind his lifelong party affiliation and that made the Democratic Party, in his estimation, the one best able to serve the broad interests of the American people. Written with an eye on the upcoming 1956 presidential election, Acheson hoped to fill an intellectual void in the current political climate by upholding the historic traditions and strengths of the party of Andrew Jackson, Woodrow Wilson, and Franklin Roosevelt. The book not only sold well but received mostly positive reviews. In one, Pulitzer Prize–winning biographer William S. White praised both the book and its author lavishly. He called *A Democrat Looks at His Party* "a memorable work, far more than a perceptive analysis of a political party. Unobtrusively and perhaps unintentionally it is also the uncomplaining testament of a man who has borne in dignity and strength lashes of a kind that few have known in the history of the country."[20]

Acheson endorsed Adlai Stevenson early as his favored Democratic nominee for the 1956 presidential election. In February 1955, during a joint press conference with Harry Truman in Independence, Missouri, Acheson said that Stevenson was his "strong choice." That unqualified endorsement sprang more from his conviction that Stevenson had the best chance of stopping Eisenhower's reelection bid than from a genuine admiration for the former Illinois governor's leadership capabilities. In one of those gratuitous quips that Acheson had trouble suppressing, he had remarked at Harvard University three years earlier, "Adlai has a third-rate mind that he can't make up." That cutting assessment of Stevenson's shortcomings had not changed in the intervening years; Acheson simply could not imagine another Democratic politician who stood a chance of besting the popular Eisenhower. At the same time, he realized that the odds against any Democratic candidate were long.[21] "It looks as though we might have another four years of Ike, Foster and foolishness," he wrote the MacLeishes in March 1956, "while the world goes to pieces around our happy and prosperous country."[22]

The 1956 election campaign coincided with the drawn-out Suez crisis, precipitated by Egyptian leader Gamal Abdel Nasser's seizure of the Suez Canal in July 1956. Acheson went on the offensive against what he characterized as an inept U.S. policy that endangered all-important relations with Great Britain and France, berating the Eisenhower administration for the incoherence of its Middle East policy. Privately, he bemoaned the weakness of the UK and U.S. response to what he saw as a wholly illegal expropriation. "Force could quite justifiably have been used to prevent this and restore the status quo ante," he commented to friend Frank Altschul in early October. "Meanwhile," he complained, "vast damage is being done to the Western alliance—which is probably more serious than any risks from Nasser in the canal."[23] When the British, French, and Israelis at the end of October mounted a military operation against Egypt, designed deliberately to coincide with the final days of the

American presidential campaign, the Eisenhower administration condemned its allies' resort to force–accepting the risk of a serious rupture within the Atlantic alliance. Acheson found that, too, a foolishly counterproductive policy. "Our allies were taught that, not only would we make no sacrifice to help them in a matter of vital interest, but that we would join the opposition to them," he complained in a high-profile lecture series at Tufts University the next year.[24] "In the Suez Crisis Dulles couldn't have done worse," he told an interviewer years later. "He ended up siding with the Russians and attacking our friends. A complete mess."[25]

A combative Acheson thrust himself into the presidential campaign directly with the delivery of a major speech, on September 26, that blasted the administration's foreign policy in extraordinarily harsh terms. In one of the speech's most memorable and oft-quoted phrases, he charged, "This administration has been playing Russian roulette with an atomic pistol." The *New York Times* published the speech in full, guaranteeing it wide notice.[26] Acheson thought that he had showed Stevenson that a sustained foreign policy critique could win the Democratic nominee votes. The cautious Stevenson, to his dismay, chose not to follow Acheson's lead. Instead, he concentrated most of his fire on domestic policy issues. Acheson was not surprised with Ike's landslide victory on November 5. He subsequently complained in a private letter that Stevenson's advisers wrongly concluded that "there was no mileage in foreign policy."[27]

In the wake of the Democrats' second consecutive presidential election setback, Acheson assumed an even more prominent public role as a key figure within the Democratic Party's leadership circle. The Democratic National Committee, anxious to regroup after the 1956 debacle, formed the Democratic Advisory Council (DAC) immediately following the election. Party elders wanted to craft coordinated policy positions in order to challenge the Republicans more effectively in 1960. On June 12, 1957, the council leaders named Acheson chairman of the DAC's freshly minted Committee on Foreign Policy. He eagerly accepted the new assignment. Truman, whose opinion they solicited, had enthusiastically recommended his former secretary of state. "There is only man for the job–Dean Acheson," he told them unequivocally. Acheson quickly named Paul Nitze, whose Cold War views mirrored his own, to serve as vice chairman. The former secretary of state now occupied a key institutional platform from which to promulgate his strongly held foreign policy positions.

Within the DAC, a tussle soon ensued between the hard-line Cold War stance advocated unapologetically by Acheson and Nitze and the softer, more accommodationist stance represented by the Stevenson–Chester Bowles wing of the party. The policy fights between the two wings were frequently fierce. Acheson relished the intellectual combat that raged for the foreign policy soul of the Democratic Party–and he plainly excelled at it. No one within the leadership group could match his incomparable knowledge of international affairs; few, if any, could match his intellectual firepower. In view of the near-pariah status that he held upon leaving office in 1953, Acheson's rise to the position of the Democratic Party's chief foreign policy strategist and spokesman represented more than redemption. It was the culmination of a most remarkable, and most unlikely, comeback.[28]

George F. Kennan's public espousal, in late 1957, of America's disengagement from Europe served to thrust Acheson forward even further into the public spotlight. The preeminent Soviet specialist, author, and intellectual considered Acheson a friend, despite sharp differences in temperament and style between the two. They had of course famously clashed over the issue of German rearmament while Kennan was serving as Acheson's director of policy planning in 1949–1950, shortly before the latter left government service. Kennan, who was spending the 1957–1958 academic year as a visiting professor at Oxford University, accepted the BBC Radio's invitation to deliver the Reith Lectures on international affairs. He used that prestigious forum to expound his deeply felt views about European policy in a series of six half-hour radio broadcasts, the first of which aired on November 10, 1957. Kennan's Reith Lectures were widely disseminated, and much debated, across Europe. The former foreign service officer argued that only a mutual withdrawal of U.S. and Soviet troops from Europe and the simultaneous forging of a reunified, neutral Germany could lead to a stable Europe, free from the threat of nuclear annihilation. The excessive Western military buildup on the European continent, in Kennan's confident assessment, increased the likelihood of war. The lectures, which could not have challenged official U.S. and NATO policy any more directly, were very well received in a Western Europe becoming increasingly wary of its role as a pawn in superpower politics. Social democratic circles in Germany, France, Great Britain, and elsewhere proved especially receptive to Kennan's disengagement message.[29]

Acheson, for his part, was horrified by the favorable publicity that quickly enveloped a position that he considered the height of irresponsibility, naïveté, and folly. When asked by Christopher Emmet of the American Council on Germany if he would be willing to prepare a riposte to Kennan's proposals, Acheson leaped at the opportunity. On January 12, 1958, he issued a two-page "Reply to Kennan" that was printed in most leading U.S. and European newspapers. It strongly reiterated the orthodox Cold War justification for the presence of U.S. troops in Western Europe as providing the essential deterrent to Soviet aggression. In a frequently cited passage that some thought unusually harsh and overly personal, Acheson declared, "Mr. Kennan has never, in my judgment, grasped the realities of power relationships but takes a rather mystical attitude toward them. To Mr. Kennan there is no Soviet military threat in Europe." A host of prominent Democrats, including Truman, Stevenson, Harriman, and Senators Estes Kefauver, John F. Kennedy, and Lyndon B. Johnson, offered statements endorsing Acheson's position, helping distance the party from Kennan's unorthodox views. Acheson even received plaudits from an unexpected quarter: John Foster Dulles and Richard Nixon each wrote to congratulate him for challenging Kennan and thus bolstering current NATO policy.[30]

The Kennan-Acheson brouhaha about Germany and the U.S. troop presence in central Europe, with its highly personal overtones, generated substantial publicity on both sides of the Atlantic. "Next to the Lincoln Memorial in moonlight," joked the *New York Times*'s James Reston, "the sight of Mr. Dean G. Acheson blowing his top is without doubt the most impressive view in the capital."[31] At the invitation of the prestigious journal *Foreign Affairs*, Acheson elaborated on his views in an essay, titled "The Illusion of Disengagement," that appeared in its April 1958 issue. He decried the isolationist instincts lurking behind the false hope of an American withdrawal from Europe. "It was the same futile—and lethal—attempt to crawl back into the cocoon of history," he charged, that characterized the isolationism of the interwar years. "The

Illusion of Disengagement" would be one of his most reprinted and frequently cited articles.[32] "I can quite understand that the Kennan-Acheson brawl causes pain to our mutual friends," Acheson conceded in a personal letter to Philip Jessup. "But the self-deprecating garnishment of his lectures did not minimize their damaging, indeed reckless, content," he said in his defense. The German people formed the prime audience he sought to reach, Acheson told Jessup. He was trying "to destroy as effectively as I could the corroding effect of what [Kennan] had said and the belief that he was a seer in these matters. . . . The great danger is that the West . . . will come to believe its own bunk."[33]

Acheson's convictions regarding the indispensability of Western Europe to U.S. security in the Cold War had remained unaltered since his years in high office. They lay at the heart of his virulent rejection of Kennan's disengagement thesis. Europe's importance derived for him from a classic realist appreciation of the relationship between economic strength and military power. As he explained in his 1958 book, *Power and Diplomacy*, Europe contained "the largest aggregation of skilled workers in the world," critical and abundant natural resources, and an industrial base "second only to our own." Consequently, "if Europe should, by evil chance, become subject to Soviet domination, the remainder of the non-communist world would become unmanageable." Even more ominous, the Soviet bloc would then be in control of an industrial-military base greater than that of the United States and exceeding that achieved by Nazi Germany at the pinnacle of its power nearly two decades earlier. In the event, the balance of world power would tip decisively in Moscow's direction.

Without American assistance, Acheson was convinced, the Europeans simply could not withstand Soviet aggression. Joint U.S.-European defense efforts thus formed the linchpin of any effective Western Cold War strategy. "The North Atlantic Treaty, its organization, and its military forces," he emphasized, "are recognition of the truth that no balance of power in Europe, or elsewhere, adequate to restrain Soviet power is possible unless the weight of the United States is put into the scales. Without association with the United States, the European powers cannot prevent the leaders of the Soviet Union from having their way in Western Europe." For him, the key to containing the Kremlin's expansionist inclinations was the maintenance of an effective military deterrent. That was, in turn, dependent on the clearly expressed–

and, above all, *credible*–determination of the United States to unleash a full-scale nuclear attack on the Soviet Union, if need be, to prevent any military incursion into central Europe. Given the enormous stakes that Acheson believed to be at play in Western Europe–nothing less than the future physical safety of the American homeland–his categorical condemnation of Kennan's loose talk about disengagement and a neutralized Germany comes into clearer focus. That is equally true, of course, for his vehement denunciations of the Eisenhower administration's massive retaliation tenet and its concomitant failure to cultivate stronger bonds within the Atlantic alliance.[34]

THE DEMOCRATS' FOREIGN POLICY SAGE

As the 1960 election drew near, Acheson redoubled his efforts to help the Democrats regain the White House. He used his perch as the DAC's chief foreign policy oracle to craft party positions aimed at providing a distinctive Democratic alternative to what he considered the lassitude of the Eisenhower years. "More than any other person, Acheson deserves the credit, for better or for worse, for shifting the Democratic Party's foreign-policy agenda away from Stevensonian liberalism and back to the conservative, unyielding cold war tradition of Harry Truman," biographer Douglas Brinkley has rightly noted. "John F. Kennedy would be the benefactor of the swing back to the tough-minded, action-oriented, European-dominated, anti-communist foreign-policy principles of the Truman-Acheson heyday."[35] At first, Acheson was unimpressed by Kennedy, a Georgetown neighbor, albeit one he counted more as an "acquaintance" than a friend. In a letter to Frankfurter, in December 1958, Acheson suggested that someone other than Stevenson or Kennedy "should be our boy."[36] His initial preference was, in fact, for Missouri Senator W. Stuart Symington, a like-minded Cold War stalwart. Acheson thought JFK too young and too inexperienced for the presidency. He also harbored a deep disdain for JFK's father, Joseph P. Kennedy, whose unscrupulous methods and freewheeling style Acheson loathed and whose past support both for appeasement and McCarthyism he deplored. Those biases spilled over onto the entire Kennedy clan. Senator Kennedy's call for Algerian independence and his simultaneous broadside against French colonial policy in a 1957 speech also greatly irked Acheson, who devoted several pages in *Power and Diplomacy* to upbraiding the younger Kennedy for his brashness and presumptuousness.[37]

As Kennedy proved himself an adept political operator during the Democratic primaries and one with tough-minded Cold War views akin to his own, Acheson softened his stance. He came increasingly to see the Massachusetts senator as a viable, even an admirable–if still less than ideal–presidential aspirant. Acheson went so far as to dissuade Truman from releasing a statement critical of Kennedy's candidacy in the midst of the primary campaign. It would be "most uncharacteristic to call names and run away," he pleaded to the former president–to good effect.[38] Although he played no direct role in the campaign, other than responding to several JFK phone calls asking for foreign policy advice on different subjects, Acheson was certainly pleased with the result. Shortly after Kennedy's razor-thin victory over Nixon, he shared his generally positive outlook on the president-elect with a number of foreign correspondents. "I believe he has qualities which will make him an able, vigorous, but tactful, leader," Acheson forecast, "and that, after he has had the opportunity over a year or so to demonstrate these qualities, the country will respond and follow him because of them."[39]

At Kennedy's request, the president-elect called on Acheson at his P Street home within weeks of his electoral triumph. The specific reason for the visit was to solicit Acheson's views about some of the key cabinet and other senior appointments that the new chief executive needed to make, especially in the realm of foreign and defense policy. The tête-a-tête served a useful symbolic purpose for Kennedy as well; a publicized consultation with the diplomatic éminence grise of his party–and a throng of reporters camped out in front of the Acheson residence prior to Kennedy's arrival–helped create the image of a seamless link between the Kennedy and Truman administrations. Although JFK startled Acheson by refusing to join him in a cocktail, requesting tea instead, the meeting went well. Asked his advice about whom he should name to head the State Department, Acheson recommended first David Bruce and then John McCloy. When Kennedy did not bite, he next suggested Dean Rusk, his loyal underling during the Truman administration and current head of the Rockefeller Foundation. Acheson also highly recommended C. Douglas Dillon, the Republican financier and diplomat, for the Treasury Department. Kennedy, who heard similar praise for Rusk and Dillon in a subsequent meeting with Robert Lovett, shortly thereafter appointed them as his secretaries of state and treasury, respectively.

Toward the close of their conversation, JFK asked Acheson if he would be willing to consider an appointment as ambassador to NATO. The former secretary of state graciously declined, likely seeing such a post as too trifling for a person of his stature. Perhaps he would have considered becoming Kennedy's secretary of state, had the incoming president offered him his old post. He did not. Kennedy possessed more than enough political acumen to recognize that proposing the still controversial Acheson for a second stint at Foggy Bottom would have alienated not just numerous Republicans but key constituencies within his own party as well. Acheson told Kennedy that there was no formal governmental appointment that he wanted but that he "would be glad to help him in any way that [he] could with advice."[40]

He soon had the opportunity. In early February 1961 Secretary of State Rusk asked Acheson if he would conduct a wholesale review of NATO policy for Kennedy's benefit. Acheson threw himself into the choice assignment with great eagerness and zest. For the first time in eight years, he was back at the center of the foreign policy fray. During the administration's early weeks, Acheson's new responsibilities made him a frequent visitor to the State Department, Pentagon, and White House and a regular participant at high-level meetings. The return to the action had a tonic effect on his spirits. "DA is buoyed up by it all," observed Barbara Evans, his longtime secretary, "and looks better and younger than I have seen him in years."[41] Acheson's advisory committee on NATO policy completed its report in March. Consistent with its principal author's longstanding views, the Acheson Report advocated a broad-scale buildup of NATO's conventional forces. He reasoned that a more formidable conventional force would give the West the capability of resisting a Soviet attack in central Europe without immediately resorting to nuclear weapons. That would, in turn, reduce the likelihood of such an attack. A stronger conventional deterrent, in Acheson's assessment, would thus lessen the risk of a nuclear blowup, just as a continuation of the Dullesian reliance on massive retaliation would increase it. That conclusion dovetailed well with the Kennedy administration's emerging strategic doctrine of "flexible response." Acheson must have felt vindicated after his long years in the policy wilderness when, on April 21, JFK adopted a slightly revised version of the Acheson Report as the government's official NATO policy.[42]

Kennedy asked Acheson also to prepare an analysis of possible U.S. and NATO responses in the event that Soviet leader Nikita S. Khrushchev renewed his threat to the allied position in West Berlin. A possible showdown with the Soviets in isolated and vulnerable West Berlin, located a hundred miles from the West German border, constituted one of Kennedy's greatest fears. In late 1958 Khrushchev had triggered the first crisis over Berlin since Stalin's blockade when he suddenly announced Moscow's intention to sign a new treaty with East Germany. That move would, in effect, nullify the World War II agreements that formed the legal basis for joint occupation of the former German capital. In a subsequent declaration, Khrushchev gave the Western powers six months to negotiate directly with East Germany if they wanted to maintain their presence within and transit rights to and from Berlin. The latter prospect was anathema to U.S. policymakers since it would have seriously undercut the West German government, which adamantly refused to recognize the legitimacy of the Soviet-sponsored German Democratic Republic. Acheson instantly appraised the Khrushchev ultimatum as the gravest Soviet challenge to the West since the Korean War. On December 11, 1958, he gave a blistering address at Johns Hopkins University's School for Advanced International Studies in which he castigated the Eisenhower administration for failing to ensure the presence of sufficient ground troops in central Europe to discourage Soviet adventurism. That was a consequence, in his savage assessment, of its all-or-nothing dependence on nuclear weapons. "The truth is," Acheson told his audience, "we have to stay [in West Berlin] because to get out will destroy us all."[43] In a private letter to Frankfurter, following that public talk, he ruminated on the grim set of options the West faced: "Should we start nuclear war rather than leave Berlin? Answer. No. . . . Should we insist that present communications to West Berlin be maintained, and use force to remove obstacles? Answer. Yes. This is dangerous. But there is some elasticity here."[44]

The crisis could be resolved, Acheson was convinced, only if the Kremlin became persuaded of the allies' willingness to fight to maintain the status quo in West Berlin. Then, and only then, would Khrushchev back down. He summarized his thoughts about the Berlin crisis in the aptly titled article, "Wishing Won't Hold Berlin," which appeared on March 7, 1959, in the mass-circulation *Saturday Evening Post*. Describing the Berlin flash point as a test of wills between Moscow and Washington, Acheson argued that Eisenhower must convince the Soviets that the United States was "genuinely determined to keep traffic to Berlin open, at whatever risk, rather than abandon the people and permit the whole Western position to crumble." Once again, he called for a major allied troop buildup and for a bold, unyielding policy on the part of the West.[45] "I see a major disaster ahead," he confided in private correspondence with Senator Lyndon Johnson. "The ejection of the Western powers from Berlin and its absorption, over a few months' time, into East Germany," he worried, "will vastly increase Soviet power and prestige in Europe and in Asia." Such a devastating blow could even lead to the disintegration of NATO.[46]

Although none of those worst-case scenarios had come to pass, since Khrushchev had essentially withdrawn his ultimatum by mid-1959, Acheson's fears had not lessened in the intervening two years. In a memorandum for Kennedy of April 3, 1961, which the powerful National Security Adviser McGeorge Bundy (brother of his son-in-law William Bundy) judged to be "first-rate," Acheson reemphasized the vital importance of maintaining the status quo in West Berlin. As he had in his published essay in the *Saturday Evening Post*, Acheson argued that the United States had no choice but to take forceful action if the Soviets provoked another crisis over allied rights in Berlin—and he made clear that he expected one. Acheson again underscored his guiding conviction that the national security of the United States demanded that it be prepared "to fight for Berlin."[47]

Two days later, during a meeting with visiting British prime minister Harold Macmillan, Kennedy asked Acheson to open the session with a summary of his preliminary thinking about Berlin. It was nothing short of extraordinary that a new president, in office just a few months, would have a private citizen who held no formal governmental position brief a key allied leader on the most serious issue facing the West. Acheson seized the opportunity with characteristic aplomb, dominating the early portion of the Kennedy-Macmillan meeting with a chilling recitation of the military actions he considered imperative to meet an anticipated Soviet challenge. He delineated with penetrating logic the reasons why Berlin remained "of the greatest importance" to the West and why, consequently, "some sort of military response" would be needed to meet any Soviet effort to impede allied transit routes. The former secretary of state plainly unnerved Macmillan and his party with his matter-of-fact discussion of the need to prepare for a head-on military clash with Soviet and East German forces, up to the division-level, in order to demonstrate the allies' resolve to maintain their rights in West Berlin. Kennedy, for his part, did nothing to contradict any of the dire scenarios Acheson sketched.[48]

Shortly after his "bloodcurdling" disquisition to the British prime minister, as White House aide Arthur M. Schlesinger Jr. described it, Acheson departed on a presidentially sanctioned diplomatic mission to Western Europe. At JFK's personal request, he met with German chancellor Adenauer and French president Charles de Gaulle. Acheson then addressed a private session of the North Atlantic Council, in Paris. In each of those settings, Acheson strove to reassure America's major NATO partners that the new administration, despite its strong push for the buildup of conventional forces, had no intention of withdrawing nuclear weapons from Europe—or of weakening the U.S. nuclear deterrent that had long served as the ultimate guarantor of European security. Indeed, he told the NATO Council that "there is absolute certainty that if there is nuclear attack in Europe, [the] US will respond with all weapons at its command."[49] Kennedy doubtless chose Acheson for the task not just because of his finely honed diplomatic skills and unsurpassed experience with NATO issues. As a founder of the Atlantic pact and one of its best-known proponents, Acheson also gave JFK a personal emissary whose mere presence evoked a sense of continuity in U.S. policy. That symbolic link conveyed a reassuring signal during an unsettling period of change in the Cold War and in European-American relations.

Upon his return to Washington, Acheson was thrust even more fully into the administration's contingency planning for Berlin. That planning took on special urgency following the stormy Kennedy-Khrushchev summit meeting at Vienna in early June. The Soviet leader's renewal of his threat, during the Vienna talks, to terminate the agreements that still governed allied access to West Berlin, had triggered a full-blown Cold War crisis. In so acting, Khrushchev also confirmed Acheson's earlier prediction, thereby burnishing the latter's reputation for foresight and shrewdness among the coterie of much less seasoned strategic analysts surrounding Kennedy. Although still merely a private attorney, and one who at sixty-eight was already past the traditional retirement age, Acheson suddenly began exercising nearly as much power at this early stage of the crisis as those within Kennedy's inner circle.

On June 16 he dominated the discussion and largely set the terms of debate during a key meeting of the newly created interdepartmental group charged with contingency planning for a Berlin showdown. Then, and later, Acheson took an exceptionally hard-line stance. Operating from the core premise that West Berlin, as he phrased it, "was very, very important indeed, certainly involving deeply the prestige of the United States and perhaps its very survival," Acheson stressed that the United States simply could not compromise allied rights there without jeopardizing its entire global position. Given such lofty stakes, he asserted that the United States must convince Khrushchev that it was willing to use the full range of its military might–all the way up to, and including, nuclear weapons–to defend the allied position in West Berlin. "Our problem was [how] to increase his fear that we would use nuclear weapons if necessary," Acheson reasoned. Since mere bluff would not suffice, persuading Moscow to back down hinged on "our determination to use nuclear weapons if we had to." Of course, Acheson had no desire to spark a nuclear confrontation. Since a withdrawal from West Berlin would in his judgment "destroy our power position," however, Acheson insisted that a willingness to risk nuclear war must be accepted. Any negotiation, in his adamant opinion, would be a self-defeating sign of weakness–tantamount to surrender.[50]

Those chilling conclusions ran through the lengthy Berlin memorandum that he submitted for the president's consideration on June 28. "West Berlin has been protected, in the last analysis, by the fear that interference with the city, or with access to it, would result in war between the United States and the Soviet Union," Acheson emphasized. "War, as used here," he clarified–lest there be no confusion–"means eventually nuclear war." Acheson surmised that Khrushchev's evident willingness to court substantial risks with his latest challenge to the Western position in the former German capital meant that the deterrent power of the West's nuclear arsenal had somehow declined in his eyes. The challenge for the United States, accordingly, was to begin making sufficiently concrete preparations for war so as to convince Khrushchev that its resolution had, in fact, not wavered. If that firm course of action succeeded, and it was the one Acheson strongly advocated, the Soviet leader would then most likely recognize "that what he wants is not possible without war," and that would "cause him to change his purpose." However, Acheson admitted, "There is, also, a substantial possibility that war might result."[51]

Acheson's deeply held and forcefully articulated views made him a commanding figure during the Kennedy administration's tense deliberations over Berlin. On June 29, at a meeting of the National Security Council, he dominated the discussion in a manner almost certainly unprecedented for any private citizen in an international crisis of such magnitude. Acheson held fast to his core positions: that negotiations must be avoided at all costs and that the risks of nuclear war must be borne with equanimity. The former State Department chief also weighed in on the related issue of whether to deploy medium-range ballistic missiles in Western Europe. Acheson opposed the idea, currently being weighed within the administration, as needlessly divisive at a time when maintaining NATO unity was imperative in the face of Khrushchev's provocations. "The Berlin crisis," he wrote Secretary of Defense Robert S. McNamara, "seems to me the period, above all others, when we do not want to stir up British fears of Germany or divisive issues between the French and ourselves."[52]

W. Averell Harriman, Kennedy's ambassador-at-large, was left aghast by his former classmate's hawkish views on Berlin. "How long is our policy to be dominated by that frustrated and rigid man?" he complained to Arthur Schlesinger. "He is leading us down the road to war." Abram Chayes, the State Department's legal adviser, later recalled, "Dean was riding high. He had the feeling that he was in control."[53]

But, appearances aside, Acheson was not in control; he was no longer secretary of state but a mere private citizen. And he almost certainly overplayed his hand. Kennedy, Bundy, and McNamara might even have been using Acheson as a kind of devil's advocate, ensuring that the most hawkish views were given a hearing while they groped for less extreme alternatives. All three were appalled by the prospect that the current crisis over Berlin could culminate in a catastrophic nuclear war that neither superpower wanted, with potentially tens of millions of casualties on each side.

At an NSC meeting of July 13, Acheson found almost no support for his recommendation that the president declare a national emergency. When, on

July 25, Kennedy delivered a nationally televised speech on the Berlin crisis that called for the mobilization of reserve units, Acheson privately grumbled that it constituted too weak a counter to the Soviet challenge. Distressed to see his support ebbing, Acheson gradually began withdrawing from his unusual role of outside adviser and freelance policy advocate. In a letter to Truman, on July 14, he voiced disdain for the administration's preoccupation with "our image" while bemoaning the absence of "vigorous leadership" at the top.[54]

In early August Acheson retreated to Martha's Vineyard, where each of his daughters maintained summer homes, for a vacation. He wrote Frankfurter that he was leaving Washington "in a rather depressed condition." "I have had my full quota of the New Frontier," he announced.[55] Upon his return, Acheson remained glum. Khrushchev's decision, in mid-August, to erect a wall to stem the exodus of East Berliners to the West, appalled him. "I believe that this autumn we are heading for a most humiliating defeat over Berlin," he predicted in a letter to Truman. "I am now going to—in the current jargon—'phase out' for a while," he added. "To work for this crowd is strangely depressing. Nothing seems to get decided."[56]

Acheson's notoriously caustic tongue and penchant for tart comments about public figures also contributed to his growing estrangement from the Kennedy administration. In June he told an audience of retired foreign service officers that observing Kennedy was like watching a gifted young performer with a boomerang knock himself out. When the remark got back to JFK, as it inevitably did, he was infuriated. Not until August 18 did Acheson extend an apology. "I am most distressed," he wrote the president. "I continually err in regarding my humor as less mordant and more amusing than the facts warrant."[57]

Over the next year Acheson had minimal involvement with foreign policy issues. He represented the Cambodian government as chief counsel in a dispute with Thailand over ownership of a ninth-century temple that straddled the two countries' border. That assignment temporarily revived his legal practice. The case brought him on a delightful trip to Cambodia, Japan, and Australia, followed by a month in the Netherlands successfully arguing the case before the International Court of Justice in The Hague. With the conclusion of the Cambodian case, which turned him into a veritable national hero in

Cambodia, Acheson found himself back in Washington, and at loose ends. "This summer, I must figure out something to do," he wrote Alice, who was then traveling in Europe. "The speech, the only one I ever make, is beginning to pall. Another book has not yet begun to gestate. I have no cases and no job. . . . So I must think of something, but not until we get back from Europe."[58] Having just ended a twenty-five-year stint on Yale's governing board, Acheson did not even have the affairs of "my university" to absorb his still prodigious energies. Frankfurter's recent stroke also contributed to Acheson's melancholy mood; he saw the justice almost daily and found it painful to watch his dear friend's indomitable vitality slowly recede.

That May he met Alice in London, attended a conference in the Netherlands, and visited friends in Sweden and elsewhere in Europe, maintaining the hectic traveling schedule that marked his post–secretary of state years. The overseas travel helped lift his spirits, as it so often did. Yet one suspects that Acheson would have canceled any of those trips at a moment's notice for another crack at what he found most exhilarating: "the responsibility" that "goes with the power of decision."[59]

The Kennedy administration's shocking discovery, in October 1962, that the Soviets had been surreptitiously shipping nuclear missiles into Cuba gave him that opportunity. On October 16, the same day that U-2 photographs confirmed the Soviet activity, Kennedy again summoned Acheson to the White House to assume the role of policy adviser. The next day he participated in two meetings of the hastily established NSC Executive Committee (ExCom), Kennedy's ad hoc advisory sounding board. Acheson, by then apprised of the basic facts surrounding Khrushchev's brazen effort to establish medium-range and intermediate-range nuclear missile sites on Fidel Castro's Cuba, immediately sided with the hawks who were advocating a military response. "We should proceed at once with the necessary military actions and should do no talking," Acheson recommended with typical self-assurance. "The Soviets will react some place," he predicted. "We must expect this; take the consequences and manage the situations as they evolve. We should have no consultations with Khrushchev, Castro, or our allies, but should fully alert our allies in the most persuasive manner by high level people." He worried especially that the "political effect" of Soviet missiles in Cuba would be "terrible," particularly "in

Latin America and among our allies abroad." Acheson, accordingly, called for a prompt, surgical air strike to destroy the missile sites, with no attempt at prior negotiations with Moscow. Yet he disagreed vehemently with the uniformed military's advocacy of an all-out invasion of Cuba as certain to cause massive civilian casualties.[60]

On the morning of October 18, JFK invited Acheson to outline his thinking during a private, one-hour meeting. The former secretary of state reiterated his opinion that an immediate air strike without prior warning to the Soviets represented the best of a set of bad options. An invasion would be too risky, Acheson reasoned; a naval blockade was an ineffectual tool for getting missiles *out* of Cuba. He dismissed out of hand Attorney General Robert F. Kennedy's concern that a U.S. air strike would represent a "Pearl Harbor in reverse." Acheson later ridiculed that view as "high school thought unworthy of people charged with the government of a great country."[61]

His role in the most perilous crisis of the nuclear age then suddenly shifted from participant in ExCom deliberations to diplomatic envoy. Kennedy asked Acheson to represent him on a secret mission to inform the leaders of France and West Germany of the actions he intended to pursue. On October 22 Acheson arrived in Paris, U-2 photographs in tow, and was quickly ushered into the Élysée Palace for a private discussion with President de Gaulle. In a meeting that has become encased in legend in the intervening years, de Gaulle listened intently to Acheson's presentation and, at first, declined the American visitor's offer to inspect the photographic evidence of Soviet missile sites. The French leader stressed that he had absolutely no reason to question the veracity of the evidence Acheson brought with him—though he did, in fact, later scrutinize closely the fruits of U.S. aerial reconnaissance, marveling at a technological wonder with which he was unfamiliar. After Acheson provided de Gaulle with considerable detail about JFK's proposed action—the naval quarantine that he had personally opposed—the former general remarked that "certainly France can have no objections to that since it is legal for a country to defend itself when it finds itself in danger." Ironically, de Gaulle voiced some of the same misgiving that Acheson himself had earlier expressed, though in his role as presidential emissary Acheson necessarily kept his personal views under wraps.[62] Upon escorting the former secretary of state to the door at the conclusion of their one-hour conversation, de Gaulle paid Acheson the ultimate compliment. "It would be a pleasure to me if things were all done through you," he said.[63] "De Gaulle could not have been better," Acheson gushed soon after to a favorite correspondent. "We could not have had a more satisfactory talk."[64]

The peaceful resolution of the Cuban missile crisis days later left Acheson deeply ambivalent. Kennedy's forceful rhetoric and tight enforcement of the quarantine, along with an American pledge not to invade Cuba and a secret promise to remove its Jupiter nuclear missiles from Turkey, led Khrushchev to back down and remove Soviet missiles from Cuba. Acheson attributed that outcome more to "plain, dumb luck," though, than to any particularly wise crisis management on Kennedy's part. "Mr. K's effort in Cuba gave the real measure of his contempt for Mr. Kennedy," he wrote to Jean Monnet that November. "It was a real gamble; it came close to coming off. But it just missed."[65] Acheson believed that Kennedy's demonstrated irresolution in previous crises, such as Berlin, had brought on the Cuban missile showdown by tempting the Soviets to take advantage of the American leader's vulnerability. "My own desire was for more vigorous action than was taken," he told another correspondent. "I never quite believed that my younger colleagues really understood the nature of the decision. . . . So I was in favor of destroying the missiles and the [Soviet] IL 28 bombers by low level conventional bombing and then dealing with the consequences."[66]

LBJ AND VIETNAM: AN OLD WARRIOR'S LAST BATTLE

Kennedy's assassination in November 1963 shocked Acheson, as it did so many Americans. "This nation was truly shattered," he wrote his English friend Pamela Berry in early December. "It was not bewilderment at the loss of a great and tried leader, as with F.D.R., for J.F.K. was not that," he remarked. "It was fear from the utter collapse of all sense of security which lay at the bottom of the emotion. No one knew what had happened. We were like victims of an earthquake. Even the ground under our feet was shaking. . . . It all conspired to produce a terrifying shock." The ascension of Vice President Lyndon Johnson, a man Acheson had long admired for his consummate political skills and vast legislative experience, to the presidency reassured him. "In the change of leaders we have not suffered a loss," he confided to Berry. "We have a leader whom

I shall be happy to follow into what promises to be a battle worth fighting."[67] Johnson had been in the Oval Office less than two months when Acheson wrote to James F. Byrnes, his old boss, "Isn't Lyndon doing a great job? If he will only not kill himself he bids fair to be among the top class of presidents."[68] In a similar vein, he enthused to Philip Jessup, "Our new president is impressive. . . . The whole town is again crackling with life."[69]

Johnson reciprocated Acheson's warm embrace. He had assiduously courted Acheson throughout the previous decade with flattery and regular correspondence, trying to win over an establishment luminary; it was a tactic this most ambitious and calculating of politicians employed routinely with those who might be a position to help him. LBJ phoned Acheson to invite him to a private luncheon meeting at the executive mansion less than two weeks after assuming the presidency.[70] As had Kennedy, Johnson frequently invited Acheson to the White House, soliciting his advice on important international issues and vying to gain the unequivocal backing of his party's most eminent foreign policy hand. To suggest that Acheson enjoyed the attention would be a major understatement.

When Greece and Turkey nearly came to blows over the status of the island of Cyprus in the early summer of 1964, Johnson asked Acheson to serve as a mediator. He reasoned that the man so closely identified with the Greek-Turkish aid program of 1947 might be able to exert some influence on NATO's most disputatious members. Once again Acheson threw himself into the assignment with gusto and his familiar take-charge style, wearing his seventy-one years lightly. He devoted two months to ultimately fruitless negotiations, held at Geneva, that were aimed at devising an equitable solution to the daunting Cyprus problem through a complicated partition plan that he helped design. Acheson placed blame for the failure almost entirely on the shoulders of Greek prime minister George Papandreou, who, he despaired in a cable to Undersecretary of State George Ball, "has not made one attempt toward the agreement he could have and which would give him nine-tenths of all he hoped for."[71] In a letter to old Yale classmate Ranald MacDonald that September, Acheson referred flippantly to his two months of mediation in Geneva as "the worst rat race I have ever been in—trying to deny Greeks and Turks their historic recreation of killing one another."[72] He was even more

Acheson at the Lyndon Johnson White House, July 1965. Photo by Yoichi R. Okamoto, courtesy of the Lyndon Baines Johnson Library and Museum

scathing in a letter to close confidante Archibald MacLeish. "You know nothing of the deeper frustration of life," Acheson joked, "until you spend two months keeping Greeks and Turks from killing one another while hoping all the time, not only that they would do just that, but make a pretty thorough job of it."[73] Still, he earned LBJ's gratitude for his efforts and the two men found themselves in essential accord on the particulars of the vexing Cyprus question.

In 1965, as the deepening U.S. intervention in Vietnam began to overshadow virtually all other foreign policy priorities, Johnson increasingly drew on Acheson for advice and perspective. What LBJ craved most of all, however, was what he expected from all his confidantes: steadfast support and unwavering loyalty. After advancing an abortive peace plan, with Undersecretary Ball, that aimed at precluding the need for U.S. combat forces, the former secretary of state fell in line. He offered wholehearted–and unqualified–backing for Johnson's decision to escalate U.S. involvement, both publicly and privately. Acheson viewed the ongoing conflict between the U.S.-supported South Vietnamese regime and the North Vietnamese–backed National Liberation Front, however wrongly, as a challenge analogous to the one he had faced in Korea. Communist aggression–and he saw Hanoi as a puppet of Moscow and Beijing, much as Pyongyang had been–demanded a firm American response lest America's credibility worldwide suffer. "I have been drawn in to some aspects of the Vietnam situation and have come to know a good deal about it," he pontificated to Lucius Battle in June 1965. "The Administration is wholly right and the intellectuals wholly wrong."[74] The next month Acheson joined a group of former senior officials–Johnson's so-called "Wise Men"–for a discussion of Vietnam and other international flash points. He grew impatient with the president's lengthy whining about the burdens of office and about how "he had no support from anyone at home or abroad" on Vietnam. "Finally I blew my top and told him that he was wholly right in the Dominican Republic and Vietnam," Acheson recounted in a letter to Truman, "that he had no choice except to press on, that explanations were not as important as successful action. . . . With this lead, my colleagues came thundering in like the charge of the Scots Greys at Waterloo."[75]

Acheson stoutly opposed negotiations with the Communist side, as he nearly always did. Talks with Hanoi should take place, he insisted in a private letter, only after the United States achieves "the drastic suppression of the belligerency instigated, directed, and supplied from the north." Comparing the Vietnam conflict to that in Korea, always his basic point of reference, he remarked, "Now, as then, we must weigh considerations beyond the area of immediate conflict. I think the Government has weighed them correctly."[76] In November 1965, following the major buildup of U.S. combat forces, Acheson stated with trademark bravado, "There is, I think, every reason to expect that we are on the way to accomplishing our purpose."[77]

His major misgiving about Johnson's foreign policy, at this juncture, was not that it was failing in Vietnam but that the president was ignoring equally important challenges in Europe. When one of those festering challenges reached a boiling point, with de Gaulle's announcement in early March 1966 that France was about to leave NATO's integrated military command, Johnson asked Acheson to chair a NATO crisis management committee. A still vigorous Acheson, whose new duties gave him a temporary State Department office and staff, carefully explored various options for limiting the damage that France's independent course would inflict on the alliance he continued to extol as essential to U.S. security. In the end, he found that four-month assignment nearly as frustrating as his stint as chief Cyprus negotiator. Acheson grew frustrated with both the White House and the State Department, believing that they were falsely depicting him as stubbornly and unreasonably anti–de Gaulle with unflattering leaks to the press. Johnson's kid-glove treatment of the prickly French leader also grated on Acheson. After a few martinis at a Washington dinner party, he blurted out to Francis Bator, one of the administration's top Europeanists, "You made the greatest imperial power the world has ever seen kiss de Gaulle's arse."[78] Acheson directed his fire at the president himself shortly thereafter. As he recounted the episode to Anthony Eden, "This all blew up at a White House meeting when, at some crack of LBJ's, I lost my temper and told him what I thought of his conduct and I was not prepared to stand for any more of it. Rusk and McNamara dove for cover while Ball and I slugged it out with Mr. Big. . . . It was exhilarating and did something to clear the air."[79]

The intemperate outburst also led, not surprisingly, to a temporary falling out between "Mr. Big" and the former secretary of state. Acheson confided to friends and family members that he had quite had his fill of the vain, thin-skinned, and imperious Johnson. "My frustration quotient was too high for an old man," he quipped to Archibald MacLeish.[80] LBJ could focus on only one or two issues at a time, he vented in a letter to Truman, and currently Vietnam and balance of payments issues crowded out everything else. "So Europe is forgotten," Acheson lamented, "and a good deal that you, General Marshall and I did is unraveling fast. For the Chief of the world's greatest power and the only one capable of world responsibility, this is a disaster."[81]

In November 1967, with the Vietnam War mired in stalemate, the public growing restive, and his own secretary of defense privately expressing doubts about the U.S. war effort, Johnson again turned to Acheson and a group of distinguished former policymakers for advice and support. The Wise Men, who included McGeorge Bundy, George Ball (now out of government), Clark Clifford, W. Averell Harriman, and C. Douglas Dillon, among others, received intensive briefings from military officials. Then, as the president had hoped, they counseled that the United States must persevere—and ultimately prevail—in Vietnam. They regarded the stakes there as extremely high: Vietnam was a critical theater in the broader struggle to contain the expansion of communism, and U.S. credibility and deterrent power were at risk there. "If we keep up the pressure on them, gradually the will of the Viet Cong and the North Vietnamese will wear down," said Clifford. Acheson, who assumed a leadership role within the group, agreed. He remarked that the war was "going well" for the United States. "When these fellows decide they can't defeat the South, then they will give up," he proclaimed with characteristic self-assurance. "This is the way it was in Korea. This is the way the Communists operated."[82] Acheson repeated those views the next month in a television interview, in which he described Vietnam as the same as Korea and insisted that the United States would win there once U.S. resolution compelled the Communists to change their objectives, as it had in Korea.[83]

That winter Acheson gradually began rethinking his views about the Vietnam conflict, spurred especially by the bold, countrywide Communist offensive that began in late January 1968, coincident with the Vietnamese Tet holiday. Before then, Harriman had visited Acheson at his home in Georgetown and tried to persuade his old colleague and friend that there were stark differences between the Korean and Vietnamese cases. The dovish Harriman, who also participated—but remained silent—during the Wise Men meetings in November—urged Acheson to keep an open mind and to keep his channels of communication with the president open. He gained the sense, from their encounter, that the former secretary was not quite so rigid in his support of Johnson's policies as he appeared.[84] Acheson was in Antigua for his annual winter vacation when the Tet offensive broke. He heard vigorous antiwar sentiments from many of his closest friends there. One of them, John Cowles, the publisher of the *Minneapolis Star and Tribune* and a man whom Acheson had come to have great respect and affection for, regaled his prominent friend with passionate arguments in favor of total U.S. disengagement from Vietnam.

On February 27, shortly after Acheson's return to Washington, Johnson summoned the former secretary to meet with him in the White House. Their forty-five minute session formed part of LBJ's desperate effort to maintain backing for his increasingly embattled Vietnam policy. Liberal Democrats were increasingly turning against the war in the wake of an enemy offensive that appeared to shatter the illusion of American progress. The meeting went poorly. Acheson had to endure a Johnson monologue about his troubles, which irritated the former secretary. Before Johnson could even complete his monologue, Acheson abruptly left to return to his law office at the Union Trust Building, just two blocks from the White House. When Walt Rostow, LBJ's national security adviser, phoned him to inquire why he had departed so suddenly, Acheson said with unusual bluntness, "You can tell the president—and you can tell him in precisely these words—that he can take Vietnam and stick it up his ass." The president himself then took the phone and persuaded Acheson to walk back to the White House to complete their conversation. Acheson asked Johnson if he could have full access to classified information and briefings from knowledgeable officials so that he could conduct his own investigation of the war. Desperate for support from the traditional centers of power within his own party, LBJ assented.[85]

Acheson's immersion in Vietnam issues over the next several weeks led him to question in fundamental ways many of his earlier views. On March 14 he wrote Cowles that he had "completed the second stage (High School) of my Vietnam education" and that it "has confused some of my earlier simple conclusions and shown the difficulties to be even greater than I thought." That same day he met again with Johnson and made it clear that he could no longer believe the false optimism being pedaled by the military.[86]

On March 25 Johnson summoned Acheson and the Wise Men to another meeting at the White House. After receiving a series of candid briefings from leading military and civilian experts throughout that day and into the next morning, the Wise Men met alone with LBJ on the afternoon of March 26. What ensued surely ranks among the more remarkable, and frank, conversations that a president has ever held with a collection of nongovernmental consultants on a matter of such enormous significance. "There is a very significant shift in our position," began former National Security Adviser Bundy solemnly. "When we last met we saw reasons for hope. We hoped then that there would be slow but steady progress. Last night and today the picture is not so hopeful[,] particularly in the country side." Acheson had summed up the opinion of the majority of the group's members, Bundy continued, when he said that "we can no longer do the job we set out to do in the time we have left and we must begin to take steps to disengage." Only three of the Wise Men disagreed, two of whom were career military officers who were willing to defer to Commanding General William Westmoreland's recent request for additional troops.

Acheson, whose own doubts about the wisdom of current policy had been mounting steadily ever since the outbreak of the Tet fighting, was particularly forceful. He insisted that time was of the essence. "Time is limited by reactions in this country," he observed. "We cannot build an independent South Vietnam; therefore, we should do something by no later than late summer to establish something different." When Supreme Court Justice and Johnson intimate Abe Fortas ventured that this was not the time for a bombing halt, Acheson disagreed sharply. "The issue is not that stated by Fortas," he snapped. "The issue is can we do what we are trying to do in Vietnam. I do not think we can."[87]

The Wise Men's firm support for a policy of disengagement clearly shook Johnson. Although he knew in advance of Acheson's recent dovish turn, he had not expected the vehemence of the once staunchly pro-war Democrat's objections. Neither had he anticipated so dramatic a switch in the views of so many other experienced foreign policy hands—and certainly not in so short a period. Reflecting on that climactic meeting decades later, Clifford well captured the wider significance of the Wise Men's advice to LBJ. "The men who had helped lay down the basic line of resistance to the expansion of communism in the world, the statesmen of Berlin and Korea, had decided they had had enough in Vietnam," he recalled. "The price was not commensurate with the goal." He hastened to add, correctly, that the men who confronted Johnson in the White House on March 26 still supported the overall strategy of containing the Soviet Union and China. That certainly held true for Acheson. He—and they—were hardly signaling an abandonment of basic Cold War policies and commitments. Rather their "opposition to the war was based solely on the belief that Vietnam was weakening us at home and in the rest of the world," he noted. "And," Clifford added pointedly, "they were right."[88] Secretary of State Rusk put it more succinctly. "The political tide had clearly moved against the war," he recorded in his memoir, "when Dean Acheson abandoned ship."[89]

Vietnam War specialists find themselves in rare agreement on the signal influence of the Wise Men's intervention on Johnson's announcement, just days later, of a partial bombing halt over North Vietnam and his simultaneous call for immediate negotiations with Hanoi. With those moves, LBJ essentially signaled that the United States was no longer seeking to achieve a military victory. Clearly, Acheson's deep skepticism about the prospects for success in Vietnam, his forceful articulation of that stance, and the former secretary's natural assumption, as if by birthright, of a leadership role within the group contributed immeasurably to that epochal turning point. Without Acheson's galvanizing presence at those critical meetings, the dynamic between LBJ and the Wise Men could well have played out in a different way, with the outside consultants' recommendations packing less punch—and carrying less weight—with a stubborn and still determined president.

We will never know. What we do know is that Acheson, on the eve of his seventy-fifth birthday, proved sufficiently supple and open-minded to shift his position on the war virtually 180 degrees. If a mounting rigidity of view and a reflective hawkishness had become characteristic traits of the Acheson of the 1960s, as critics have fairly noted, then this startling about-face on the most momentous foreign policy crisis since the early Cold War becomes especially significant to an appreciation of his life and career. "We had been wrong in believing that we could establish an independent, non-communist state in South Vietnam," he wrote his daughter Jane that April, a remarkably blunt admission of error for an aging statesman rarely plagued by self-doubt or troubled by second thoughts about his instinctual judgments on strategic questions.[90] In similar fashion, he admitted to President Richard Nixon during a private meeting a year later that, although he had supported Johnson's decision to deploy substantial numbers of U.S. troops in 1965, "I had been wrong."[91] One can imagine how, in his reassessment of the U.S. military commitment in Vietnam, Acheson might have remembered Brandeis instructing him so long ago always to be guided by the facts of the matter at hand and to adjust one's opinions to those facts—never the reverse. One can imagine as well how, in that rethinking, he might have heard the echoes once again of his hero Holmes's famous admonition that general propositions cannot settle particular cases.

It is tempting to view the final arc of this remarkable man's life as mere postscript. Acheson's central role in the post–Tet offensive decisions that set the Johnson administration on the course toward military disengagement from Vietnam, after all, constituted Acheson's last, great battle in the public arena. It was a noble battle, moreover, and one that he helped win. But Acheson did not retreat to the sidelines in the aftermath of the climactic Wise Men's showdown with Johnson. To have done so would have been wholly out of character. Instead, Acheson continued fighting to enhance the security and advance the best interests of his country, as he saw them, for the next three and a half years—until a massive stroke finally claimed his life on October 12, 1971.

He even mended fences with Nixon, a man he had long found contemptible. In December 1967 he told an interviewer, "I have never met Mr. Nixon. . . . I have no respect for him at all. And I would be sad indeed if he became President of the United States."[92] When Nixon and his national security adviser, Henry A. Kissinger, courted the grand old man of U.S. diplomacy, however, Acheson responded favorably to the attention and flattery. Throughout 1969 and 1970, he became a regular visitor, for the first time, to a Republican White House. Acheson freely offered Nixon and Kissinger advice on Vietnam, U.S.-Soviet relations, NATO, the Middle East, southern Africa, and a range of other pressing issues. He agreed to serve as national cochair, in the spring of 1970, of a citizen's committee supporting Nixon's push for an antiballistic missile system, and the next year he led a group opposing the Mansfield Amendment, which would have cut U.S. troop commitments to NATO in half. In each of those confrontations, he took the side of a Republican president against liberal Senate Democrats whom he considered "woolly-headed."[93] He wrote a friend, by way of partial explanation, that "Nixon is a definite relief from L.B.J., not out of definable positive virtues, but from the absence of a swinish, bullying boorishness which made his last years unbearable."[94]

His wife was less willing to forgive Nixon's past transgressions, telling an interviewer in 1987 that she felt Nixon had simply used her husband to gain political advantage.[95] Acheson himself soon soured on Nixon as well, breaking with him on the controversial decision to invade Cambodia in April 1970, among other matters. A letter to close friend John Cowles, in January 1971, reflected how dramatically his views had shifted. "My sad current conclusion," Acheson said, "is that the present administration is the most incompetent and undirected group I have seen in charge of the U.S. government since the closing years of the Wilson administration."[96]

There were few in Washington policy circles by then, of course, who had any firsthand memory of the Wilson years. That Acheson did offers testimony both to his staying power and to his advancing years. When the *New York Times*'s C. L. Sulzberger, in an admiring tribute to "the Sage of Sandy Spring," referred to Acheson as "an old man," he accepted the term with good humor.[97] "So I agree that I am an old man—and sometimes feel like one," he wrote Anthony Eden.[98] Yet Acheson, despite nagging health problems, continued to keep abreast of international affairs as keenly as most specialists several decades his junior. His observations in personal correspondence about the implications of Nixon's opening to China, for example, are studded with astute insights.[99]

In the early autumn of 1971 Acheson was eagerly preparing for his first trip to southern Africa, a journey he was slated to make with Anthony Eden. His support of the white minority regimes in Rhodesia and South Africa, which was based on a narrowly legalistic understanding of how international law protected national sovereignty, had become one of the odd passions of the last years of his life—to the dismay of some friends as well as his own daughters and daughter-in-law. Acheson bristled at the suggestion that racism lay behind his position, though a longstanding paternalist attitude toward peoples of color certainly did.[100] On October 12, following a day given over to preparing his garden at Harewood for winter, Acheson sat down at his desk to write Eden about their impending trip. An hour later, he suffered a major stroke and died instantly. He was seventy-eight.

CONCLUSION

By almost any measure, Dean Acheson ranks as one of the most important, accomplished, and consequential diplomats in the entire sweep of U.S. history. During the 1940s and early 1950s, a seminal period both in U.S. foreign policy making and in modern world history, Acheson served in a number of key State Department positions. As assistant secretary of state for economic affairs and then for congressional affairs (1941–1945), as undersecretary of state (1945–1947), and finally as secretary of state (1949–1953), he played an active and sometimes decisive part in the conceptualization and creation of a new, American-dominated world order. The economic, strategic, and political foundations of that order, forged out of the ashes of humanity's most devastating conflict, owe as much to Acheson's vision, perspicacity, and diplomatic skill as to those of any other individual.

The overall strategy adopted by the United States to meet the Soviet challenge of the immediate postwar years, while simultaneously rebuilding the military, economic, social, and political strength of the West, likewise bears Acheson's indelible imprint. More than any other Western statesman, he was responsible for developing, and implementing, the essential Cold War strategy pursued by the United States and its NATO partners over the next four decades. Acheson had a hand in nearly all of the pivotal Western initiatives of the early Cold War years: from the Truman Doctrine, the Marshall Plan, NATO, and West Germany's rehabilitation and reconstruction to the Korean intervention,

America's massive post-Korea rearmament program, its efforts to promote Western European unity and integration, and its early attempts to channel and control developments in an increasingly turbulent third world.

His engagement with and influence on U.S. foreign relations, as the preceding pages have shown, were not confined simply to the years in which the Washington-based attorney held official positions of governmental responsibility. In the critical year and a half that followed the outbreak of war in Europe, in September 1939, Acheson assumed a lead role in the intense public debate about U.S. national security needs in a world at war, a debate that reverberated across the nation's airwaves, print media, and assembly halls. His proved an unusually eloquent and articulate pro-interventionist voice during that watershed period. He offered a sharp, forceful, and tightly reasoned rebuke to isolationists' emotional appeals. During Acheson's brief return to the private sector, between mid-1947 and early 1949, his vigorous personal lobbying campaign on behalf of the Marshall Plan showed once again that a private citizen could remain fully engaged in an ongoing foreign policy question of singular importance.

January 1953 might have brought his formal State Department career to an end, but the former secretary of state never ceased his efforts to shape the wider public discourse about the direction of American foreign policy. Neither, right up to his death in 1971, did Acheson ever stop trying to influence the diplomatic decisions of those presidents, secretaries of state, and other high-ranking officials who proved receptive to his counsel—or even, in some cases, to those who did not. Acheson's active participation in a series of internal deliberations during the administrations of John F. Kennedy and Lyndon B. Johnson extended to some of the most dangerous crises of the entire Cold War. His involvement, as the Democrats' wise and wizened elder statesman, in high-stakes meetings about Berlin, Cuba, Vietnam, and other international flash points constitutes a notable final chapter in Acheson's long career on the public policy stage.

Acheson's credentials as one of the major "Shapers of International History" also extend well beyond his deserved stature as a leading architect of U.S. foreign policy. As much as any modern diplomat, he helped craft the international institutions and multilateral alliances that have exerted an enduring impact on the international system as a whole. Acheson was quite literally "present at the creation" of the International Monetary Fund, the World Bank, the United Nations, and the North Atlantic Treaty Organization, among other iconic institutions. Further, he helped inscribe a set of liberal, Wilsonian principles into the very marrow of world diplomacy. Those ranged from measures promoting nondiscriminatory trade agreements, free flows of investment capital, and easy currency convertibility to habits of openness and transparency in state-to-state negotiations—especially, in the latter case, in the conduct of inter-allied relations. In the pains he took to foster bonds of unity among the Western powers, Acheson helped enshrine the practices of consultation, compromise, and multilateralism as foundational principles of the Western alliance. He even helped codify the notion of the "West," a construction based at first on a kind of imagined community of European and North American nation-states that presumably shared not just interests and values but also a common civilizational heritage as well. Over time the construction took root. It became real partly because statesmen and ordinary citizens alike from Washington to Paris to Bonn to Rome accepted and internalized the notion of an idealized West that Acheson, as effectively as any contemporary, helped promulgate.

It is a central premise of this book that individual historical actors matter. Without question, impersonal structural forces made possible the epoch of American global predominance that was coterminus with the second half of the twentieth century—and which has continued into the early years of the twentieth-first century. In 1945 the United States possessed not just air and naval capabilities that dwarfed those of its nearest rivals, along with a complete monopoly on the atomic bomb, but it was also producing an astonishing 50 percent of the world's goods and services. Some form of Pax Americana struck many knowledgeable observers, then as now, as a well-nigh inevitable by-product of such massive relative power. In conjunction with the global devastation and dislocation caused by a war that had claimed as many as sixty million lives, the possession of that degree of power might make such an outcome appear almost overdetermined. Yet, as Oliver Wendell Holmes liked to say, in a line that Acheson frequently repeated, "The mode by which the inevitable came to pass is called effort."[1] Individuals seized on those historic opportunities, and none did so more astutely than Acheson.

A small group of strong-minded and historically conscious individual policymakers, Acheson prominent among them, struggled to mold the contours of a new world order that would both enable and constrain American power. Members of that group labored to gain broad international assent, and hence legitimacy, for the rules that would govern that order. In the process, through a complex blend of multilateral negotiations and unilateral initiatives, they helped put in place a workable and durable international system. That Acheson and his compatriots constructed a global order that reflected U.S. values and protected U.S. material and security interests hardly surprises. That an international system rooted in American predominance achieved global legitimacy—at least outside the Sino-Soviet bloc—stands as one of their, and his, grandest achievements.

For Acheson, power had to be harnessed to purpose. Without power, he realized that one's purpose—however noble—was rendered ineffectual and meaningless. A careful student of power, Acheson proved himself a master in the attainment and purposive use of it. His close relationship with the president he served allowed Acheson to dominate the foreign policy decision-making process within the Truman administration to a degree that has rarely been matched, before or since, by a U.S. secretary of state. "The relationship between Truman and Acheson was probably the best between a president and his secretary of state in this century," Paul Nitze has observed. "They knew each other's thoughts and, more importantly, they had the deepest respect for each other. Mr. Truman realized that he needed someone with Dean's foreign policy experience and analytical mind, while Acheson realized that he needed Mr. Truman's down-to-earth commonsense qualities. . . . They worked together as a team."[2] The deep divisions and personal animosities that have characterized the national security teams of almost all U.S. presidential administrations over the past half century simply did not exist during the Truman administration, the short-lived reign of the combative Louis Johnson at the Pentagon excepted. Acheson strove assiduously to prevent such rifts from developing, all the while working to retain his enviable status as Truman's most valued and trusted adviser.

From 1949 to 1953 Truman deferred to Acheson on virtually all matters of strategic and diplomatic import. Earlier, during Acheson's tenure as undersecretary of state, he had become perhaps the most powerful number two man in the State Department's history. James Byrnes's frequent travels and rocky relationship with Truman strengthened Acheson's hand within the president's inner circle. With Brynes's dismissal at the end of 1946 and the ascension of George Marshall, Acheson became even more powerful. Marshall elevated him to the role of de facto chief of staff, leaving Acheson as an uncommonly influential undersecretary, a status buttressed by the former general's hectic travel schedule and his penchant for delegating responsibility to his trusted deputy on most key policy matters.

Acheson's power base at home derived as well from the effective working relationship that he cultivated with Congress, especially with senior leaders of both parties and with the ranking members of the Senate Foreign Relations Committee. The McCarthyite assault on his integrity from early 1950 onward harmed Acheson's relations with the legislative branch, to be sure, but never to the extent assumed by popular legend. His ability to gain strong congressional backing for almost all the major initiatives he lobbied Capitol Hill on behalf of, including the massive post–Korean War rearmament program and the long-term stationing of U.S. troops in Western Europe, offers unmistakable evidence of Acheson's undiminished skills as both lobbyist and policy salesman.

Viewing international history through a biographical lens allows author and reader alike to consider connections between a subject's policy decisions and that individual's personal makeup, background, formative influences, biases, values, and the like. In Acheson's case, as this narrative has suggested, that connection is strong. It cannot be emphasized enough that Acheson's overall worldview, his general habits of thought, and his approach to analyzing problems and reaching informed decisions about complex matters were all shaped at a tender age by three of the giants of American legal thought, and of modern intellectual life more broadly. Felix Frankfurter, Louis Brandeis, and Oliver Wendell Holmes influenced the young lawyer in countless ways. Collectively, the three men—each a dynamic, charismatic, and intellectually imposing figure in his own right—taught Acheson lessons about the law, politics, and life that would stand him in good stead throughout his career.

From them, he learned to approach issues, legal or otherwise, on their own terms, allowing the weight of the evidence about any particular question to be determinative. In Holmes's famous formulation, one that Acheson quickly took to heart and never forgot, general principles cannot decide concrete cases. Dogmatism and rigidity of thought, in short, were always to be avoided; instead, pragmatism, experience, and a rigorous analysis of the relevant facts at hand should be granted pride of place in the examination of any legal, political, or public policy matter. All three of these eminent legal scholars, two of whom were already on the Supreme Court and one of whom would be before long, took the young law student and clerk under their wings before he had even reached his mid-twenties. It is unlikely that any major twentieth-century statesman had the opportunity to learn at the feet of more eminent mentors than those who guided and inspired the young Acheson. His approach to diplomatic challenges throughout his career derived in significant measure, as this biography has argued, from modes of analysis and patterns of thought developed a generation before the Cold War came to dominate international affairs. Yet Acheson's approach to that Cold War, it bears emphasizing, cannot fully be understood without reference to the formative influences of those earlier years.

Acheson is commonly portrayed as the archetypal foreign policy realist of the Cold War era. Insofar as he believed that effective diplomacy meant the art of the possible, and that desired ends and available means needed at all times to be kept in balance, that characterization appears apt. As his hero Holmes is often tagged a legal realist, so Acheson—in similar fashion—can be termed a diplomatic realist. He certainly believed that the intentions and capabilities of adversaries and potential adversaries must be appraised with great care and that strategies must be devised to counter any potential hostile action that an opponent might undertake, given that opponent's available capabilities. Acheson frequently quoted Holmes to the effect that "the judgment of nature upon error is death." He found in that aphorism support for the notion that certain risks, in the life of a nation as in the life of an individual, simply should not be tempted when the consequences of guessing wrong could be fatal. When dealing, as in the case first of Nazi Germany and later of Soviet Russia, with an adversary of formidable military power, Acheson insisted that the United States must first build up its own military and productive strength. In typical realist fashion, Acheson was convinced that only a nation's existing military capabilities could serve to deter an adversary from aggressive action and, relatedly, that strength could pay diplomatic dividends by conferring leverage at the conference table.

Yet as appropriate as it might be to brand Acheson a realist, the label obscures as much as it reveals. The identification of a broad framework of analysis employed by certain historical actors cannot by itself explain why those individuals reacted as they did to particular issues and events. George F. Kennan is also commonly labeled a realist. Yet on some of the most important issues of the early Cold War—none more basic than the issue of German reunification—Acheson the realist and Kennan the realist found themselves on opposite sides. A framework sufficiently elastic to include Acheson and Kennan within it thus has severe limitations for the student of foreign policy. There can be no one "realist approach" to any truly complex issue, anymore than there can be a single "American approach."

A certain amount of romanticism and nostalgia inhered in Acheson's realism as well, a facet of his approach to international politics that contradicts classic precepts of realism and neorealism. Those precepts, as commonly theorized by international relations scholars, hold that policymakers, or "state actors," typically seek security for their state by striving to sustain a balance of power. Power-balancing, in this formulation, is rooted in the fundamental interests of states in preventing other individual states, or coalitions, from gaining a preponderance of power within the international system. A practitioner of realpolitik, consequently, aims at an equilibrium within the international system, an essentially amoral goal. For a scholar examining world affairs through a realist theoretical prism, as well presumably for most national leaders, the internal character of states rarely determines external behavior and hence need not be weighed as a major variable in strategic decision making. Yet Acheson does not fit that mold. He always strove, in the most fundamental sense, to re-create something approximating the Pax Britainica of the nineteenth century, which he often cited as the ideal of a functioning, inclusive world order. The international order he labored to construct grew, in part, from his nostalgic longing for the world of his youth, a pre–World War I era that he knew could never be restored. What he strove to help foster, in its place, was what he saw as the next best alternative: not a modern state system predicated on an amoral equilibrium of states with inherently conflicting interests, as a genuine realist would aspire to create, but rather "an environment in which our national life and individual freedom can survive and prosper."[3]

Such a world required not a balance of power, in the standard meaning of that concept, but a preponderance of *American* power. It required a truly global economic system, governed by the rule of law and the free flow of goods, investment capital, and ideas. Acheson believed it could be held in place only by a combination of superior American military power and international institutions dominated by liberal norms and lubricated by American capital. Such a global order would protect what Acheson liked to call a "political economy of freedom"–at home and abroad.

Toward the end of his first year as secretary of state, Acheson engaged in a quiet conversation with a friend, in the living room of his Georgetown home, about family life. "When you come right down to it, the purpose of foreign policy is to preserve the freedom of our homes," he said, "and also the freedom to do one's work, or move on and do one's work somewhere else. There are millions throughout the world with the same aspirations–to be allowed to live out their lives in their own way." Then, he suddenly shifted gears and brought up the greatest threat to that liberal vision of a free, orderly world. "War would end all this," he reflected. "War would mean regimentation–every man assigned to a hard task, dispersed industries, human beings living underground in caves like beasts, a nightmare. It would mean the very end of all freedom. Peace is freedom, and freedom is our life."[4]

It is tempting to end a biography of Acheson with some reductionist score-card on his diplomatic accomplishments and failures, strengths and weaknesses, prescience and short-sightedness. I will not succumb to that temptation. Ample evidence has been presented in the present narrative to enable readers to draw their own conclusions about where he succeeded and where he failed–both on his own terms and in the broader sweep of history. Acheson's story is not his story alone, at any rate; rather, it is the story of America's encounter with the wider world writ large, during a period in which the United States achieved the zenith of its power and influence. Acheson's presumptuousness, arrogance, and conceit about remaking the world in America's image were, in a broader sense, also those of the country that he so loved and whose interests he strove so mightily, if imperfectly, to advance. Some of his concrete achievements, however, were ones for which he, as much as anyone, deserves singular commendation. He helped forge durable multilateral institutions; fostered a historic Franco-German rapprochement; promoted effectively Western European unity; and, perhaps most of all, recognized and worked to counter the horrendously oppressive and illiberal consequences that Nazi or Soviet hegemony would surely have brought to the world as a whole. Those initiatives owe much to an outsized, iconoclastic, and irreverent man of uncommon wisdom, vision, and forthrightness.

NOTES

Chapter 1: Years of Preparation

1. For Acheson's family background, see especially Dean Acheson, *Morning and Noon: A Memoir* (Boston: Houghton Mifflin, 1965). See also David McLellan, *Dean Acheson: The State Department Years* (New York: Dodd, Mead, 1976); *Hartford Courant,* January 29, 1934.

2. Acheson, *Morning and Noon,* 1.

3. Ibid., 2–3, 23.

4. Ibid., 18–19, 24

5. Ibid., 25–26.

6. Quoted in Philip Hamburger, "Mr. Secretary–I," *New Yorker* 25 (November 12, 1949): 39.

7. Walter Isaacson and Evan Thomas, *The Wise Men: Six Friends and the World They Made: Acheson, Bohlen, Harriman, Kennan, Lovett, McCloy* (New York: Simon & Schuster, 1987), 55–56; James Chace, *Acheson: The Secretary of State Who Created the American World* (New York: Simon & Schuster, 1998), 22–25.

8. Acheson, *Morning and Noon,* 27–39.

9. Quoted in Isaacson and Thomas, *Wise Men,* 85.

10. Gaddis Smith, *Dean Acheson* (New York: Cooper Square, 1972), 4–6; Chace, *Acheson,* 33–34.

11. Isaacson and Thomas, *Wise Men,* 86.

12 Quoted in Philip Hamburger, "Mr. Secretary–II," *New Yorker* 25 (November 19, 1949): 41.

13. Quoted in McLellan, *Dean Acheson,* 10.

14. John Lamberton Harper, *American Visions of Europe: Franklin D. Roosevelt, George F. Kennan, and Dean G. Acheson* (New York: Cambridge University Press, 1994), 245.

15. McLellan, *Dean Acheson,* 12.

16. Quoted in Hamburger, "Mr. Secretary–I," 39.

17. Quoted in Isaacson and Thomas, *Wise Men,* 87.

18. Ibid., 89–90; McLellan, *Dean Acheson,* 13.

19. Quoted in McLellan, *Dean Acheson,* 16.

20. Acheson, *Morning and Noon,* 78–103.

21. Quoted in McLellan, *Dean Acheson,* 19.

22. Acheson to Frankfurter, November 16, 1920, folder 139, box 11, Dean Acheson Papers, Manuscripts and Archives, Yale University, New Haven, CT.

23. Remarks delivered at Brandeis's funeral service, October 7, 1941, in Dean Acheson, *Fragments of My Fleece* (New York: Norton, 1971), 213–15.

24. Acheson speech, May 25, 1956, folder 11, box 38, Acheson Papers, Yale.

25. Holmes to Harold Laski, November 29, 1919, in *Holmes-Laski Letters: The Correspondence of Mr. Justice Holmes and Harold J. Laski, 1916–1935,* ed. Mark De Wolfe Howe (New York: Atheneum, 1963), 1: 171.

26. Acheson, *Morning and Noon,* 62–65; Acheson to Michael Janeway, May 24, 1960, in *Among Friends: Personal Letters of Dean Acheson,* ed. David S. McLellan and David C. Acheson (New York: Dodd, Mead, 1980), 182–83.

27. Acheson to Ranald MacDonald, September 29, 1937, in *Among Friends,* 33.

28. Brandeis to Frankfurter, November 25, 1920, in *"Half Brother, Half Son": The Letters of Louis D. Brandeis to Felix Frankfurter,* ed. Melvin I. Urofsky and David W. Levy (Norman: University of Oklahoma Press, 1991), 66.

29. Acheson to John H. Vincent, December 27, 1919, in *Among Friends,* 4.

30. Acheson to Frankfurter, March 31, 1931, folder 141, box 11, Acheson Papers, Yale; Chace, *Acheson,* 56–57; Hamburger, "Mr. Secretary–II," 44–46.

31. Quoted in McLellan, *Dean Acheson,* 21.

32. Acheson, *Morning and Noon,* 155–59.

33. Ibid., 159–60.

34. Ibid., 161.

35. Ibid., 162; Brandeis to Frankfurter, April 26, 1933, in *"Half Brother, Half Son,"* 519.

36. *Newsweek,* October 7, 1933; *Baltimore Sun,* May 3, 1933; Acheson, *Morning and Noon,* 186–93.

37. Acheson, *Morning and Noon,* 163–65.

38. Ibid., 186–93; *Baltimore Sun,* November 15, 1933; *The Times* (London), November 15, 1933; Acheson to Roosevelt, November 1933, folder 165, box 13, Acheson Papers, Yale.

39. Acheson, *Morning and Noon,* 191.

40. Quoted in McLellan, *Dean Acheson,* 21.

41. Acheson to Prentiss B. Gilbert, February 13, 1934, folder 165, box 13, Acheson Papers, Yale.

42. Acheson to the editor, *Baltimore Sun,* October 17, 1936, folder: "Democratic Party: National Politics [1]," box 93, Dean Acheson Papers, Harry S. Truman Library (HSTL), Independence, MO; Acheson to Grenville Clark, October 31, 1936, ibid.

43. Acheson, *Morning and Noon,* 199–214.

44. Ibid., 215.

45. Acheson speech, "An American Attitude Toward Foreign Affairs," November 28, 1939, reprinted in ibid., 267–75.

46. His letters to law partner George Rublee offer some clues to his evolving views. See, for example, Acheson to Rublee, September 29, 1938, November 29, 1938, and January 17, 1939, folder 340, box 27, Acheson Papers, Yale.

47. Acheson speech, September 16, 1946, folder: "Classified Off the Record Speeches," box 73, Acheson Papers, HSTL.

48. Acheson speech, "Do You Mean Those Words?" June 4, 1940, reprinted in *Morning and Noon,* 217–22.

49. Ibid., 222–23; Acheson and others, letter to the *New York Times,* August 11, 1940, "Letter to the *New York Times* Regarding the Transfer of U.S. Destroyers" folder, box 134, Acheson Papers, HSTL; David Reynolds, *From Munich to Pearl Harbor: Roosevelt's America and the Origins of the Second World War* (Chicago: Ivan R. Dee, 2001), 85–87.

50. Acheson to McCloy, September 12, 1940, folder 261, box 21, Acheson Papers, Yale.

51. Acheson statement, "Shall We Give Further Aid to Great Britain?" Mutual Broadcasting System, American Forum of the Air, October 6, 1940, "American Forum of the Air" folder, box 134, Acheson Papers, HSTL.

52. Acheson to Alfred Winslow, October 28, 1940, folder 1, box 38, Acheson Papers, Yale.

53. Acheson, *Morning and Noon,* 225–26.

54. Quoted in Harper, *American Visions of Europe,* 260.

55. Acheson, *Morning and Noon,* 226–27.

Chapter 2: From World War to Cold War

1. *Washington Post,* January 24, 1941; *New York Times,* January 24, 1941; Dean Acheson, *Present at the Creation: My Years in the State Department* (New York: Norton, 1969), 17.

2. Acheson, *Present,* 15–16.

3. Ibid., 18.

4. Ibid., 19

5. Jonathan Utley, *Going to War With Japan, 1937–1941* (New York: McGraw-Hill, 1985).

6. Acheson, *Present,* 37–39.

7. Ibid., 48–63.

8. Acheson to Sir Frederick Leith-Ross of the British Treasury, July 22, 1941, "File #2, Post War–ER&EP," Records Relating to Wartime Relief, Acheson Records, Lot 1, Department of State Records, Record Group (RG) 59, National Archives (NA), College Park, MD; State Department memorandum to Acheson, Welles, and Hull, August 4, 1941, ibid.; Keynes to Acheson, July 29, 1941, folder 224, box 8, Acheson Papers, Yale; Acheson, *Present*, 29–33; Robert Skidelsky, *John Maynard Keynes*, vol. 3, *Fighting for Freedom, 1937–1946* (New York: Viking, 2000), 126–31.

9. Acheson, *Present*, 33.

10. Ibid., 34, 68–69; memorandum of conversation between Acheson and Litvinov, December 20, 1943, "File #2: Post War–ER & EP, May 7," Acheson Records, Lot 1, NA.

11. Acheson speech, "Post-War Economic Policy," undated (probably delivered in mid-1943), "Publication File, Draft File, 1941–1945, Correspondence General" folder, box 137, Acheson Papers, HSTL; Acheson testimony, November 30, 1944, U.S. House, Subcommittee on Foreign Trade and Shipping of the Special Committee on Post-War Economic Policy and Planning, *Post-War Economic Policy and Planning*, 78th Cong., 2nd sess. (Washington: U.S. Government Printing Office, 1944), 1071–98.

12. Acheson to Noel Hall, August 1, 1944, folder 188, box 15, Acheson Papers, Yale; Acheson testimony, June 13, 1945, U.S. Senate, Committee on Banking and Currency, *Bretton Woods Agreements Acts*, 79th Cong., 1st sess.(Washington: U.S. Government Printing Office, 1945), 37–38; Acheson, *Present*, 82–84.

13. Acheson, *Present*, 89–93, 101; Acheson to Donald Hiss, August 2, 1944, Miscellaneous folder, Committee on International Conferences, Acheson Records, Lot 56 D 419, NA.

14. Acheson to David Acheson, April 30, 1945, in *Among Friends*, 51.

15. Acheson, *Present*, 104.

16. Ibid., 88; Acheson to Mary Bundy, May 23 and 28, in *Among Friends*, 55; Acheson to Mary Bundy, July 20, 1945, folder 52, box 4, Acheson Papers, Yale.

17. Acheson to Mary Bundy, July 1, 1945, in *Among Friends*, 58.

18. Acheson, *Present*, 120.

19. Isaacson and Thomas, *Wise Men*, 322; Robert Beisner, "Patterns of Peril: Dean Acheson Joins the Cold Warriors, 1945–46," *Diplomatic History* 20 (Summer 1996): 324.

20. Acheson testimony, June 12 and 13, 1945, Senate Committee on Banking and Currency, *Bretton Woods Agreements Act*, 20–22, 37–38, 49.

21. Acheson, *Present*, 113.

22. Beisner, "Patterns of Peril," 326–29; Acheson, *Present*, 123–25; Isaacson and Thomas, *Wise Men*, 324–25.

23. Quoted in Beisner, "Patterns of Peril," 329.
24. Acheson speech, "American Soviet Friendship," November 14, 1945, *Vital Speeches of the Day* 12 (December 1, 1945): 110–12; Isaacson and Thomas, *Wise Men*, 339–40; Smith, *Dean Acheson*, 30–31; Beisner, "Patterns of Peril," 348–49.
25. Quoted in Beisner, "Patterns of Peril," 330.
26. Ibid., 330–31; Acheson, *Present*, 151–54.
27. Acheson to Joseph V. Machugh, October 23, 1947, "Atomic Energy, 1947–1948" folder, box 2, Acheson Papers, HSTL.
28. Acheson to Byrnes, August 15, 1946, *Foreign Relations of the United States*, 1946, 7: 840–42 (hereafter cited as *FRUS*, with the year and volume); Acheson to Truman, August 16, 1946, ibid., 843; Forrestal Diary Entry, August 15, 1946, *The Forrestal Diaries*, ed. Walter Millis (New York: Viking, 1951), 192; Melvyn P. Leffler, *A Preponderance of Power: National Security, the Truman Administration, and the Cold War* (Stanford, CA: Stanford University Press, 1992), 123–25.
29. Robert L. Beisner, *Dean Acheson: A Life in the Cold War* (New York: Oxford University Press, 2006), 43.
30. Transcript of Proceedings, Department of State, June 4, 1947, folder 13, box 47, Acheson Papers, Yale.
31. Acheson to the Embassy in Greece, October 15, 1946, *FRUS*, 1946, 7: 235–37.
32. Acheson, *Present*, 192; Felix Frankfurter diary entries, October 15 and 18, 1946, *From the Diaries of Felix Frankfurter*, ed. Joseph Lash (New York: Norton, 1975), 269.
33. Acheson, *Present*, 192.
34. Ibid., 200.
35. Ibid.
36. Acheson to Michael Janeway, May 24, 1960, in *Among Friends*, 182. For Acheson's admiring portrait of Marshall, see Dean Acheson, *Sketches From Life of Men I Have Known* (New York: Harper, 1959), 147–66.
37. Quoted in Isaacson and Thomas, *Wise Men*, 391.
38. Acheson, *Present*, 217.
39. Acheson to Marshall, February 21, 1947, *FRUS*, 1947, 5: 29–31; Acheson, *Present*, 217.
40. Quoted in Isaacson and Thomas, *Wise Men*, 393; Acheson to Marshall, February 24, 1947, *FRUS*, 1947, 5: 44–45.
41. Acheson, *Present*, 219.
42. Quoted in Isaacson and Thomas, *Wise Men*, 396. For the text of the Truman Doctrine, see *Public Papers of the Presidents* (*PPP*), Harry S. Truman, 1947 (Washington: U.S. Government Printing Office, 1948): 176–80.
43. Acheson statements, March 20, 1947, U.S. House, Committee on Foreign Affairs, and March 24, 1947, U.S. Senate, Committee on Foreign Relations, folder 12, box 47, Acheson Papers, Yale; Acheson testimony, March 13, April

1, and April 3, 1947, U.S. Senate, Committee on Foreign Relations, *Legislative Origins of the Truman Doctrine*, Hearings held in Executive Session, 80th Cong., 1st sess., Historical Series (Washington: U.S. Government Printing Office, 1973), 1–20, 78–98, 165–201; Acheson, *Present*, 224–25.

44. Acheson draft letter for Truman, May 5, 1947, "Memos for the President, January–July 1947" folder, Records of the Executive Secretariat, Acheson Records, Lot 53 D 444, RG 59, NA.

45. Acheson, *Present*, 226.

46. Ibid., 212.

47. Clayton to Acheson, May 27, 1947, *FRUS*, 1947, 5: 230–32.

48. Acheson speech, Department of State *Bulletin* 16 (May 11, 1947): 920, 924; Acheson, *Present*, 227–29.

49. Dean Acheson, *This Vast External Realm* (New York: Norton, 1973), 19.

50. Acheson, *Present*, 237.

51. Transcript of Proceedings, Department of State, June 4, 1947, folder 13, box 47, Acheson Papers, Yale.

52. Acheson, *Present*, 239.

Chapter 3: Constructing an Atlantic Community

1. Acheson, *Present*, 238–39.

2. Acheson to Philip W. Watts, December 9, 1957, in *Among Friends*, 133.

3. Michael Wala, "Selling the Marshall Plan at Home: The Committee for the Marshall Plan to Aid European Recovery," *Diplomatic History* 10 (Summer 1986): 247–65; Acheson, *Present*, 240–41.

4. Acheson talk, "Town Hall of the Air," October 14, 1947, "Marshall Plan Talks: Town Hall" folder, box 8, Acheson Papers, HSTL.

5. Rauh to Acheson, November 21, 1947, "Marshall Plan Talks: California, etc. [2]" folder, ibid.

6. Acheson speech, December 3, 1947, ibid.

7. *Report of the Portland Committee on Foreign Relations*, November 30, 1947, ibid.; Acheson speech, Atlantic City, January 21, 1948, "Atlantic City" folder, ibid.; Acheson press conference, December 22, 1947, folder 14, box 47, Acheson Papers, Yale.

8. *Report of the Portland Committee on Foreign Relations*.

9. *San Francisco Examiner*, November 29, 1947.

10. *New York Times*, November 29, 1947.

11. *Report of the Portland Committee on Foreign Relations*.

12. Acheson, testimony before the House of Representatives, January 28, 1948, "Com. for the MP–Press Releases [2]" folder, box 5, Acheson Papers, HSTL.

13. Butler to Truman, December 3, 1947, "Marshall Plan Talks: California, etc. [2]" folder, ibid.

14. Acheson, *Present*, 241–42.
15. Acheson address, Lansing, Michigan, September 30, 1948, folder 15, box 47, Acheson Papers, Yale; Acheson speech, National War College, September 16, 1948, "Classified Off the Record Speeches" folder, box 73, Acheson Papers, HSTL.
16. Isaacson and Thomas, *Wise Men*, 462.
17. Acheson, *Present*, 249–50.
18. Marshall to Acheson, January 7, 1949, folder 280, box 22, Acheson Papers, Yale; Acheson to Marshall, January 10, 1949, ibid.
19. Acheson, *Present*, 257, 259.
20. Leffler, *Preponderance*, 277–79; Acheson memorandum of conversation with Truman, January 24, 1949, Acheson's Memoranda of Conversations, Acheson Papers, HSTL.
21. Acheson statement, January 26, 1949, Department of State *Bulletin* 20 (February 26, 1949): 160.
22. Acheson, *Morning and Noon*, 40–41, 109, 121–22.
23. Acheson statement, January 26, 1949.
24. Dirk U. Stikker, *Men of Responsibility: A Memoir* (New York: Harper and Row, 1965), 223.
25. Memorandum of conversation between Acheson and Bonnet, February 14, 1949, *FRUS*, 1949, 4: 107–08.
26. Acheson to Caffrey, February 25, 1949, ibid., 122–24.
27. Memorandum of conversation between Truman and Acheson, February 28, 1949, ibid., 125.
28. Acheson memorandum of discussion with Truman, March 2, 1949, ibid., 141; Dean Acheson Oral History Interview, July 30, 1971, HSTL; memorandum of conversation between Acheson, Connally, and Vandenberg, February 28, 1949, Acheson's Memoranda of Conversations, Acheson Papers, HSTL.
29. Minutes of Fourteenth Meeting of the Washington Exploratory Talks on Security, March 1, 1949, *FRUS*, 1949, 4: 126–35; Hume Wrong (Canadian ambassador to the United States) to Canadian foreign minister Lester B. Pearson, March 1, 1949, *Documents on Canadian External Relations*, 15, 1949 (Ottawa: Minister of Supply and Services, 1995): 553–54 (hereafter cited as *DCER*).
30. Acheson memorandum of discussion with Truman, March 2, 1949, *FRUS*, 1949, 4: 141–42.
31. Escott Reid, *Time of Fear and Hope: The Making of the North Atlantic Treaty, 1947–1949* (Toronto: McClelland and Stewart, 1977), 58. For a similar observation, see Lester B. Pearson, *Mike: The Memoirs of the Right Honourable Lester B. Pearson*, vol. 2, *1948–1957* (Toronto: University of Toronto Press, 1972), 56–57.
32. Minutes of the Sixteenth and Eighteenth Meetings of the Washington Exploratory

Talks on Security, March 7, 1949, *FRUS,* 1949, 4: 166–74, 213–24; Acheson to Truman, March 8, 1949, ibid., 174.

33. Acheson address, "The Meaning of the North Atlantic Pact," March 18, 1949, Department of State *Bulletin* 20 (March 27, 1949): 384–88.

34. Truman telegram, March 19, 1949, ibid., 388.

35. Acheson remarks, April 4, 1949, Department of State *Bulletin* 20 (April 17, 1949): 471. The "Lincolnesque" compliment was from British ambassador Lord Halifax, in Halifax to Acheson, April 7, 1949, folder 187, box 15, Acheson Papers, Yale.

36. Truman address, April 4, 1949, Department of State *Bulletin* 20 (April 17, 1949): 481–82.

37. Memorandum of conversation between Acheson, Bohlen, Connally, and Vandenberg, February 14, 1949, *FRUS,* 1949, 4: 109.

38. Kennan paper, March 8, 1949, *FRUS,* 1949, 3: 96–102

39. Wilson D. Miscamble, "Rejected Architect and Master Builder: George Kennan, Dean Acheson and Postwar Europe," *Review of Politics* 58 (Summer 1996): 437–68; Melvyn Leffler, "Negotiating From Strength: Acheson, the Russians, and American Power," in *Dean Acheson and the Making of U.S. Foreign Policy,* ed. Douglas Brinkley (New York: St. Martin's, 1993), 188–90.

40. Acheson, *Sketches,* 1–59.

41. Memorandum of conversation between Truman, Acheson, Bevin, and Schuman, *FRUS,* 1949, 3: 173–75; William I. Hitchcock, *France Restored: Cold War Diplomacy and the Quest for Leadership in Europe, 1944–1954* (Chapel Hill: University of North Carolina Press, 1998), 110–12.

42. Acheson to Truman, April 8, 1949, *FRUS,* 1949, 3: 176.

43. Memorandum of conversation between Jessup and Malik, April 11, 1949, ibid., 717–20; Leffler, *Preponderance,* 282–84.

44. Acheson to Jessup, May 18, 1949, *FRUS,* 1949, 3: 884–85; Leffler, *Preponderance,* 283–84.

45. Acheson testimony, May 19, 1949, U.S. Senate, Committee on Foreign Relations, Hearings held in Executive Session, *Reviews of the World Situation, 1949–1950,* 81st Cong., 1st and 2nd sess., Historical Series (Washington: U.S. Government Printing Office, 1974), 2–22.

46. Diary entry, May 19, 1949 in *The Private Papers of Senator Vandenberg,* ed. Arthur H. Vandenberg Jr. (Boston: Houghton Mifflin, 1952), 485.

47. Acheson to Truman and Webb, June 11, 1949, *FRUS,* 1949, 3: 977–79; Acheson testimony, January 10, 1950, Senate Committee on Foreign Relations, *Reviews of the World Situation,* 114; Acheson, *Present,* 297.

48. Acheson, *Present,* 301.

49. Acheson remarks, June 22 and 23, 1949, Department of State *Bulletin* 21 (July 4, 1949): 858–61.

50. Leffler, *Preponderance*, 385; Acheson testimony, June 22, 1949, Senate Committee on Foreign Relations, *Reviews of the World Situation*, 23–49.
51. Acheson, *Present*, 308.
52. Acheson testimony, August 8, 1949, U.S. Senate, Committee on Foreign Relations, and U.S. House, Committee on Armed Services, *Military Assistance Program*, 81st Cong., 1st sess. (Washington, DC: U.S. Government Printing Office, 1949), 10, 12–13.
53. Acheson testimony, August 5, 1949, U.S. Senate, Joint Committee on Armed Services and Foreign Relations, Joint Hearings held in Executive Session, *Military Assistance Program: 1949*, 81st Cong., 1st sess., Historical Series (Washington, DC: U.S. Government Printing Office, 1974), 51.

Chapter 4: Into the Cauldron

1. Dean Rusk, *As I Saw It* (New York: Norton, 1990), 422.
2. Department of State *Bulletin* 16 (May 11, 1947): 920, 924.
3. On Japan's centrality for Acheson, see especially Michael Schaller, *The American Occupation of Japan: The Origins of the Cold War in Asia* (New York: Oxford University Press, 1985); Ronald McGlothlen, *Controlling the Waves: Dean Acheson and U.S. Foreign Policy in Asia* (New York: Norton, 1993), 17–49.
4. Acheson, *Present*, 257.
5. Quoted in Isaacson and Thomas, *Wise Men*, 5.
6. Acheson testimony, March 18, 1949, U.S. Senate, Committee on Foreign Relations, Hearings Held in Executive Session, *Economic Assistance to China and Korea*, 81st Cong., 1st sess., Historical Series (Washington: U.S. Government Printing Office, 1974), 27–28.
7. Quoted in Nancy Bernkopf Tucker, *Patterns in the Dust: Chinese-American Relations and the Recognition Controversy, 1949-1950* (New York: Columbia University Press, 1983), 165.
8. Quoted in Chace, *Acheson*, 217.
9. Ibid.; Beisner, *Acheson*, 178–79.
10. Acheson testimony, March 18, 1949, Senate Committee on Foreign Relations, *Economic Assistance to China and Korea*, 38–40.
11. Quoted in Tucker, *Patterns in the Dust*, 163.
12. Tang Tsou, *America's Failure in China, 1941-50* (Chicago: University of Chicago Press, 1963), 2: 501.
13. Department of State, *United States Relations With China: With Special Reference to the Period 1944-1949* (Washington: U.S. Government Printing Office, 1949); letter of transmittal from Acheson to Truman, July 30, 1949, Department of State *Bulletin* 21 (August 8, 1949): 279–84.
14. Quoted in Chace, *Acheson*, 220.
15. Quoted in Tang Tsou, *America's Failure*, 2: 509.

16. Beisner, *Acheson*, 188.

17. Acheson, *Present*, 302–03.

18 *United States Relations With China*; Acheson statement, Department of State *Bulletin* 21 (August 15, 1949): 236–37; Leffler, *Preponderance*, 295–97.

19. Quoted in Keith D. McFarland and David L. Roll, *Louis Johnson and the Arming of America: The Roosevelt and Truman Years* (Bloomington: Indiana University Press, 2005), 256–57.

20. Acheson, *Present*, 345.

21. Department of State *Bulletin* 21 (October 3, 1949): 487.

22. Leffler, *Preponderance*, 325–26; Leffler, "Negotiating From Strength," 193–94.

23. Memorandum of conversation between Acheson, Schuman, and Bevin, *FRUS*, 1949, 3: 599–603.

24. Acheson to Schuman, October 30, 1949, ibid., 622–25.

25. Acheson to Truman and Acting Secretary of State James Webb, November 11, 1949, ibid., 635.

26. Konrad Adenauer, *Memoirs, 1945–1953*, trans. Beate Ruhm von Oppen (Chicago: H. Regnery, 1966), 206.

27. Acheson, *Present*, 341–42; memorandum of conversation between Acheson and Adenauer, November 13, 1949, *FRUS*, 1949, 3: 308–11; Kai Bird, *The Chairman: John J. McCloy, the Making of the American Establishment* (New York: Simon & Schuster, 1992), 325–26.

28. Acheson, *Present*, 338; Acheson testimony, June 22, 1949, Senate Committee on Foreign Relations, *Reviews of the World Situation, 1949–1950*, 42; Adenauer, *Memoirs*, 206–8.

29. Acheson, *Present*, 345–46.

30. Beisner, *Acheson*, 232; Steven L. Rearden, "Frustrating the Kremlin Design: Acheson and NSC 68," in *Dean Acheson and the Making*, 159–75.

31. Lilienthal Diary entry, January 31, 1950, *The Journals of David E. Lilienthal*, vol. 2, *The Atomic Energy Years, 1945–1950* (New York: Harper & Row, 1964), 623–33; Paul H. Nitze, *From Hiroshima to Glasnost: At the Center of Decision: A Memoir* (New York: G. Weidenfeld, 1989), 87–91; Beisner, *Acheson*, 233.

32. Rearden, "Frustrating the Kremlin Design."

33. Study prepared by Nitze, February 8, 1950, *FRUS*, 1950, 1: 145–47.

34. Memorandum of conversation between Acheson, Webb, Nitze, and others, March 7, 1950, Acheson's Memoranda of Conversations, Acheson Papers, HSTL.

35. Memorandum of conversation between Acheson and Herter, March 24, 1950, *FRUS*, 1950, 1: 206–09.

36. Record of meeting of the State-Defense Policy Review Group, March 16, 1950, ibid., 196–99.

37. For the full text of NSC 68, see ibid., 235–92.

38. Michael J. Hogan, *Cross of Iron: Harry S. Truman and the Origins of the National Security State, 1945-1954* (New York: Cambridge University Press, 1998), 303–04; Leffler, *Preponderance*, 355–60.

39. Quoted in Beisner, *Acheson*, 305.

40. Quoted in ibid.

41. James T. Patterson, *Mr. Republican: A Biography of Robert A. Taft* (Boston: Houghton Mifflin, 1972), 442–43.

42. Acheson testimony, January 10, 1950, Senate Committee on Foreign Relations, *Reviews of the World Situation, 1949-1950*, 130–34; Beisner, *Acheson*, 198–99.

43. Quoted in Patterson, *Mr. Republican*, 453.

44. Department of State *Bulletin* 22 (January 23, 1950): 111–16.

45. See, for example, William W. Stueck, *Rethinking the Korean War: A New Diplomatic and Strategic History* (Princeton, NJ: Princeton University Press, 2002).

46. Acheson, *Present*, 359–61; Beisner, *Acheson*, 281–98; Lilienthal Diary entry, January 26, 1950, *Journals of David E. Lilienthal*, 2: 58–63.

47. *Newsweek*, February 6, 1950.

48. McLellan, *Acheson*, 220; Richard M. Fried, *Men Against McCarthy* (New York: Columbia University Press, 1976), 14.

49. Quoted in Fried, *Men Against McCarthy*, 43.

50. Quoted in David M. Oshinsky, *A Conspiracy So Immense: The World of Joe McCarthy* (New York: Oxford University Press, 2005), 108–09; Beisner, *Acheson*, 305.

51. Quoted in Beisner, *Acheson*, 306.

52. Clifford to Acheson, March 21, 1950, folder 78, box 6, Acheson Papers, Yale.

53. Acheson to Stimson, March 27, 1950, in *Among Friends*, 68.

54. Lilienthal Diary entry, January 6, 1951, *Journals of David E. Lilienthal*, vol. 3, *Venturesome Years, 1950-1955* (New York: Harper & Row, 1966), 58–63.

55. Isaacson and Thomas, *Wise Men*, 494; Eric Sevareid comment, CBS radio, January 14, 1953, Scrapbook Items folder, box 59, Acheson Papers, HSTL.

56. David C. Acheson, *Acheson Country: A Memoir* (New York: Norton, 1993).

57. Quoted in Beisner, *Acheson*, 276.

58. Acheson to Oliver Franks, December 24, 1949, *FRUS*, 1949, 7: 927.

59. Acheson testimony, January 10, 1950, Senate Committee on Foreign Relations, *Reviews of the World Situation, 1949-1950*, 152–54; Schaller, *American Occupation*, 193, 213–14.

60. Quoted in Patrick J. Hearden, *The Tragedy of Vietnam* (New York: HarperCollins, 1991), 41.

61. Quoted in Andrew J. Rotter, *The Path to Vietnam: Origins of the American Commitment to Southeast Asia* (Ithaca, NY: Cornell University Press, 1987), 54.

62. Robert J. McMahon, *Colonialism and Cold War: The United States and the Struggle for Indonesian Independence, 1945-49* (Ithaca, NY: Cornell University Press, 1981).

63. Memorandum of conversation between Acheson and Stikker, March 31, 1949, *FRUS*, 1949, 4: 258–61; memorandum of conversation between Acheson and Bevin, April 4, 1949, *FRUS*, 1949, 6: 51–54; McMahon, *Colonialism and Cold War*, 292–94; Cees Wiebes and Bert Zeeman, "United States 'Big Stick' Diplomacy: The Netherlands Between Decolonization and Alignment, 1945–1949," *International History Review* 14 (February 1992): 45–70.

64. Acheson, *Present*, 673.

65. Editorial note, *FRUS*, 1950, 6: 711; Problem Paper prepared in the State Department, ibid., 711–15.

66. Department of State *Bulletin* 22 (February 20, 1950): 291–92; memorandum of conversation between Acheson and Romulo, *FRUS*, 1950, 6: 752–53.

67. Mark Atwood Lawrence, *Assuming the Burden: Europe and the American Commitment to War in Vietnam* (Berkeley: University of California Press, 2005), 272.

68. Acheson to the State Department, May 8, 1950, *FRUS*, 1950, 3: 1007–1013; Lawrence, *Assuming the Burden*, 272–73.

69. Department of State *Bulletin* 21 (October 31, 1949): 668.

70. Acheson testimony, October 12, 1949, Senate Committee on Foreign Relations, *Reviews of the World Situation, 1949–1950*, 90.

71. Acheson, *Present*, 402–4; memorandum of telephone conversation between Acheson and Truman, June 24, 1950, George M. Elsey Papers, HSTL.

72. Acheson, *Present*, 405.

73. Ibid.

74. Acheson testimony, January 30, 1950, U.S. House, Committee on International Relations, *United States Policy in the Far East, Pt. 2*, Selected Executive Session Hearings of the Committee, 81st Cong., 2nd sess., Historical Series (Washington, DC: U.S. Government Printing Office, 1976), 8: 406–07.

75. Acheson dictation, May 10, 1951, "MacArthur–Testimony Re" folder, box 64, Acheson Papers, HSTL.

76 Quoted in Robert J. Donovan, *Tumultuous Years: The Presidency of Harry S Truman, 1949–1953* (New York: Norton, 1982), 197.

77. Memorandum of Blair House meeting, June 25, 1950, *FRUS*, 7: 157–61.

78. Bruce to Acheson, June 26, 1950, ibid., 175–76.

79. Memorandum of Blair House meeting, June 26, 1950, ibid., 178–83; Acheson, *Present*, 407–08.

Chapter 5: The Crucible of War

1. Acheson remarks, July 21, 1950, Department of State *Bulletin* 23 (July 31, 1950): 171–72.

2. Hogan, *Cross of Iron*, 267–68, 283–85.

3. McFarland and Roll, *Louis Johnson*, 224–25, 231–33; Nitze, *From Hiroshima to Glasnost*, 105.

4. Schaub to James Lay, Executive Secretary of the NSC, *FRUS*, 1950, 1: 299–305; McFarland and Roll, *Louis Johnson*, 224–25, 231–33.

5. Quoted in Leffler, *Preponderance*, 366.

6. Acheson, *Present*, 374. See also Robert Jervis, "The Impact of the Korean War on the Cold War," *Journal of Conflict Resolution* 24 (December 1980): 563–92.

7. Symington to the NSC, July 6, 1950, *FRUS*, 1950, 1: 338–41.

8. Record of cabinet meeting, July 14, 1950, Acheson's Memoranda of Conversations, Acheson Papers, HSTL; Hogan, *Cross of Iron*, 344–46.

9. Truman message, July 19, 1950, *PPP*, 1950: 527–37.

10. Acheson statement, August 2, 1950, U.S. House, Armed Services Subcommittee of the Committee on Appropriations, in *Documents on American Foreign Relations, 1950*, eds. Raymond Dennett and Robert K. Turners (Princeton, NJ: Princeton University Press, 1951), 12: 146–49.

11. Acheson memorandum of meeting with congressional leaders, August 14, 1950, Acheson's Memoranda of Conversations, Acheson Papers, HSTL.

12. Truman statement, August 1, 1950, *PPP*, 564–66; Hogan, *Cross of Iron*, 305–6.

13. Acheson's notes for congressional testimony, undated, *FRUS*, 1950, 1: 393–97.

14. Acheson testimony, August 31, 1950, U.S. Senate, Committee on Appropriations, *Supplemental Appropriations for 1951*, 81st Cong., 2nd sess. (Washington, DC: U.S. Government Printing Office, 1950), 268–69.

15. Acheson testimony, September 11, 1950, U.S. Senate, Committee on Foreign Relations, *Reviews of the World Situation: 1949–1950*, 342–43.

16. Acheson testimony, U.S. Senate, Committee on Appropriations, *Supplemental Appropriations for 1951*, 271.

17. Acheson, *Present*, 436; Douglas to Acheson, July 12, 1950, *FRUS*, 1950, 3: 130–32.

18. Acheson to certain diplomatic officers, July 22, 1950, ibid., 138–41.

19. Bruce to Acheson, July 28, 1950, ibid., 151–59; McCloy to Acheson, August 3, 1950, ibid., 180–83.

20. Acheson testimony, May 1, 1950, U.S. Senate, Committee on Foreign Relations, *Reviews of the World Situation, 1949–1950*, 291; Acheson testimony, June 5, 1950, U.S. House, Committee on Foreign Affairs, *To Amend the Mutual Defense Assistance Act of 1949*, 81st Cong., 1st sess. (Washington, DC: U.S. Government Printing Office, 1950), 22; Acheson, *Present*, 436–37.

21. Memorandum by Acheson of conversation with Truman, July 31, 1950, *FRUS*, 1950, 3: 167–68.

22. Memorandum of conversation between Acheson and Schuman, September 12, 1950, ibid., 287–88; memorandum of conversation between Acheson, Schuman, and Bevin, September 14, 1950, ibid., 299–300; Acheson to Truman, September 14, 1950, ibid., 301–02.

23. Acheson's remarks, contained in telegram from Acheson to Webb, September 17, 1950, ibid., 316–20.

24. Memorandum of conversation between Webb and Truman, September 25, 1950, ibid., 353–54

25. Acheson testimony, June 2, 1950, in McGeorge Bundy, ed., *The Pattern of Responsibility, from the Record of Secretary of State Dean Acheson* (Boston: Houghton Mifflin, 1951), 115.

26. Memorandum of conversation between Acheson, Marshall, and others, October 5, 1950, *FRUS*, 1950, 3: 358–61; Acheson's notes of a meeting with Lovett, October 10, 1950, Acheson's Memoranda of Conversations, Acheson Papers, HSTL.

27. Acheson testimony, cited in Bundy, *Pattern*, 119–20.

28. Paul-Henri Spaak, *The Continuing Battle: Memoirs of a European, 1936–1966* (Boston: Little, Brown, 1971), 155.

29. Acheson testimony, November 28, 1950, Senate Committee on Foreign Relations, *Reviews of the World Situation*, 376–78.

30. JCS Directive to MacArthur, contained in Webb to the U.S. Mission at the UN, September 26, 1950, *FRUS*, 1950, 7: 781–82; Acheson, *Present*, 452–53.

31. Acheson, *Present*, 445.

32. CIA memorandum, October 12, 1950, *FRUS*, 7: 933–34.

33. Quoted in Chace, *Acheson*, 299.

34. Bevin to Franks, November 14, 1950, *Documents on British Policy Overseas*, Series 2, eds. H. J. Yasamee and K. A. Hamilton (London: Her Majesty's Stationery Office, 1991): 4: 202–04; Bevin to Franks, November 22, 1950, ibid., 212–14; Pearson, *Memoirs*, 2: 159–61, 64.

35. Acheson, *Present*, 447.

36. Quoted in Isaacson and Thomas, *Wise Men*, 530.

37. Acheson to Truman, July 25, 1955, in *Among Friends*, 103.

38. Quoted in Isaacson and Thomas, *Wise Men*, 541.

39. Notes on NSC meeting, November 28, 1950, *FRUS*, 1950, 7: 1246–47; notes of a meeting at the Pentagon, December 3, 1950, ibid., 1324–26.

40. Acheson, *Present*, 487; Chace, *Acheson*, 325–26; minutes of NAC meetings, December 18 and 19, 1950, *FRUS*, 1950, 3: 585–604.

41. Department of State *Bulletin* 24 (January 1, 1951): 3–6.

42. Truman statement, December 1, 1950, *PPP*, 564–66; Hogan, *Cross of Iron*, 305–06.

43. Quoted in Hogan, *Cross of Iron*, 311. See also the revised policy statement approved by the president at that meeting: NSC 68/4, December 14, 1950, *FRUS*, 1950, 1: 467–74.

44. Acheson off-the-record remarks, December 14, 1950, "Classified Off the Record Speeches [1]" folder, Box 73, Acheson Papers, HSTL.

45. Study by the Joint Chiefs of Staff, January 15, 1951, *FRUS*, 1951, 1: 62–75.

46. Notes of a meeting at the Pentagon, December 3, 1950, *FRUS*, 1950, 7: 1326.

47. Minutes of meeting on MacArthur testimony, May 18, 1951, "MacArthur–Testimony Re" folder, Box 64, Acheson Papers, HSTL.

48. Quoted in Oshinsky, *Conspiracy So Immense*, 194–96.

49. Acheson statement, June 1, 1951, U.S. Senate, Hearings before the Committees on Armed Services and Foreign Relations, *Military Situation in the Far East*, 82nd Cong., 1st sess. (Washington, DC: U.S. Government Printing Office, 1951), 1714 ff.

50. Chace, *Acheson*, 260–62; Acheson, *Present*, 431–32.

51. Dulles to Acheson, December 8, 1950, *FRUS*, 1950, 6: 1359–60; Ronald Pruessen, *John Foster Dulles: The Road to Power* (New York: Free Press, 1982), 467–68.

52. Acheson to Louis Johnson, September 7, 1950, with enclosure, *FRUS*, 1950, 6: 1293–96; Acheson, *Present*, 434–35.

53. Acheson to Marshall, with enclosures, January 9, 1951, *FRUS*, 1951, 6, pt. 1: 787–89; editorial note, ibid., 137.

54. Acheson, *Present*, 540; *FRUS*, 1951, 6, pt. 1: 790–967.

55. Memorandum by Dulles, April 12, 1951, ibid., 972–76.

56. Memorandum by Acheson of a meeting with Gen. Omar Bradley and Robert Lovett, June 29, 1951, ibid., 1163–64.

57. Acheson to Truman, June 28, 1951, ibid., 1159–61; Acheson to Truman, August 29, 1951, ibid., 1300–1301.

58. Acheson, *Present*, 542–48.

59. *Conference for the Conclusion and Signature of the Treaty of Peace With Japan: Record of Proceedings* (Washington, DC: U.S. Government Printing Office, 1951), 308–9.

60. Acheson speech, "The International Scene," August 27, 1951, "Classified Off the Record Speeches" folder, box 73, Acheson Papers, HSTL.

61. Peter Hahn, *The United States, Great Britain, and Egypt, 1945–1956: Strategy and Diplomacy in the Early Cold War* (Chapel Hill: University of North Carolina Press, 1990), 93–130; Leffler, *Preponderance*, 286–91, 419–26.

62. Quoted in Hahn, *United States, Great Britain, and Egypt*, 136–37.

63. Quoted in David S. Painter, *Oil and the American Century: The Political Economy of U.S. Foreign Oil Policy, 1941–1954* (Baltimore: Johns Hopkins University Press, 1986), 175.

64. Statement of U.S. Position on the Iranian Oil Situation, May 18, 1951, in *Documents on American Foreign Relations, 1951*, eds. Raymond Dennett and Katherine D. Durant (Princeton, NJ: Princeton University Press, 1953) 13: 588–89

65. NSC 107/2, June 27, 1951, *FRUS*, 1952–1954, 10: 71–76.

66. Harriman's handwritten notes, undated, "Iran: Diary & Notes, 1951" folder, box 292, W. Averell Harriman Papers, Library of Congress (LC), Washington,

DC; Harriman's memoranda of conversations with Mosaddeq, July 16–August 24, 1951, "Iran–Memoranda of Conversations, 1951" folder, ibid.

67. Memorandum of conversation between Acheson and Truman, October 10, 1951, *FRUS*, 1952–1954, 10: 222–24.

68. Memorandum of conversation between Churchill, Eden, Truman, Acheson, and others, January 6, 1952, Acheson's Memoranda of Conversations, Acheson Papers, HSTL.

69. Memorandum of conversation between Acheson and Eden, January 9, 1952, *FRUS*, 1952–1954, 10: 311–20.

70. Acheson, *Present*, 766–67; Hahn, *United States, Great Britain, and Egypt*, 140–43.

71. Acheson address, December 22, 1950, Department of State *Bulletin* 24 (January 1, 1951): 3–6.

72. Acheson statement, U.S. Senate, Committees on Foreign Relations and Armed Services, February 16, 1951, in ibid. (February 26, 1951): 323–28. See also Leffler, *Preponderance*, 407; Bundy, *Pattern*, 83–100.

73. Acheson statement, February 16, 1951. For the full hearings, see U.S. Senate, Committee on Foreign Relations, *Assignment of Ground Forces of the United States to Duty in the European Area*, 82nd Cong., 1st sess. (Washington, DC: U.S. Government Printing Office, 1951).

74. Acheson to Griswold, June 27, 1951, in *Among Friends*, 71.

75. Quoted in Harper, *American Visions of Europe*, 308.

76. Acheson memorandum, July 6, 1951, *FRUS*, 1951, 3: 813–19.

77. Memorandum of conversation between Acheson, Marshall, and others, July 16, 1951, ibid., 836–38.

78. Acheson and Lovett to Truman, July 30, 1951, ibid., 849–52; editorial note, ibid., 847–49.

79. Acheson, *Present*, 558.

80. Records of Acheson, Bevin, and Schuman meetings, September 12, 13, and 14, 1951, *FRUS*, 1951, 3: 1268–90.

81. Acheson to Truman, November 30, 1951, ibid., 747–51.

82. Pearson, circular dispatch on the Rome meeting, December 8, 1951, *DCER*, 17, 1951: 993.

83. Acheson, *Present*, 609.

84. Harper, *American Visions of Europe*, 314.

85. *FRUS*, 1952–1954, 5, pt. 1: 150–175; Final Communiqué of the 9th Session of the NAC, February 26, 1952, ibid., 177–79.

86. Acheson to Truman, February 26, 1952, ibid., 175–76; Acheson, *Present*, 625–26.

87. McCloy to Acheson, April 15, 1952, folder 261, box 21, Acheson Papers, Yale.

88. Acheson to the Embassy in France, March 17, 1952, *FRUS*, 1952–1954, 7, pt. 1: 183–84.

89. Acheson to Truman, May 26, 1952, ibid., 680–84; memorandum of conversation between Truman and Acheson, May 22, 1952, ibid., 671–72.

90. Acheson, *Sketches*, 53–55.

91. Acheson to Dunn, November 8, 1952, *FRUS*, 1952–1954, 6, pt. 2: 1276–78.

92. Pearson to the Delegation at the UN General Assembly, November 22, 1952, *DCER*, 18, 1952: 1372–74; Acheson memorandum of meeting with the Canadian cabinet, November 22, 1952, Acheson Memoranda of Conversations, Acheson Papers, HSTL.

93. Memorandum of conversation between Acheson and Monnet, December 14, 1952, *FRUS*, 1952–1954, 6, pt. 1: 254–55.

94. Acheson, *Present*, 720–21.

Chapter 6: Elder Statesman

1. Acheson to Philip and Lois Jessup, February 17, 1953, Acheson folder, box 3, Philip C. Jessup Papers, Library of Congress, Washington, DC.

2. Acheson to Ned Burling, February 2, 1953, in *Among Friends*, 77.

3. Acheson to Jeffrey C. Kitchen, February 13, 1953, in ibid., 79.

4. Acheson to Burling, March 8, 1953, folder 270, box 21, Acheson Papers, Yale.

5. Acheson to David and Pat Acheson, February 7, 1953, folder 4, box 1, ibid.

6. Acheson to the Jessups, February 17 and 24, 1953, Acheson folder, Jessup Papers.

7. Acheson to the MacLeishes, March 26, 1953, folder 270, box 21, Acheson Papers, Yale.

8. Acheson to Truman, April 14, 1953, in *Among Friends*, 82–83.

9. Acheson to Truman, May 28, 1953, in ibid., 83–84.

10. Acheson to Battle, August 6, 1953, in ibid., 89.

11. Acheson to Truman, July 21, 1953, in ibid., 85–88.

12. Acheson speech, October 1, 1953, in *Documents on American Foreign Relations, 1953*, ed. Peter V. Curl (New York: Harper and Brothers, 1954), 15: 114–20.

13. Douglas Brinkley, *Dean Acheson: The Cold War Years, 1953–71* (New Haven: Yale University Press, 1992), 19; Acheson to Battle, December 4, 1953, folder 26, box 2, Acheson Papers, Yale.

14. Chase, *Acheson*, 368–69.

15. Acheson to Oliver Franks, December 28, 1953, folder 148, box 12, Acheson Papers, Yale; Acheson to Battle, December 4, 1953, folder 26, box 2, ibid.

16. Quoted in Brinkley, *Cold War Years*, 21; Dean Acheson, "Instant Retaliation: The Debate Continued," *New York Times Magazine*, March 28, 1954.

17. Acheson to Charles B. Gary, February 25, 1955, folder 161, box 13, Acheson Papers, Yale.

18. Frankfurter to Acheson, January 7, 1957, folder 289, box 23, ibid.

19. Acheson to Battle, May 2, 1955, folder 28, box 2, ibid.

20. Brinkley, *Cold War Years*, 39–40.
21. Ibid., 38–39, 47.
22. Acheson to the MacLeishes, March 1, 1956, folder 270, box 21, Acheson Papers, Yale.
23. Acheson to Frank Altschul, October 4, 1956, in *Among Friends*, 116–17.
24. The lectures were subsequently published as Dean Acheson, *Power and Diplomacy* (Cambridge: Harvard University Press, 1958). The quote is on p. 114.
25. Quoted in Brinkley, *Cold War Years*, 45.
26. *New York Times*, March 26, 1956.
27. Acheson to Francis and Priscilla O. Allen, undated (probably early 1957), folder 7, box 1, Acheson Papers, Yale.
28. Brinkley, *Cold War Years*, 54–58.
29. George F. Kennan, *Russia, the Atom, and the West* (New York: Harper, 1958).
30. *Washington Post*, January 12, 1958; Brinkley, *Cold War Years*, 82–84.
31. Quoted in Brinkley, *Cold War Years*, 82.
32. Dean Acheson, "The Illusion of Disengagement," *Foreign Affairs* 36 (April 1958): 371–82.
33. Acheson to Jessup, March 25, 1958, Acheson folder, box 3, Jessup Papers.
34. Acheson, *Power and Diplomacy*, 7.
35. Brinkley, *Cold War Years*, 106–07.
36. Acheson to Frankfurter, December 7, 1958, folder 146, box 11, Acheson Papers, Yale; Acheson Oral History Interview, April 27, 1964, by Lucius Battle, 1–2, Oral History Program, John F. Kennedy Library (JFKL), Boston, MA.
37. Acheson, *Power and Diplomacy*, 121–27.
38. Memorandum by Acheson of a conversation with Truman, June 30, 1960, folder 11, box 68, Acheson Papers, Yale; Acheson to Truman, August 12, 1960, in *Among Friends*, 190–91; Acheson Oral History Interview, 2–3, JFKL.
39. Quoted in Brinkley, *Cold War Years*, 112.
40. Acheson Oral History Interview, JFKL, 5–9; Chace, *Acheson*, 382–83; Acheson to Dirk U. Stikker, December 27, 1960, in *Among Friends*, 200–201.
41. Quoted in Isaacson and Thomas, *Wise Men*, 609.
42. Policy Directive, "NATO and the Atlantic Nations," April 20, 1961, *FRUS*, 1961–1963, 13: 285–91.
43. Quoted in Brinkley, *Cold War Years*, 94.
44. Acheson to Frankfurter, December 12, 1958, in *Among Friends*, 151–52.
45. Dean Acheson, "Wishing Won't Hold Berlin," *Saturday Evening Post*, March 17, 1959.
46. Acheson to Johnson, March 17, 1959, folder 215, box 17, Acheson Papers, Yale.
47. Acheson to Kennedy, April 3, 1961, *Declassified Document Reference Service* (1985), 2547.
48. Memorandum of conversation, April 5, 1961, *FRUS*, 1961–1963, 14: 36–40.

49. Acheson to Kennedy and Rusk, April 10, 1961, ibid., 13: 269–72; Acheson to Kennedy and Rusk, April 20, 1961, ibid., 291–95; NATO Mission to the State Department, April 22, 1961, ibid., 295–99.

50. Record of NSC meeting, June 16, 1961, *FRUS*, 1961–1963, 14: 119–24.

51. Acheson Report, June 28, 1961, ibid., 138–59.

52. Acheson to McNamara, July 19, 1961, folder 45c, Records of the NATO Adviser, 1957–1961, RG 59, NA.

53. Quoted in Isaacson and Thomas, *Wise Men*, 610–11.

54. Acheson to Truman, July 14, 1961, in *Among Friends*, 208; record of NSC meeting, July 13, 1961, *FRUS*, 1961–1963, 14: 192–94.

55. Acheson to Frankfurter, August 3, 1961, folder 148, box 12, Acheson Papers, Yale; Isaacson and Thomas, *Wise Men*, 614.

56. Quoted in Isaacson and Thomas, *Wise Men*, 615–16.

57. Acheson to Kennedy, August 18, 1961, Dean Acheson folder, Special Correspondence, President's Office Files, John F. Kennedy Papers, JFKL; Acheson Oral History Interview, 14, JFKL.

58. Acheson to Alice Acheson, April 28, 1961, in *Among Friends*, 229–30.

59. Acheson to Patrick Devlin, undated (probably early 1963), in ibid., 245.

60. Memorandum of meeting, October 17, 1962, *FRUS*, 1961–1963, 11: 97–98; Acheson Oral History Interview, 23, JFKL.

61. Dean Acheson, "Dean Acheson's Version of Robert Kennedy's Version of the Cuban Missile Affair," *Esquire*, February 1969. This essay was reprinted as "Homage to Plain Dumb Luck," in *The Cuban Missile Crisis*, ed. Robert A. Divine (Chicago: Quadrangle, 1971). See also Brinkley, *Cold War Years*, 156–64; Nitze, *From Hiroshima to Glasnost*, 123–24.

62. Embassy in France to Rusk, October 22, 1962, *FRUS*, 1961–1963, 11: 165–67.

63. Acheson Oral History Interview, 23–24, JFKL.

64. Acheson to Pamela Berry, December 3, 1962, folder 32, box 2, Acheson Papers, Yale.

65. Acheson to Monnet, November 1962, folder 288, box 23, ibid.

66. Acheson to Patrick Devlin, undated (probably early 1963), in *Among Friends*, 244–45.

67. Acheson to Berry, December 10, 1963, folder 32, box 2, Acheson Papers, Yale.

68. Acheson to Byrnes, January 14, 1964, folder 55, box 4, ibid.

69. Acheson to Jessup, "Dean Acheson–2" folder, box 3, Jessup Papers.

70. Transcript of a telephone conversation between Johnson and Acheson, December 4, 1963, in *Lyndon B. Johnson: The Kennedy Assassination and the Transfer of Power, November 1963–January 1964*, vol. 2, *December 1963*, ed. David Johnson and David Shreve (New York: Norton, 2005), 127–28.

71. Acheson to Ball, August 7, 1964, *FRUS*, 1964–1968, 16: 223–25. See also H. W.

Brands, *The Wages of Globalism: Lyndon Johnson and the Limits of American Power* (New York: Oxford University Press, 1995), 76–82.

72. Acheson to MacDonald, September 6, 1964, folder 264, box 21, Acheson Papers, Yale.

73. Acheson to MacLeish, September 6, 1964, Dean Acheson folder, box 1, Archibald MacLeish Papers, Library of Congress.

74. Acheson to Battle, June 15, 1965, folder 26, box 2, Acheson Papers, Yale.

75. Acheson to Truman, July 10, 1965, in *Among Friends*, 272–73.

76. Acheson to E. A. Burtt, October 14, 1965, folder 54, box 4, Acheson Papers, Yale.

77. Acheson to Burtt, November 2, 1965, ibid.

78. Thomas Alan Schwartz, *Lyndon Johnson and Europe: In the Shadow of Vietnam* (Cambridge: Harvard University Press, 2003), 103–11. The quote is on p. 109.

79. Acheson to Eden, June 29, 1966, in *Among Friends*, 279.

80. Acheson to MacLeish, August 8, 1966, Dean Acheson folder, box 1, MacLeish Papers.

81. Acheson to Truman, October 3, 1966, in ibid., 281–82.

82. Jim Jones (assistant to the president) to Johnson, November 2, 1967, *FRUS*, 1964–1968, 5: 954–70.

83. Acheson interview by the Public Broadcast Laboratory, December 3, 1967, Acheson folder, box 429, Harriman Papers.

84. Harriman memorandum of meeting with Acheson, December 12, 1967, ibid.

85. Chace, *Acheson*, 424; Brinkely, *Cold War Years*, 255–58.

86. Acheson to Cowles, March 14, 1968, folder 84, box 6, Acheson Papers, Yale; memorandum of a meeting with Johnson, March 14, 1968, in *Among Friends*, 292–94.

87. Notes of meeting, March 26, 1968, *FRUS*, 1964–1968, 6: 471–74.

88. Clark Clifford, *Counsel to the President: A Memoir*, with Richard Holbrooke (New York: Random House, 1991), 518–19.

89. Rusk, *As I Saw It*, 481.

90. Acheson to Jane Acheson Brown, April 13, 1968, April 13, 1968, in *Among Friends*, 296–97.

91. Record of meeting between Acheson and Nixon, March 19, 1969, folder 12, box 68, Acheson Papers, Yale.

92. Acheson interview by the Public Broadcast Laboratory, December 3, 1967, Acheson folder, box 429, Harriman Papers.

93. "Safeguard: America's Nuclear Defense, May 18, 1970, "Citizens' Committee to Safeguard America [1]" folder, box 3, Acheson Papers, HSTL; Chace, *Acheson*, 431–32, 435–36.

94. Acheson to Pamela Berry, June 24, 1969, folder 33, box 2, Acheson Papers, Yale.

95. Brinkley, *Cold War Years*, 282–83.

96. Acheson to Cowles, January 12, 1971, in *Among Friends*, 321–22.

97. C. L. Sulzberger, "The Sage of Sandy Spring," *New York Times*, September 9, 1970.

98. Acheson to Eden, September 23, 1970, folder 119, box 9, Acheson Papers, Yale.

99. Acheson to Eden, September 9, 1971, ibid.

100. Brinkley, *Cold War Years*, 303–28.

Conclusion

1. Acheson speech, June 4, 1946, in Acheson, *Fragments*, 19.

2. Nitze, *From Hiroshima to Glasnost*, 83.

3. Acheson, *This Vast External Realm*, 19.

4. Quoted in Hamburger, "Mr. Secretary–II," 61.

BIBLIOGRAPHIC ESSAY

For anyone researching the life and career of Dean Acheson, two archival collections are indispensable. Acheson's personal papers are housed in the Manuscripts and Archives Division at Yale University's Sterling Memorial Library, in New Haven, Connecticut. The correspondence files are especially rich. Acheson's official papers, covering his government service in the Roosevelt and Truman administrations, are located at the Harry S. Truman Presidential Library, in Independence, Missouri. Among other crucial files in those papers are Acheson's official memoranda of conversations for the entirety of his tenure as secretary of state.

A valuable published collection of Acheson's private letters is *Among Friends: Personal Letters of Dean Acheson*, edited by David S. McLellan and David C. Acheson (New York: Dodd, Mead, 1980).

National Archives II, in College Park, Maryland, contains a wide range of documents produced by or sent to Acheson during his years as assistant secretary of state (1941–1945), undersecretary of state (1945–1947), and secretary of state (1949–1953). Much of this material is not duplicated in the Truman Library documentation. State Department Lot Files 1 and 56 D 419, each termed "Acheson Records," contain especially interesting documentation for his early years in the State Department. The College Park holdings also include papers pertaining to Acheson's post–secretary of state diplomatic activities.

The most valuable collection of published documents for Acheson's State Department career remains the numerous, relevant volumes in the *Foreign Relations of the United States* series, which were used extensively in this biography. Prepared in the State Department, the ongoing series is published by the U.S. Government Printing Office. The annual volumes for 1945–1947 and 1949–1951, along with the triennial volumes for 1952–1954, contain literally tens of thousands of pages of documentation germane to Acheson's diplomatic career. They are essential to any critical engagement with it.

Texts of nearly all of the major speeches Acheson delivered during his terms as undersecretary of state and secretary of state have been published in the Department of State *Bulletin.* Written copies of those and many other speeches delivered throughout his life can be found in the speech files in his papers at Yale and at the Truman Library, as well as in some published collections. Among the latter, Dean Acheson, *This Vast External Realm* (New York: Norton, 1973), and Dean Acheson, *Fragments of My Fleece* (New York: Norton, 1971) are recommended.

Acheson's extensive remarks during congressional hearings, both extemporaneous and prepared, offer another exceptionally rich source for anyone examining his record as a policymaker. Relevant hearings are cited throughout the present study, particularly in chapters 3, 4, and 5. Acheson's comments during executive sessions of the Senate Foreign Relations Committee and the House Committee on Foreign Affairs and the House Armed Services Committee, published as the "Historical Series," are especially revealing. A useful selection of Acheson's testimony in open congressional hearings can be found in *The Pattern of Responsibility*, edited by McGeorge Bundy (Boston: Houghton Mifflin, 1951).

Two useful oral history interviews with Acheson are located in the Truman Library and in the John F. Kennedy Presidential Library, in Boston, Massachusetts.

Acheson's published writings, which are extensive, offer an exceptionally valuable window into his life and career. *Morning and Noon: A Memoir* (Boston: Houghton Mifflin, 1965) covers his life up to his initial State Department appointment in 1941. *Present at the Creation: My Years in the State Department* (New

York: Norton, 1969) is his Pulitzer Prize–winning account of his governmental service from 1941 to 1953. As with all memoirs, they should be used with caution since they naturally represent the author's version of events. Among Acheson's other notable reminiscences are *Sketches From Life of Men I Have Known* (New York: Harper, 1959). For a sentimental and entertaining account of the Acheson family by Dean's son, see David C. Acheson, *Acheson Country: A Memoir* (New York: Norton, 1993).

Acheson has attracted substantial interest from biographers and historians. The two earliest biographies, each of which was written before the bulk of the relevant diplomatic papers had been declassified, are Gaddis Smith, *Dean Acheson* (New York: Cooper Square, 1972); and David McLellan, *Dean Acheson: The State Department Years* (New York: Dodd, Mead, 1976). James Chace, *Acheson: The Secretary of State Who Created the American World* (New York: Simon & Schuster, 1998) is a lively, if somewhat superficial, full-length biography by an accomplished journalist. The premier Acheson biography, although it concentrates almost exclusively on the 1945–1953 period, is Robert L. Beisner, *Dean Acheson: A Life in the Cold War* (New York: Oxford University Press, 2006), a comprehensive, well-researched, and carefully argued study. A fine account of Acheson's post–secretary of state years is Douglas Brinkley, *Dean Acheson: The Cold War Years, 1953–71* (New Haven: Yale University Press, 1992).

Two intelligent studies that compare Acheson with a group of contemporary policymakers are Walter Isaacson and Evan Thomas, *The Wise Men: Six Friends and the World They Made* (New York: Simon & Schuster, 1986); and John Lamberton Harper, *American Visions of Europe: Franklin D. Roosevelt, George F. Kennan, and Dean G. Acheson* (New York: Cambridge University Press, 1994).

More specialized studies of Acheson's statecraft include Douglas Brinkley, ed., *Dean Acheson and Making of U.S. Foreign Policy* (New York: St. Martin's, 1993); Ronald McGlothlen, *Controlling the Waves: Dean Acheson and U.S. Foreign Policy in Asia* (New York: Norton, 1993); and John T. McNay, *Acheson and Empire: The British Accent in American Foreign Policy* (Columbia: University of Missouri Press, 2001).

The secondary literature dealing with U.S. foreign relations during Acheson's tenure in the State Department is vast, complex, and highly contentious, especially for the early Cold War period. Some of the books and articles that I have found most helpful are cited in the notes. For state-of-the-art essays on this era in international history, see especially Melvyn P. Leffler and Odd Arne Westad, eds., *The Cambridge History of the Cold War,* vol. 1, *Origins (1917–1962)* (New York: Cambridge University Press, forthcoming).

INDEX

ABOUT THE AUTHOR

Robert J. McMahon is the Mershon Distinguished Professor of History at Ohio State University. He is the author of several books on U.S. foreign relations, including *The Cold War: A Very Short Introduction, The Limits of Empire: The United States and Southeast Asia Since World War II*, and *The Cold War on the Periphery: The United States, India, and Pakistan.* He served as the president of the Society for Historians of American Foreign Relations in 2001. He lives in Columbus, Ohio.